INCEPTION MINDSET

The Contextual Art and Science of Leading
in a Permanently Complex World

Robert Radi, Ph.D., MBA

LiveLifeHappy
Publishing

LiveLife**Happy**
Publishing

Published and Distributed in The United States of America by Live Life Happy Publishing.

www.livelifehappypublishing.com

Library of Congress Cataloging-in-Publication Data

Robert Radi

Inception Mindset.

Management & Leadership > Leadership, Management & Leadership > Strategic Planning, Business Culture > Workplace Culture

ISBN Paperback Book 978-1-990461-50-7

ISBN Hard Cover 978-1-990461-51-4

Live Life Happy Publishing

Publisher's Note & Author DISCLAIMER

CONTENTS

DEDICATION

*To my wife, Charlotte, my son Max,
and my late mother, Rina.*

I love you.

*This book is dedicated to all those amazing individuals
who are willing to do, give, serve, and create value.
And when they come up short, they try again.*

ACKNOWLEDGMENTS

HUMBLY GRATEFUL

There are so many people who have contributed to my growth and development as an individual. I always thought, "What a cliché!" when someone writes or says, "There are too many to mention," until I found myself in their place while writing this section. Indeed, there are too many to mention, and the risk of forgetting someone is too significant. You know who you are and how much you mean to me. Many authors have influenced the shaping of my perspectives and are recognized in the bibliography, and while some are long gone ahead, I want to express my gratitude to them all.

I want to acknowledge all the dedicated and hard-working individuals I met and collaborated with over the last 38 years since I naively ventured for my first working experience in the Alps of Italy at age 14. The business owners, executives, and managerial leaders in the private sector, I have engaged with while working with some of the most respected and valuable brands. Colleagues in academia -- resolute and unwilling to give up their integrity. Leaders and those entrusted in their care dedicating their lives to public service, often unsung heroes, giving it all to public safety and local, state, and federal agencies. May they always remember that perfect landings don't make the news. With much gratitude, I want to thank those in the U.S. military and federal law enforcement for always giving me a fair shot at expressing my perspectives in the context of leadership. Thank you for your service.

In acknowledging how this book came to fruition, I want to thank my wife, Charlotte, for fiercely believing in me and telling me, "I want you to write that book!" When prompted by my "But who is going to read it?" she always replied, "I will!" As I write this book, you are working through your dissertation, and I am so proud of you. Your research will bring value to primary education and beyond.

I want to thank Dr. Kurt Motamedi. I cannot count the times he encouraged me to write this book over the many meals we were blessed to share at the end of a long day of teaching and learning together. It has been a privilege working with him.

My appreciation to Tamika McCuistion, an exemplary builder of enterprises, for graciously accepting the daunting task of reading the unedited manuscript as it was being written and for providing insightful feedback. I would also like to thank Dr. John Scully for his encouraging comments on the manuscript, Dr. John Carnesale for the challenging questions he posed about the concepts, John Hoffner for his recommendations at the start of this endeavor, Kathleen Fitzpatrick for her input on the many conceptual papers I wrote in preparation to writing this book, Kimber Maderazzo for lending her kitchen table where the last three chapters of this book came alive (and espresso machine to make that happen), Victory and Richard Grund for their encouragement and affection.

To my publisher, Andrea Seydel, thank you for encouraging me to author the book I wanted and needed to write. I trust this is the inception of many future collaborations.

To my Lord, thank you for giving me life and teaching me how to live it daily. I know I am a work in progress. Thank You for your Fatherly patience. May this book be valuable and meaningful for others and find its way to those who need it.

FOREWORD

The mosaics of knowledge and experiences that shape our world are intricate, diverse, amorphous, and evolving. I have explored the evolving contextual facets of wisdom, insight, and prudent action throughout my career and recently investigated and authored perspectives on the intersection of contextual intelligence and contextual competency.

In my many years as an educator, researcher, and practitioner in the field of strategic leadership and management, I have explored a plethora of insightful ideas and philosophies. Inception Mindset unfurls the many facets of contextual art and science for leadership in our unfolding complex world. It is a captivating thoughtful work synergizing scholarship and real-world action.

I recall vividly the day Dr. Radi, my esteemed colleague, and former student, first shared with me the inklings of what would later blossom into his insightful work on the Inception Mindset. I recognized then the power of his idea and encouraged its growth, understanding that it was a perspective sorely needed in today's challenging times. I encouraged its development, sensing its pivotal role in addressing the complex challenges of our modern epoch.

Inception Mindset is more than just a testament to the author's intellect and dedication. It extends an open invitation to leaders of all stripes – the aspiring, the emergent, and the established – to look upon the world through a transformative cognitive lens. It offers a novel paradigm for leadership in an age of burgeoning complexity and unrivaled change.

Inception Mindset is a beacon of enlightenment in the turbulent sea of complexity. It brings to the forefront the importance of going beyond adapting to complexity by thriving within it. The world's reality may be imbued with complexity and unpredictability, but the responses we elicit do not have to mirror this disorder. They can, instead, be guided by discernment, strategic wisdom, and an unwavering commitment to personal and organizational evolution.

It serves as a platform for introspection and discovery. It takes you on a voyage through the corridors of the self, the organization, and the broader environment. Drawing from a wealth of empirical research and real-world experiences, it presents a thought-provoking examination of our contextual realities. It provides a careful blend of analysis and practicality and navigates the reader toward insightful strategies and prudent actions in a turbulent, evolving, complex world.

Robert's ability to interlace academic rigor with practical insights is admirable. His intellectual honesty, a trait I've always admired in him, is palpable in each chapter. The result is a piece of literature that is as enlightening as it is relatable, as invigorating as it is instructive.

Inception Mindset has been a personal journey of insight and introspection for me. I am certain that its readers, regardless of their executive role or level of leadership, embark on a similar journey. The narratives, strategies, and insights encapsulated within these pages serve as a compass, guiding individuals through the labyrinth of complexities inherent in today's world.

To have been part of the genesis of this exceptional work is an honor. Witnessing its transition from a nascent idea to a concrete contribution to leadership literature has been a remarkable experience. I am certain that it will significantly impact the field of leadership and serve as a beacon for those charting their course through our intricate world.

Kurt Motamedi, Ph.D., MBA, MSEE
Professor of Strategy and Leadership
Pepperdine Graziadio Business School
Author of Contextual Competence (2018). International Journal of Business and Management, Vol. VI(1), pp. 26-35., 10.20472/BM.2018.6.1.003

INTRODUCTION

FOR YOUR CONSIDERATION

"I cannot teach anything to anyone, all I can do is help them think."
— Socrates

I will start by restating Socrate's quote. Not only can I not teach anything to anyone, but all I can do is **think along** with them. I also tell the participants in the leadership development seminars, workshops, and courses I facilitate that I am not there to "fix" them because, number one, they are not broken. Number two, I would start by "fixing" myself if I knew how to "fix" people. This book is not a biography. Trust me, I am not that interesting, albeit at times intriguing. It is not meant to tell "my story," although there are references to my experiences only when relevant in framing the topic to facilitate the thinking. This book is meant to provide a sandbox for you to think and wonder, "What if?" **This is not a self-help book.** I never liked the term and found it difficult to digest. The term makes it sound as if individuals are helpless and without agency. "Here, I have it all figured out, and now I am giving it to all to you for $xx.95 so you can self-help!" Give me a break!

However, in my assessment, too many people are getting too comfortable with "outsourcing" their thinking. René Descartes proclaimed: "I think, therefore I am." This statement reminds us that thinking is essential to the fabric of our existence and, therefore, our identity. When his father challenged his choice of pursuing physics instead of an income-generating career in engineering, Albert Einstein allegedly told his father, "I will think for the sake of thinking!" **This is a "thinking book." Think and implement.** I invite you to think with me, with the sincere hope that this book will honor the time and energy you will invest in reading it. Together we can move the needle.

If you have ever traveled on Sunset Blvd in Los Angeles, California, where I lived for sixteen years, you may have seen at a particular time of the year large billboards promoting a movie that was in theaters months before, and you may have noticed in large letters:

FOR YOUR CONSIDERATION

Well, if you are going to watch or stream that movie again is all gravy for the production company, but that billboard is there for the Members of the Academy who will vote for the various categories for the OSCARS®.

All I am proposing in this book is the result of a myriad of experiences in the trenches, academic research, empirical data extrapolated from inter-actions, teaching, learning, wonderments, many proverbial 2 X 4's to my face, and curiosities, but above all an earnest attempt to bring value in all I do. We all have an epistemology, which is, our individual theory of know-ledge concerning its methods, validity, and scope, as well as the distinction between justified belief and mere opinion. My epistemology blends Prag-matism and Constructivism. I value ideas not solely for their theoretical elegance, but for their practical utility. This represents the Pragmatic as-pect of my epistemological framework. Concurrently, I also uphold Con-structivism's tenet: while certain facts are absolute, knowledge is primarily constructed rather than transmitted, especially when dealing with complex systems. So, paint me as a Pragmatic Constructivist.

I often use the following example in my lectures. Let's step back thou-sands of years to consider how mushroom knowledge was formed. How did we learn that the striking red mushroom with white spots (Fly Agaric), though visually appealing, can be fatally poisonous? Or that its relative in a white coat (Amanita phalloides, commonly known as the death cap) is most definitely deadly? This knowledge was not innate or obvious; it was painstakingly constructed over time. People, regrettably, lost their lives, providing the empirical data from which the surrounding community could construct this vital piece of knowledge. This knowledge was then socially constructed and passed down through generations via the human practice of narrative. This exemplifies the principle of Constructivism: knowledge emerges from our interactions with our environment and is subsequently integrated into our social consciousness.

So, knowledge is constructed and socially negotiated over time, especially in the face of complexity, and there the function of time plays a role. Throughout this book, you will find that I mention other authors and their work, and at times I point out alignments and divergences with the perspectives I offer. This practice is not meant to refute any of the work but to approach each concept I propose with curiosity and intellectual honesty while acknowledging those who had the fortitude to bring their perspectives into the dialogue of their time so that we can engage in the dialogue of our time.

This is not a book from someone who figured it all out and now bestows their wisdom upon you. In channeling Confucius, I can say that at 52, I am doing my best to continue my growth as a human being first to be a better leader. I am an ongoing project, continuously learning and adapting. One of the most significant quotes for me is from Dr. Martin Luther King: "Life's most persistent and urgent question is, 'What are you doing for others?'" I try to address that question every day and come up short every day. And the next day, I will try again. Perhaps, a little insanity is needed when operating in complexity.

I offer it all to you FOR YOUR CONSIDERATION. So, this is a thinking book for individual and organizational development across **Four Horizons:** 1. The Environment, 2. The Self, 3. The Organization, and 4. The Three Combined.

As a companion to your journey across the four horizons, Integral Advantage® has developed the **Inception Mindset™ Inventory**. This exclusive professional development tool is a self-assessment designed to catalyze personal and professional growth—and we're offering it complimentary.

Completing the assessment by visiting InceptionMindset.com is a breeze. It involves addressing 24 items on a 5-point Likert scale. Your personalized report will be emailed to you (please check your spam folder) and available for instant download, providing immediate insights into your developmental journey. There are no right or wrong answers or good or bad results, just growth opportunities. With an Inception Mindset, we equip ourselves to navigate the unprecedented complexity of our times more effectively.

Charting Our Journey

Inception Mindset

You Are Here

Introduction For Your Consideration

Horizon 1
The Complex Environment

Chapters

1 A Permanent State of Inception
   An Inception Mindset
2 Gaining Clarity in Complexity
   Complexity is CADE

Horizon 2
The Self in Complexity

3 Clarity in Contextual Complexity
4 A Reframed Philosophy
5 Your Contextual Leadership Brand
6 Leadership Brand Authoring
7 Contextual Cultural Flow

Horizon 3
The Organization In Complexity

8 Entrusted Empowerment
9 The Practice of Entrusted Empowerment
10 Cultivating Innovation & Learning

Horizon 4
The Environment, The Self, The Org.

11 The Process of Strategic Innovation
12 Inception Mindset as the Way Forward

Conclusion A Journey Toward Wisdom

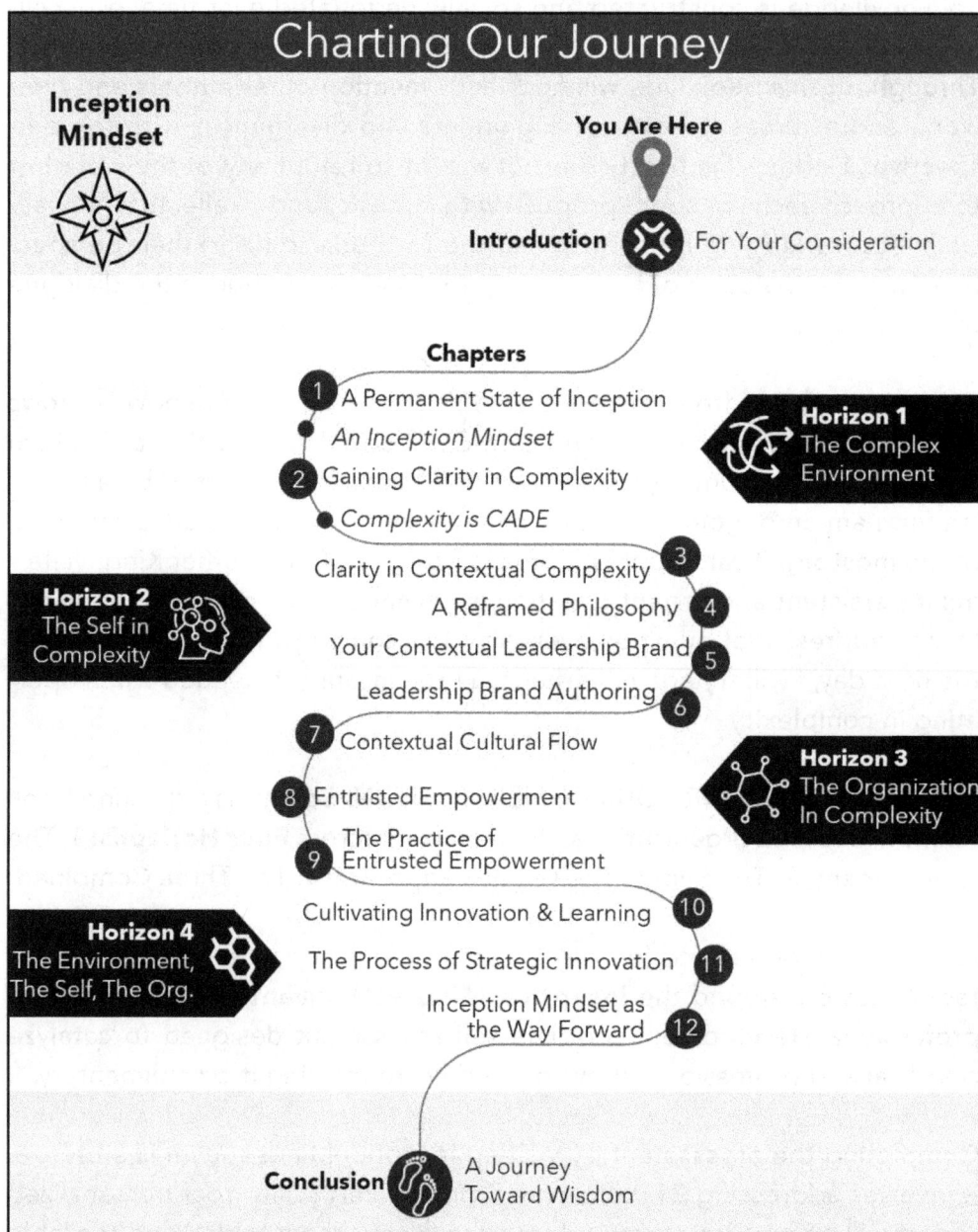

The term development is critical. Everything in this book is developmental, and none of it is "corrective or remedial" in nature. Addressing how we behave is not equivalent to changing who we are. It is the central tenet to be who we indeed are. Addressing how our organizations operate in contextual complexity is not the equivalent of changing because we did it wrong in the past, but embracing the future that has yet to be written. Knowledge may indeed be powerful, but it may be bounded in time and by time, while creativity and curiosity are boundless.

I have learned many lessons from my late Mother. The last lesson I learned was how she handled her battle with leukemia over fifteen months amid the COVID-19 pandemic. I have learned this: **Courage is Faith, and Faith is Courage**. Faith is not a denial of the prevailing logic or the dismissal of the probabilities. Faith is the courage to approach a challenge with a mindset toward the possibilities while remaining true to ourselves, our beliefs, and our purpose. Her battle ended on February 1st, 2021, and the pandemic kept us physically apart for the entire time, as millions of other people also experienced worldwide. With restricted air travel, the world was big once again. Millions of goodbyes were said over the phone during that time, all part of the human experience.

All life's transitions take courage. We are all in transition as the complexity of our environment is outpacing our current cognitive capacity. I define complexity as a constellation of new beginnings, a state of inception in which we are forced to reframe what we have known to be accurate, but it is no longer the case. A permanent state of inception requires us to develop an *Inception Mindset*. The quote, "It is not what we don't know that gets us into trouble, it is what we know for sure that ain't so," is often attributed to Mark Twain, though it's not definitively proven that he said it. The quote has also been linked to Josh Billings and Will Rogers. Regardless of the source, the quote emphasizes the danger of being overly certain about something that may not be true. The quote is widely used to emphasize the importance of questioning our assumptions and maintaining a healthy skepticism to gain clarity. It's a reminder that certainty can sometimes lead us astray if it's not based on accurate information. During a speaking engagement coinciding with the release of his book Full-Spectrum Thinking: How to Escape Boxes in a Post-Categorical Future, futurist Dr. Bob Johansen stated: "The future will reward clarity but punish certainty." He repeated "punish certainty" twice for good measure. While this quote was from his previous book, The New Leadership Literacies, it had gained salient meaning amid the COVID-19 response as I was wearing multiple hats, including the hat of an elected official. After hearing Dr. Johansen pronouncing those words, vs. reading them, I thought, "Yes, and...

gaining clarity is the equivalent of mental elbow grease." We need to do the work, and there is nothing "soft" about the commitment it takes.

For as long as I can remember, since my days in consumer product strategy when dealing with clients, I have always advocated for gaining clarity first, which goes against my nature of "getting it done." At times I did it better than others. During a call with a potential client, a company holding a utility patent, I asked the essential questions needed to assess the viability of the potential product. My questions were meant to diagnose the product's critical aspects in the consumer's context. At one point, the owner says, "Look, Robert, this project is a piece of cake!" to which I promptly responded, "If we approach the development of a product with 'it will be a piece of cake' mentality, it will only ensure that the result is a piece of crap." After a moment of awkward silence, he said, "Robert, you missed your call," to which I replied, "Oh, yeah, what would that be?" and he said, "You should have been a philosopher." Perhaps. But while I could have worded my response more elegantly, the facts of the matter remained. The U.S. Patent Office does not issue patents based on a product's manufacturability and contextual market viability. Ultimately, we didn't work on the project, and after some 15 years, the product never made it to the market, and if my remarks had anything to do with that, so be it. I apologize to the attorneys out there who would have made a hefty fee in a consumer product liability lawsuit. The certainty of a patent is no substitute for clarity in complex environmental conditions.

In complexity, Incubation is a space to gain clarity through appreciative inquiry. It goes back to thinking and, more explicitly, thinking collaboratively. It is a space to transcend the illusion of speed. As ranchers in Montana say, if you take the time it takes, it will get done faster.

Here are some guiding principles and basic tenets of this book:

1. Complexity is a permanent state.

2. Complexity is a constellation and aggregation of new beginnings.

3. In complexity, we must first see the dots before we can connect the dots.

4. Complexity is CADE— Contextualizable, Amorphous, Dynamic, and Elastic.

5. Complexity punishes linear thinking. Using linear thinking in complexity is like being told to cut the red wire in an explosive device when all wires are red.

6. Complexity Amnesia. We are designed to operate in relative complexity, but we have forgotten.

7. Complexity, yes. But Context matters.

8. Success is a byproduct of value generation, not the way around. We need to talk more about Key Value Factors rather than Key Success Factors. That is a desirable aspect of free markets.

9. We cannot get to inclusion through exclusion.

10. To lead in complexity, we must have clarity about who we are first.

11. Each one of us is unique. Our leadership brand is unique.

12. We cannot get or make others trust us. Trust is earned every day.

13. We don't get to empower others. We can foster the conditions for them to empower themselves.

14. We cannot get to innovation without controversy and calculated risk.

15. We cannot get to innovation without incubation.

16. We need to slow down to speed up.

17. We cannot adapt to complexity if we don't help others adapt.

18. We cannot get anything done if not through people and for the people.

19. We need to find our voices and leverage the power of our leadership narrative.

20. We must commit to continuing our personal growth.

This is, in essence, what we will explore together in this book. But why write the book now? The impetuousness to write this book came from the comments I received in person and written evaluations from those I share these concepts with. I realized how these concepts are gaining more saliency and are resonating more in the contemporary environment than when I first conceived them. The shaping of some of these concepts finds their genesis in my work as a Ph.D. student and some form the capstone thesis I wrote as part of my Presidents and Key Executives (PKE) MBA at Pepperdine University. Since 2011, that document has been shared with numerous executives attending the PKE program who found the original elements helpful not only for the completion of their thesis but also for their context.

A partner at one of the Big Four, who was attending the PKE MBA program, told me that they did read my document. Surprised because I was aware of the document's length and the demands on their time, I asked, "The whole thing?" They say, "Yes, the whole thing." So, with curiosity, I asked, "And? What are your thoughts, and was it helpful?" They replied that it was very well done, and he did find it helpful. Well, who can ask for anything more than that?

From time to time, remember the following, as I am telling you in my writings, I am telling myself. I don't have it all figured out. Perhaps I can bring value as you try to figure it out.

Introducing the "Thinking Point"

In the journey of exploration and discovery, this book invites you on, I recognize the importance of occasionally pausing to take in the scenery. It's akin to the Vista Points or Scenic Points that mark a journey through a fascinating landscape, where the traveler is encouraged to stop, breathe, absorb the view, and reflect on the journey so far.

This is the philosophy behind the "Thinking Point" sections you will encounter at the end of each chapter segment. Each Thinking Point is designed to serve as a vista or scenic point in our shared intellectual journey - a spot where we pause, catch our breath and reflect on the landscape of ideas we have traversed. Each is an invitation to intellectually, personally, and experientially engage with the material. As I previously stated, this is a thinking book.

Designed in the spirit of the Socratic method, each Thinking Point includes three components:

Takeaways: These are the nuggets of wisdom, the essential insights that the chapter segment has offered. They serve as a concise summary, a quick snapshot of the vista we've reached.

Reflective Questions: These are open invitations to ponder, relate the material to your own experiences, critically examine the ideas presented, or explore potential applications or implications.

Contextualization Prompt: A specific question or task that encourages you to implement ideas in a context relevant to your life or work. This is where the theoretical and conceptual meet the practice, the abstract becomes execution, and insight becomes personal revelation to gain clarity in complexity.

The Thinking Points are your opportunities to stop and think, contextualize what you have read, and to actively engage with the material. They invite you to take the insights and ideas from the book and weave them into the fabric of your thoughts, experiences, and context.

So, when you reach a Thinking Point, take your time. Savor the view, reflect on the takeaways, ponder the questions, and engage with the Contextualization Prompt. This journey is not about rushing to the destination but about savoring and making the most of it. The Thinking Points are your companions on this journey. **Enjoy the scenic route across the Four Horizons!**

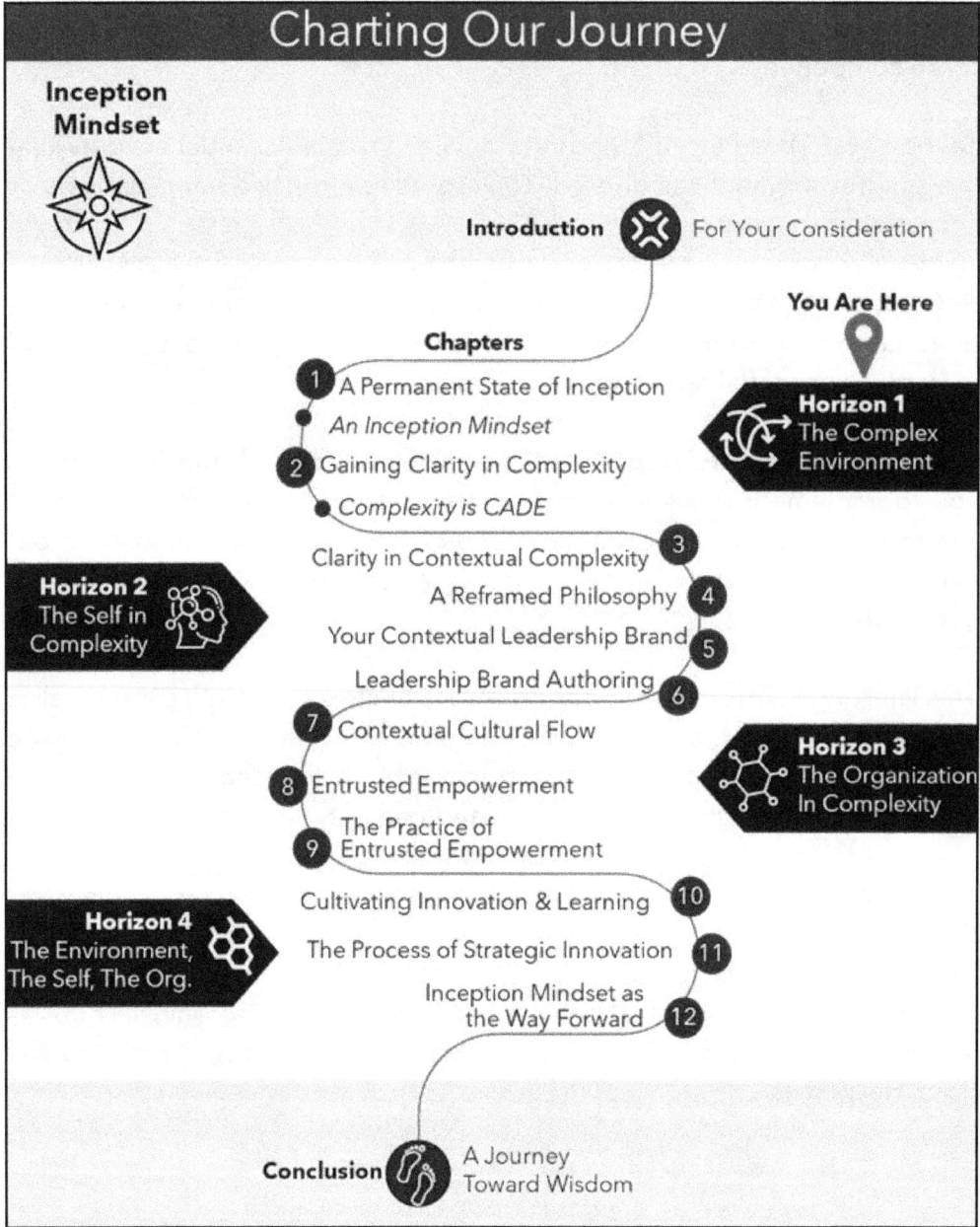

Charting Our Journey

Inception Mindset

Introduction — For Your Consideration

You Are Here

Chapters

1 A Permanent State of Inception
   An Inception Mindset

2 Gaining Clarity in Complexity
   Complexity is CADE

Horizon 1 The Complex Environment

3 Clarity in Contextual Complexity
4 A Reframed Philosophy
5 Your Contextual Leadership Brand
6 Leadership Brand Authoring

Horizon 2 The Self in Complexity

7 Contextual Cultural Flow
8 Entrusted Empowerment
9 The Practice of Entrusted Empowerment

Horizon 3 The Organization In Complexity

10 Cultivating Innovation & Learning
11 The Process of Strategic Innovation
12 Inception Mindset as the Way Forward

Horizon 4 The Environment, The Self, The Org.

Conclusion — A Journey Toward Wisdom

PART I

HORIZON 1: THE COMPLEX ENVIRONMENT

Those leading in organizations, communities and the contemporary dynamic environment face increasing complexity in their respective contexts. In this book, I define the characteristics of complexity by CADE— Contextualizable, Amorphous, Dynamic and Elastic. In this Horizon and throughout the book, I will often refer to Contextualized Complexity, as there is no 'one-size-fits-all' approach to dealing with complexity, thus reinforcing my assertion that we must contextualize complexity.

 As a result, leaders are constantly faced with the challenge of navigating through an environment in constant flux. This constant flux and adaptation can be likened to the concept of ***"inception,"*** where leaders constantly operate via various instances of new beginnings. A constellation of starting points to address plausible scenarios extrapolated through foresight or response to unforeseen environmental changes. This condition diverges from mitigating mere operational hurdles; instead, it requires a high level of creativity to build strategic capacity in the organization. **Inception**, by definition, *is the establishment or starting point of an institution or activity.*

In this context, **Inception** refers to entering and navigating through multiple layers of consciousness, each with its own emerging rules and realities. Similarly, leaders are constantly navigating through various layers of complexity, each with its challenges and realities. This complexity can be attributed to several factors, such as technological advances, global economic changes, new markets and industries, social movements, generational shifts, and collective meaning-making. The dynamics of a complex environment are not linear and demand **that leadership is contextual**, and the multitude of nodes must be recognized. Hence, organizational leadership must be reframed through an ***Inception Mindset*** as complexity requires addressing new nodes as starting points by identifying that what worked in the past cannot be linearly applied to the current context.

We are all required to operate in **a permanent state of Inception**, constantly being challenged to adapt to new realities and ways of thinking. To work in complexity, we must think creatively, be agile in decision-making, and quickly anticipate and respond to change. We must develop contextual competencies while clarifying, developing, and congruently deploying our leadership brand. Background research, methodologies, integrative frameworks, and insightful practices found throughout this book will empower individuals to operate in their contextual complexity.

CHAPTER 1

A PERMANENT STATE OF INCEPTION

"In the middle of difficulty lies opportunity."
— Albert Einstein

An Inception Mindset

The word on the street is that we are facing unprecedented complexity. But are we? If we look at the complexity of our times, it is unprecedented. But when we look at complexity in a time continuum, facing unprecedented complexity is an integral part of the human experience. Since much of the complexity of our times is humanmade, we ought to form a collective mindset that, as human beings, we are designed to operate in complexity.

Complexity demands that we develop an **Inception Mindset,** a term I coined to encapsulate the integration of the constellation of new beginnings. I define *Inception Mindset* as the holistic cognitive ability allowing individuals to perceive the complexities of our evolving world as a constellation of new beginnings. This mindset is shaped by four interconnected horizons - the environment, the self, the organization, and the integration of these three elements. It allows for a comprehensive understanding of complexity, recognizing the potential for opportunity, growth, and interconnectedness amidst every challenge.

Distinct from other mindsets, the *Inception Mindset* is not merely about identifying potential new beginnings but also about capitalizing on this potential. It enables individuals to create, implement, and execute new ideas, fostering adaptability and innovation in anticipation and response to complexity. In practical terms, *Inception Mindset* is an effective approach and practice that can be harnessed by leaders, entrepreneurs, and anyone who desires to bring about positive change in their context and the world. It paves the way for innovative problem-solving, the construction of improved organizations, and the ability to thrive amidst complexity.

In a perpetually complex world, leaders equipped with an *Inception Mindset* can adeptly navigate the challenges of constant complexity. They are set to perceive opportunities in every challenge, adapt to new realities, and consistently innovate to keep pace with an ever-evolving landscape. This mindset, therefore, is essential for those wishing to lead successfully in the unprecedented complexity of our time.

Complexity is always unprecedented at the time of its manifestation. At the beginning of the 90s, a new wave of complexity was gathering like a storm: the inception of making all our consumer products in China. At age 23, I was in the early stages of building my own business, navigating an industry known for its high business mortality rate - consumer product design and development. At that time, the "Make it in China" lure began emerging on the horizon and taking hold. One of my projects was for a brand-named Diamondback, designing a line of stationary exercise equipment, including a stationary bike, a recumbent bike, and a step-master. This was the first project I was involved in, requiring relatively sizeable plastic housing for the mechanical components of the equipment. In the two years before, I was designing smaller products with plastic housings and components. Still, I mostly designed CCTV camera security housings and other accessories made in formed sheet metal for my first client EMI (Electro-Mechanical Imagineering), in Pacoima, CA, up to that point.

The work was contracted from Diamondback by Raymond Smith of Smith-Bruni Design. Raymond was more than a client. As someone many years my senior, he had taken me under his wing, serving not just as a mentor but also as a guiding hand, helping me grow my fledgling business. Raymond was a very talented designer and value-driven businessman, his work was inspiring, and I wanted to build my chops to meet his talent.

As I worked on the project, it was conveyed to me that our designs would be sent to a manufacturer in China to create the molds, which would then be shipped to the US to produce most of the ABS plastic parts. My initial response was one of surprise: "What? What's wrong with all our mold makers in the San Fernando Valley?" The answer was simple yet impactful: **cost.**

The subsequent experience was less than optimal. The supposed cost-saving measure led to numerous revisions due to the Chinese mold makers' inability or lack of understanding. What followed was a tiring process of constant reiterations and explanations, which felt more like "educating" than designing. I found myself doing more typing and talking than designing. However, despite the hurdles, the parts eventually turned out well, meeting our expectations. I naively thought, "Been there, done that. Hopefully, this is the last time we work with China." But, as it turned out, history had other plans.

The "Made in the USA" was about to take on a new meaning. What began as outsourcing mold-making slowly expanded into other areas: molding, assembly, engineering, and eventually full-scale product development - from engineering to mold-making, manufacturing, and packaging.

And for nineteen years, I was amid this complexity until I successfully exited my business to dedicate myself to what I do to this very day. I would be lying if I said I didn't love it, at least most of the time. As the tasks grew since that Diamondback product line, so did the complexity, akin to a baby elephant rapidly maturing. What I started as a *"design business"* quickly had to evolve into a *consumer product strategy* consulting business. There was no manual, as the examples of the past were unsuitable for the present. From time to time, during our weekly calls, I would quiz my Mother regarding how my late Father, Mario, who passed away when I was 3, handled certain challenges when he was the CEO of **Rheem Radi, S.p.A,** an Italo-American joint venture and a dominating manufacturer and distributor of water heaters in Europe, ever since my grandfather Serafino Radi begun operation in 1927. As helpful and inspiring as those stories were in encouraging perseverance on my part, it was also clear that the complexities of the 60s and early 70s were not akin to the emerging complexity of the 90s. Something was amiss.

Circa 1992, I ran into a book, the first edition of The Fifth Discipline, and the notions of systems thinking resonated with me, or at least what I could cognitively comprehend in my early twenties. I liked the ideas so much that I named my business Radi System Design to convey the practice of strategically aligning all the components and stakeholders of a product development cycle. The name confused almost everyone; they thought we were a computer company. By the time I incorporated the business and filed for the trademark, the business name went with the safer and expected approach: Radi Design. This was a blessing because, as it turned out, there was no system as a stable methodology to offer to clients, as complexity demanded **a constant state of inception,** a constellation of new beginnings from technology, practices, strategies, stakeholders' engagement, you name it, it needed to be *learned, unlearned and relearned* as futurist and philosopher Alvin Toffler once wrote, a critical aspect of developing an *Inception Mindset.*

The complex dynamics of global outsourcing became all too apparent in those years. As the world's factory, China came with its set of complexities. The phrase "Made in China" was a cause for concern rather than a celebration for many consumers and brands alike. Brands had to adapt and address those concerns arising from the doubts surrounding the quality and durability of the products as issues were emerging. The initial cost-saving appeal of outsourcing often fell short when products failed to meet consumers' expectations for quality and reliability. Frequent product returns became routine, burdening the already cost-conscious companies with additional financial strain. Eventually, we collectively started to gain clarity. Rapid learning, boots on the ground, and tighter protocols emerged as practices, specifically focusing on implementing computer 3D modeling to control design from esthetical and structural design perspectives, while 3D modeling was itself limited in its capabilities as it was in an embryonic stage at best, but it rapidly matured. Learning was key, daily learning that is, especially the cultural aspects of business in China. The cultural, language, and time zone differences added further layers to the complexity. The information often got lost in translation, leading to miscommunications and errors. Not to mention the unexpected delays and cost overruns due to differences in work culture and business ethics.

This transfer of know-how and manufacturing production soon had tangible implications manifesting in job losses at home as manufacturing costs in the USA were not competitive. The repercussion of the North American Free Trade Agreement (NAFTA), an agreement signed by Canada, Mexico, and the United States, creating a trilateral trade bloc in North America, were also becoming salient to the complexity of that time. The agreement came into force on January 1, 1994. Its purpose was to eliminate barriers to trade and investment between the U.S., Canada, and Mexico. The implementation of NAFTA caused the elimination of most tariffs on products traded among the three countries.

The organizational conflict was another issue. The outsourcing model disrupted traditional workflows, creating tensions between various departments within our organizations. While the management saw it as a necessary step to remain competitive, the workforce viewed it as threatening job security. This resulted in internal conflicts, often manifesting as resistance to change, decreased productivity, and sometimes even sabotage. According to the Bureau of Labor Statistics, in 1990, there were about 17.9 million manufacturing jobs in the United States. Over the following three decades, there was a significant decline in these numbers. Periods of trade deficits, the combination of automation, globalization, and the 2008 financial crisis have resulted in the net elimination of approximately 5.6 million U. S. manufacturing jobs, or roughly a third of its manufacturing workforce.

Intellectual property was another major challenge adding to the complexity. There were instances when designs submitted to Chinese factories mysteriously appeared in the market under different brands before our official product launched. The "it fell off the truck" was a no-joke joke. This condition led to financial losses and damaged the trust and goodwill of many US brands.

When I was a teenager, age 14, I worked in a hotel located in North Italy for the summer as a chef's assistant. Long hours in hot kitchens build character. One day, the walk-in refrigerator's door in the hotel's basement malfunctioned. Unable to gain access, I ran upstairs to the kitchen and reported the issue to the chef, who was also the owner's son. With authority, he told me, "Do what the Americans do!" I said, "OK," and started to walk away, but soon I realized I didn't really grasp what he meant, so I asked, "What do the Americans do?" and he promptly responded, "They figure it out!" Eventually, I did gain access by figuring out how to get around the malfunctioning locking mechanism.

Indeed, as the nineties progressed and it was clear that China was going to play a major role, **we had to figure it out collectively**. Designers, engineers, 3D software developers, marketers, logistics experts, lawyers, banks, national brands and even consumers figured it out in a 'building the airplane while flying it' fashion. We were operating while a complex phenomenon was forming and for which (in late 2006) economic historian Dr. Niall Ferguson and economist Dr. Moritz Schularick will coin the term *Chimerica*.

A supposedly symbiotic relationship that resulted in coupling the two nations' economies - for better or for worse – and it worked…until it didn't.

Amid the contextualizable amorphous dynamic and elastic conditions, we collectively figured it out incrementally through both foresight and prompt response. Thinking in systems was vital to figuring it out. Indeed, operating in complexity was a learned and acquired strategic skill necessary for survival in those tumultuous times, and eventually, structured methodologies and good and best practices emerged. Yet, as we navigate one layer of complexity, another one will emerge because, at the end of complexity, there is more complexity.

That is why we need to develop an *Inception Mindset*. An individual operating with the *Inception Mindset* does not simply observe the potential for new beginnings but actualizes them, demonstrating creativity, agility, and anticipatory decision-making skills. The *Inception Mindset* is vital in navigating the permanent state of complexity marked by constant evolution. At its core, *inception mindset* is about recognizing and contextualizing a new beginning and approaching it with an open mind and a willingness to learn. This mindset is pivotal in the context of leadership, where the ability to anticipate, adapt, and respond to change is critical to producing value-creating outcomes.

Research has shown that the characteristics of an **Inception Mindset** are closely related to certain character strengths, such as creativity, curiosity, and open-mindedness. These strengths allow us to approach new situations with a sense of wonder and possibility rather than fear or resistance. They enable us to see opportunities where others might see only obstacles and to develop innovative solutions to complex problems. At the same time, an *Inception Mindset* requires us to be grounded in reality and to recognize the limits of our knowledge and experience. We need to balance our creativity and imagination with a sense of pragmatism and practicality and be willing to engage with the world as *it is* rather than as we wish it to be. To cultivate an *Inception Mindset*, it is important to focus on developing these character strengths and other related skills such as adaptability, resilience, and emotional intelligence.

Leaders who fail to recognize the impact of complexity on their organizations and accordingly adopt an *Inception Mindset* risk losing their competitive edge. For example, Blockbuster, a once-dominant video rental company, failed to recognize the constellation of new beginnings courtesy of the rise of streaming services like Netflix, ultimately leading to its bankruptcy. On the other hand, successful organizations such as Apple, Amazon, and Google have embraced an *Inception Mindset*, recognizing that the dynamics of a complex environment are not linear in nature and require contextual leadership. These organizations have been able to stay ahead of the curve by anticipating and responding to change quickly and by thinking creatively to build strategic capacity.

Leaders today are required to operate in a permanent state of Inception, constantly being challenged to adapt to new realities and ways of thinking. To operate in complexity, leaders must think creatively, be agile in decision-making, and quickly anticipate and respond to change. They must act in a way that allows them to move seamlessly between different layers of complexity. The *Inception Mindset* is critical for leaders to navigate through the complexities of the business environment successfully. Leaders who possess the character strengths necessary to operate effectively in a complex and ever-changing environment are better equipped to adapt to changing market dynamics and stay ahead of the curve.

This is the challenge of our time. By adopting an Inception Mindset, we can become more effective leaders, better able to navigate our environment's complexities and lead our organizations toward creating value. Our past experiences serve as a bridge to the contemporary complexity we are all trying to figure out. But it can only be figured out through new learning. Think, do, and learn...daily.

THINKING POINT

Section Takeaways

The transformation of global production and outsourcing strategies, such as the "Make it in China" era, contributed to an intricate web of complexity within organizations and in society.

The *Inception Mindset* is critical in navigating such complexity, characterized by continuous learning, adaptation, and an openness to new beginnings.

Balancing creativity and open-mindedness with practicality and realism is fundamental to cultivating an *Inception Mindset*

Despite established methodologies and best practices, each new layer of complexity demands unique strategies, further emphasizing the need for an *Inception Mindset*.

Reflective Questions

Can you recall an instance in your professional journey where you faced an unexpected shift or new beginning? How did you handle it? In what ways do you continuously learn, unlearn, and relearn in your current role? How has this shaped your approach to dealing with complexity?

Which character strengths associated with an *Inception Mindset* do you already possess, and which ones do you need to develop further?

Contextualization Prompt

Take a few moments to consider the complexity of your current professional context. Identify one aspect of your role where adopting an *Inception Mindset* could lead to better outcomes. How might you integrate this mindset into your daily practice to navigate the complexities inherent in your role more effectively?

Complexity Amnesia

Complexity is nothing new, but its contemporary characteristics, attributes, and dynamics are. When operating in complexity, linear thinking is insufficient to address contextual obstacles. Roman Emperor Tiberius (reign 14–37 A.D.) often used the expression, "I've got a wolf by the ears; for I neither know how to get rid of her nor yet how to keep her" when he encountered a critically complex issue with no apparent optimal outcome. However, the difficulty has yet to be addressed through managing the polarizing conditions, systems thinking identifying stakeholders and boundaries, or Probing, Sensing, and Responding cycles as proposed by David Snowden through his concept of the Cynefin framework, which functions as a leader's framework for decision making. The linear solution, "if we do this, that happens," is often the result of attempting to solve a complex issue as if it was a mere complication. We tell ourselves a linear story. If we ban (enter here the issue du jour), all will return to "normal." We diverge from the reality of an increasingly complex environment and fall into the trap of unintended consequences. We see our communities, organizations, and even families as islands onto themselves where everything can be regulated via on/off switches. So, we hold on or let go. "*Auribus Teneo Lupum*" (Holding a Wolf by its Ears) reminds us that there are no perfect solutions to a problem, sometimes there are no solutions at all because it is not a problem but rather a fact cemented in the environmental complexity that needs to be managed, sometimes indefinitely.

We must overcome **Complexity Amnesia**. I propose this term to capture the often-overlooked fact that complexity is not a modern phenomenon but rather a persistent aspect of human history, particularly leadership. It also emphasizes the importance of context when analyzing past events. The complexity of the 1990s was not different from the complexity faced by Emperor Tiberius. Complexity is relative to its time. The context was different, but the human experience held many commonalities.

Indeed, when we examine significant historical accomplishments like the construction of the Great Pyramids, the establishment of ancient trade routes, the organization of the first Olympic Games, or the creation of the postal service, we can clearly see that dealing with complexity is far from a modern phenomenon. The construction of the Great Pyramids required significant engineering ingenuity, resource management, and labor organization. Despite the absence of modern technology, the Egyptians devised methods to move massive stone blocks, planned the pyramid structure with incredible precision, and coordinated a large workforce over many years. The task was replete with complex challenges: logistical, human, environmental, and more. Creating networks like the Silk Road demanded an understanding and navigation of diverse political, cultural, and geographical terrains. Traders had to deal with fluctuating market dynamics, understand and respect diverse cultures, and often risk their own lives to ensure their trade missions' success. Orchestrating the First Olympic Games in ancient Greece required cooperation between often-warring city-states, adherence to a peace agreement (the Olympic Truce), and the management of logistics such as athlete accommodations, scheduling of events, and prize distribution. It was a considerable feat of diplomacy, administration, and societal organization. The inception and evolution of the postal service, from ancient courier systems to today's global networks, exemplifies dealing with complexity over centuries. The service had to adapt to changing political landscapes, advancements in transportation, evolving communication technologies, and fluctuating public needs. All these examples illustrate complexity throughout history, indicating that it isn't a condition unique to our current age. Each challenge was met with the time's available knowledge, technology, and social structures. Understanding this helps combat Complexity Amnesia and underlines the need to appreciate past complexities in their respective contexts to navigate our complex world effectively.

The Presentism Trap

Presentism contributes to Complexity Amnesia in a significant way, particularly when it comes to understanding the history and evolution of organizations and institutions. In the context of historical analysis, presentism refers to an attitude where present-day ideas, perspectives, knowledge, and values are superimposed onto past events and societies. While it's human nature to try and make sense of the past through the lens of the present, this approach can be problematic because it often results in a skewed understanding of historical events, contexts, and complexities. If we evaluate past decisions, strategies, or events solely from our current understanding and context, we are likely to misinterpret the complexity and challenges that those institutions or organizations faced at that time.

For instance, a presentist view might judge a historical business decision as faulty without considering the knowledge, cultural norms, or technology available at the time. "Steve Jobs should have done this or that…" Similarly, an organization's past strategies might seem outdated or ineffective when viewed through a presentist lens, but those strategies might have been groundbreaking or innovative. When we use it, presentism is the equivalent of playing Monday Morning Quarterback without having watched the game. Why didn't the organizers of the first Olympic Games just set up a group chat or use Zoom to meet? As ridiculous as it may sound, this is exactly why the lenses of presentism contribute to Complexity Amnesia. We are not talking about cases in which an organization's legal, ethical, and moral obligations were abandoned in favor of the short-term perspective, such as Enron, VW, Wells Fargo, WorldCom, etc. In all those instances, the lenses of the present were those of that time. Still, I would add that if all those organizations had not suffered from Complexity Amnesia, they would not have suffered from a maniacal focus on the short-term outcomes, but they would have embraced how the organization had faced and navigated the contextual complexity of their past. At the very least, they would have appreciated that as "timid" or "inadept" those past decisions and actions may have seemed through the lenses of presentism, the organization was still in existence in the present.

The failure to appreciate these complexities can lead to underestimating the past challenges faced by leaders and institutions and over-simplifying the lessons to be learned from history. Overcoming **Complexity Amnesia** requires an effort to avoid presentism, acknowledging that the complexities of the past, while different in context, were as real and impactful as the complexities we face today. This shift also contributes to the development of an *Inception Mindset*. By recognizing this, we can derive more meaningful insights from our institutional and organizational histories and better prepare ourselves for the complexities of the future by cultivating more nuanced analyses of historical events, developing contextual thinking skills, and recognizing the ongoing nature of complexity in human affairs.

In comparison, Jennifer Garvey-Berger's "Mindtraps" posits that our cognitive biases and assumptions can trap us into ineffective or damaging behaviors, especially when dealing with complexity. It's about the personal, internal mental frameworks we use to understand and interact with the world around us and how those can become misaligned in complex situations.

While this concept also acknowledges the persistent nature of complexity, it focuses more on individual responses and mindsets rather than broader historical and contextual perspectives.

In his concept of "escaping the boxes of the past," Bob Johansen discusses stepping outside our existing mental models or frameworks to tackle future challenges and complexities better. His approach suggests that existing models constrain our ability to navigate future complexities effectively.

While all these concepts share a common theme of dealing with complexity, my concept of "overcoming Complexity Amnesia" emphasizes understanding complexity's historical and contextual nature. It suggests that acknowledging and learning from the complexities of the past, relative to their time, can better prepare us for the complexities of the present and future. This perspective is more about a holistic understanding of the historical evolution of complexity and its constant presence in human life, which differs from the individual cognitive focus of Garvey-Berger's Mindtraps or Johansen's notion of escaping past models, and yet, in the "Yes, and..." world we live in, all three are relevant and worthy of your consideration. The three perspectives are complementary, providing the bigger picture by opening the aperture of our cognitive process.

David Eagleman, a neuroscientist, and the host of the PBS series The Brain, proposed in September 2021 in an episode of *Think Fast, Talk Smart* (Stanford Business) that our brains are wired for storytelling and how new senses might impact our connection and communication with others. In order to build strategic capacity and operate in complexity, we need to be comfortable thinking in abstracts to craft plausible scenarios by combining data science and system interpretation of the data. Strategy is part art and part science; when combined, you get a higher level of creativity. We need to be able to craft metaphors as means to invite others to think with us in order to break through the hardwiring of our brains that play to our fears instead of appealing to our curiosity, hopes, and creativity. While our brains are indeed hardwired to sense fear as a mechanism to respond to danger, there is something that our brains like more than fear: stories that are meaningful and saliently relevant to the context in which we operate. There is much truth in the contention in Bolman and Deal's book *Reframing Organizations* that leadership is effective when leaders are prophets and poets in the symbolic frame of organizations, and the leadership process is one of inspiration and meaning-making. In contrast, leadership is ineffective when the leaders are fanatics and charlatans, and the leadership process is one mirage and smoke & mirrors. **Linear thinking is arguably the birthplace of mirages and smoke & mirrors.**

Yet, often, we get allured by linear thinking. I directly connect linear thinking and "Ulysses and the Sirens," a famous episode from Homer's epic poem, "The Odyssey." In this part of the story, Ulysses (also known as Odysseus) and his men must navigate past the Sirens, mythical creatures who lured sailors to their death with enchanting music and voices. That is the detriment of linear thinking in complexity. Like the music of the Sirens, linear thinking is alluring and seductive, yet it can make our organizations crush onto the reefs where the Sirens are standing.

In The Odyssey, forewarned by the witch-goddess Circe, Ulysses devises a plan to save himself and his crew. He orders his men to plug their ears with beeswax so they cannot hear the Sirens' songs. However, curious to hear the Sirens' song, Ulysses has his men tie him to the mast of the ship. He orders them not to release him under any circumstances, even if he pleads and commands them to do so.

As they pass the Sirens, Ulysses hears their song and is driven nearly mad with the desire to go to them but cannot break the bonds. His men, their ears plugged with wax, cannot hear his orders to be set free and continue to row past the island of the Sirens. This story is often used as a metaphor in literature and philosophy, symbolizing the struggle between reason and emotion or the battle against destructive temptations. It can be interpreted in various ways in the context of personal discipline, resolve, and the power of foresight in overcoming challenges.

When we place the story in the **context of complexity**, its relevance is salient. The sirens represent the attractive but potentially disastrous distractions that can emerge from the complexities in our personal or professional lives. Their enchanting song can be viewed as the "noise" that often comes with complexity - the overwhelming amount of information and choices that can lead us astray if we aren't careful.

Ulysses' approach to the situation illustrates a method for handling complexity. He knew he would be susceptible to the sirens' call (distractions), so he planned, setting up safeguards (beeswax for his men's ears, being bound to the mast) to ensure he would stay on course. These aspects represent the importance of strategy, foresight, and implementing preventative measures when dealing with complex situations vs. merely attempting to apply irrelevant past experiences.

For several years, I taught an undergrad course at California State University San Bernardino - *Palm Desert Campus* (CSUSB-PD) titled Business and Society: Stakeholders, Ethics, and Public Policy. One example of an organization that suffered the consequences of Complexity Amnesia can be found in one of the case studies I assigned to my students. The British Petroleum (BP) oil spill incident, called the Deepwater Horizon oil spill, occurred in the Gulf of Mexico in 2010.

This disaster is considered one of the largest marine oil spills in history. It resulted from a blowout on the Deepwater Horizon offshore oil drilling rig, operated by Transocean under contract for BP, leading to an explosion that killed 11 workers and injured 17 others. The subsequent oil spill continued for 87 days until the well was capped, spilling an estimated 4.9 million barrels of crude oil into the Gulf of Mexico. The incident caused extensive damage to marine and wildlife habitats and the Gulf's fishing and tourism industries.

However, prior to Deepwater Horizon, BP had a solid reputation and was known for sound decisions in areas of safety and business expansion and acquisitions since their formation in 1908 as the Anglo-Persian Oil Company, which was an impressive feat of engineering and negotiation, culminating in the discovery of oil in Iran and the signing of an exclusive agreement with the Persian government. The company, later renamed Anglo-Iranian Oil Company and then British Petroleum, became one of the world's leading oil companies through several expansions and acquisitions. I don't claim that BP had a spotless record. However, BP has a long history of interest in alternative energy. In 1981, it established BP Solar, one of the first major oil companies to publicly acknowledge the threat of climate change, in a speech by the CEO at Stanford University in 1997. Prior to the Deepwater Horizon incident, BP had a generally strong reputation for safety and environmental responsibility. This was reflected in initiatives such as the "Beyond Petroleum" rebranding in 2000, where BP attempted to position itself as an environmentally friendly energy company. However, make no mistake, the signs of BP's Complexity Amnesia were already evident in the BP Texas City Refinery disaster in 2005, where 15 people lost their lives and nearly 200 were injured, in what Andrew Hopkins defined as the worst industrial disaster the US in more than a decade in the book Failure to Learn. The federal regulator, the Occupational Safety and Health Administration (OSHA), fined BP $21 million, which at that time was the largest fine ever imposed. This event occurred a mere five years prior to the Deepwater Horizon catastrophe.

Complexity Amnesia is evident in BP's approach leading up to the Deepwater Horizon disaster. Like many other organizations, BP seemed to view its operation linearly: drill for oil, extract it, refine it, and sell it. This simplistic view failed to consider the complex, interconnected system in which BP was operating, one that included not just drilling operations but also considerations around safety regulations, equipment integrity, environmental factors, human factors, stakeholder relations, and even geopolitical influences.

In the lead-up to the disaster, BP made a series of decisions that were later criticized for prioritizing cost savings and time efficiency over safety. For example, BP chose to use a type of casing for the well that was quicker to install but carried a higher risk of gas leaks. Also, despite concerns from some of their engineers, BP used fewer stabilizing devices than recommended. These decisions and others point to Complexity Amnesia, a failure to fully grasp the potential for unforeseen consequences in the complex system they were operating within.

In the aftermath of the spill, it became clear that BP had not adequately planned for such a disaster. Their response efforts were seen as slow and inadequate, and they struggled to coordinate with local, state, and federal authorities effectively. This underlined their failure to appreciate the full complexity of their operations and the potential ripple effects of a major disaster. The Deepwater Horizon disaster resulted in severe financial, reputational, and environmental consequences for BP. It is estimated that the incident cost BP more than $65 billion in clean-up costs, fines, and compensation to affected parties.

Overall, the BP Deepwater Horizon disaster serves as a sobering reminder of the potential consequences when organizations suffer from Complexity Amnesia, failing to fully appreciate and plan for the complexities and potential risks inherent in their operations and their history as an organization. Those sound decisions made since their inception in 1908 when navigating the inherent complexity of that time should have been retained in BP's modus operandi rather than been forgotten or viewed as impediments of the present.

In contrast, we can find an example of an organization that did not suffer from Complexity Amnesia in another case study I used in the same class. The Tylenol crisis in 1982 is often held up as a classic example of excellent crisis management, demonstrating how Johnson & Johnson (J&J) adhered to its core values, thus avoiding "Complexity Amnesia." Yes, J&J and Neutrogena were clients of my consumer product strategy practice, and I loved working with them, but I provide this example objectively. You'd be the judge.

In 1982, seven people in the Chicago area died after taking cyanide-laced Tylenol capsules. Panic ensued, as nobody knew whether the contamination was widespread or who was responsible. Under the leadership of CEO James Burke, Johnson & Johnson's response was swift, comprehensive, and guided by its company credo, which states that its first responsibility is to the consumers and patients it serves.

Even though Tylenol was J&J's best-selling product at the time, and even though a malicious third party clearly caused the contamination after the product had left J&J's control, the company immediately recalled all 31 million bottles of Tylenol capsules on the market—a move that cost the company over $100 million.

J&J also worked closely with law enforcement agencies to help catch the perpetrator (who was never found), kept the public informed through regular press conferences, and offered a $100,000 reward for information leading to the perpetrator's arrest. Following the incident, J&J introduced tamper-evident packaging and pushed for stricter federal regulations on over-the-counter product tampering.

This action is often seen as a textbook case of managing a complex crisis well, with J&J prioritizing public safety over short-term profit, and it helped to restore public trust in the company and its products. An exemplary avoidance of Complexity Amnesia. The brand Tylenol rebounded and continues to be a market leader, demonstrating how J&J's decision-making framework, guided by its core values and long-term thinking, helped the company successfully navigate this complex situation.

To overcome Complexity Amnesia, we must accept that we will never have the full picture when operating in complexity. Martin Luther King Jr. said, "Faith is taking the first step even when you don't see the whole staircase." This quote often encapsulates his philosophy of having faith in oneself and the courage to take the first step towards change, even if the entire path or outcome is not immediately clear.

We will never have the full picture, but we can have a bigger picture. The answer to our journey in complexity is not 42 as the answer provided by supercomputer Deep Thought in Douglas Adams' science fiction novel, "The Hitchhiker's Guide to the Galaxy." In our context, it implies that no simple, straightforward answer or guide to leading in complexity exists.

THINKING POINT

Section Takeaways

Complexity is not a new concept; it's been a persistent part of human history, but its characteristics and dynamics have evolved. Linear thinking is insufficient when complex; we need more sophisticated methods to address contextual obstacles and understand system dynamics.

Complexity Amnesia refers to the tendency to view complexity as a modern phenomenon, overlooking the historical prevalence of complexity, often due to presentism. Significant historical achievements like the construction of the Great Pyramids, the establishment of ancient trade routes, and the organization of the first Olympic Games demonstrate that dealing with complexity is not exclusive to the modern era.

Presentism can distort our understanding of past complexities, and it's crucial to appreciate past complexities in their context to learn effectively from them. It's important to avoid being entrapped by linear thinking when navigating complex situations. Overcoming Complexity Amnesia requires acknowledging past complexities and using their insights to navigate current and future complexities effectively.

Reflective Questions

Can you think of a time when you fell into the trap of Complexity Amnesia, viewing a complex situation as a novel phenomenon instead of understanding it as part of a historical continuum?

Reflect on a situation where linear thinking led you to oversimplify a complex issue. What lessons did you learn, and how might you approach a similar situation differently?

Contextualization Prompt

Consider your current professional landscape. Identify one area of complexity that you are navigating. How might acknowledging and learning from the complexities of the past help you address this challenge more effectively? Try to avoid the pitfalls of presentism and linear thinking, instead seeking to understand the issue in its unique context and developing a strategy that embraces the inherent complexity.

CHAPTER 2

GAINING CLARITY IN COMPLEXITY

*"The mind is everything. The genius is the one who takes it
to another level, and it's always the head that took them there."*
— Sir Jackie Stuart Three-time FIA Formula 1® World Champion

Complexity is CADE

Organizations that are successful in sustaining their mission can contextualize complexity and operate in it rather than attempting to respond to the entirety of the complex environment. While this book provides insights, concepts, and methods to approach and manage complexity, it's important to note that it is not a 'one-size-fits-all' rulebook or a 'magic step-by-step guide' to solve all your problems. Instead, we will look at frameworks as lenses to open the aperture and reframe complexity. We will never have the full picture, but we will have a bigger picture. Teaching has always been a companion in my professional career. At age 26, I got my first teaching assignment at Otis College of Art and Design. I would ask my students, "Who does photography?" Occasionally, a few hands would go up in the air. I would then leverage their experience to explain how we can see an object or scenery from a different perspective by moving the camera and then relate it to diverging perspectives regarding design philosophies or other socio-economic issues relevant to the design and manufacturing of new products. Today, we are all photographers because we have a smartphone in our pockets and can readily understand the analogy.

In my assessment, we should consider the unique nature of each situation and the individual or organization facing it. Therefore, I do not aim to dictate a rigid approach but to offer a framework for understanding and addressing complexity. It encourages a mindset of adaptability, resilience, and innovation, promoting continual learning, unlearning, and relearning in the face of ever-evolving circumstances. It is about embracing complexity's, contextualizable, amorphous, dynamic and elastic nature, which I have encapsulated in the CADE model. Often revelations come from "doing while thinking." In more recent years, especially as we were all experiencing the dynamics of the pandemic, I became fascinated with defining Complexity, a word I have used for almost two decades. Still, I never felt there was a definition that was also actionable.

The Future of Jobs Survey 2023, a report by the World Economic Forum, presents the view of 803 companies across 27 industries and 45 economies regarding future job trends, technology adoption, and workforce transformation strategies across the 2023-2027 timeframe. The survey finds diverging labor market outcomes globally due to economic, health, and geopolitical trends. High-income countries experience tight labor markets, while low- and lower-middle-income countries face high unemployment levels. Technology adoption and broadening digital access are the primary drivers of business transformation in the next five years. Companies anticipate significant labor market churn, predicting a net decrease of 14 million jobs due to new jobs and job displacement. The report finds that a new array of skills in the workforce is needed, but while six out of ten workers will require training, today, only half have access to adequate training opportunities. This short synopsis of a report that I would recommend reading in its entirety (see Bibliography) indicates complexity's, contextualizable, amorphous dynamic, and elastic nature.

You may be familiar with VUCA, an acronym for Volatility, Uncertainty, Complexity, and Ambiguity. It originated from the U.S. military to describe the more volatile, uncertain, complex, and ambiguous world following the end of the Cold War. The U.S. Army War College introduced the concept of VUCA in 1987, based on the leadership theories of Warren Bennis and Burt Nanus, to describe the multilateral world that emerged after the Cold War, a world characterized by rapidly changing conditions and high levels of uncertainty. Since then, the term has been adopted and expanded upon in various fields, especially in business and strategic leadership contexts, to describe the challenging and unpredictable conditions that organizations and leaders often must navigate in the modern global environment.

Warren Bennis and Burt Nanus were influential leadership scholars, and while their work doesn't directly coin the term VUCA, it certainly touches on similar themes. They emphasize the ability of leaders to navigate uncertainty, adapt to change, and guide their organizations through complex situations, all of which resonate with the ideas embodied in the VUCA concept.

One of their most well-known works is "Leaders: The Strategies for Taking Charge" (1985). In this book, they present a model of leadership based on four strategies: attention through vision, meaning through communication, trust through positioning, and the deployment of self through (positive) self-regard. These strategies could be interpreted as an approach to dealing with a VUCA environment, even though the term hadn't been coined yet.

The acronym VUCA is helpful in defining what I would call the Uber Dimension, but I often wondered what part of the acronym is actionable. In recent years I have removed from my vocabulary the expression "It is what it is" and embraced **"It Is."** The phrase "it is what it is" conveys a sense of resignation, suggesting that the situation is immutable, and one must simply accept it. It's a perspective that can encourage passivity and limit our capacity to envision alternative paths.

In contrast, the phrase "it is" acknowledges the reality of the situation but doesn't impose any judgments or conclusions about it. It encourages acceptance of the present moment as *it is* without denying the potential for change or action. This shift can promote a more proactive approach, highlighting personal agency and the ability to influence outcomes. Volatility, Uncertainty, Complexity, and Ambiguity belong in the "It Is." Furthermore, the Complexity part of the acronym captures my attention as I deem it actionable. This shift is another essential aspect in developing an *Inception Mindset*.

By defining the nature of complexity through an actionable framework, we can conceptualize methodologies and lenses through which we can build strategic capacity in our organizations. While I did take a stab at defining the Uber Dimension through an actionable framework, I ultimately realized that the key to an actionable conceptual or theoretical framework resided in refocusing my efforts to develop lenses to understand Complexity and support the organizations I serve in operating in their contextual complexity. Through my research and many less-than-satisfactory whiteboard attempts, I concluded that **Complexity is CADE**:

Contextualizable: This term underscores the profound influence of surrounding conditions or environment on understanding and interpreting complexity. It emphasizes that there is no 'one-size-fits-all' approach to dealing with complexity, thus reinforcing my assertion that we must contextualize complexity.

Amorphous: This term reinforces the notion that complex systems continually evolve and lack a definitive shape or form. It underscores the unpredictable and emergent nature of complexity. Love jigsaw puzzles? Well, complexity is like a jigsaw puzzle, with the distinction that there's no box displaying the final product's image, and the pieces do not interlock perfectly because they are not cut out from the same image. Yet, they somehow fit together. In this sense, yes, complexity is just like a jigsaw puzzle.

Dynamic: This term emphasizes the non-static, ever-changing nature of complex systems. It acknowledges that complexity involves multiple variables interacting over time, often in a non-linear fashion. The most significant fallacy we can introduce in our organizations and communities is the attempt to address complexity with linear thinking. Simplistic approaches such as "stop this, start that!" or "It's either this or that!" are akin to taking cyanide to cure a headache. Yes, the headache would cease and never be experienced again, but at what cost?

Elastic: This term stresses the inherent resilience and adaptability of complex systems. It suggests that such systems can stretch and adapt in response to changes and then revert or evolve when conditions permit. Notably, these systems often consist of individuals or groups of people. In many ways, the system's adaptability reflects the individuals' abilities to adapt.

The **CADE acronym** provides a richer, more nuanced depiction of complexity that acknowledges its dynamic, adaptable, context-dependent, and unpredictable characteristics. The four lenses, Contextualizable, Amorphous, Dynamic and Elastic, are not sequential. Instead, the four are superimposed to produce the final image. This means we cannot choose which lens to acknowledge and which to ignore, as CADE is a compounded effect. Using this definition, I underscore the need for a flexible and responsive approach to navigating complexity in leadership, organizational dynamics, or beyond. In essence, CADE outlines the need for flexibility, adaptability, and contextual understanding when dealing with complexity. Ultimately, in complexity, there is no "we have always done it this way" because we don't get to do it long enough even to consider saying that. By adopting an *Inception Mindset* and leveraging CADE as a compounded lens, we **gain clarity in complexity**.

If we fail to gain clarity, we will approach complexity as something to solve linearly and because it needs to be solved within a set of artificial parameters. We will devise the most complicated methodologies we can consciously or unconsciously conceptualize. We must avoid complicating complexity by approaching it with a set of cognitive lenses allowing us to build strategic capacity in our organizations.

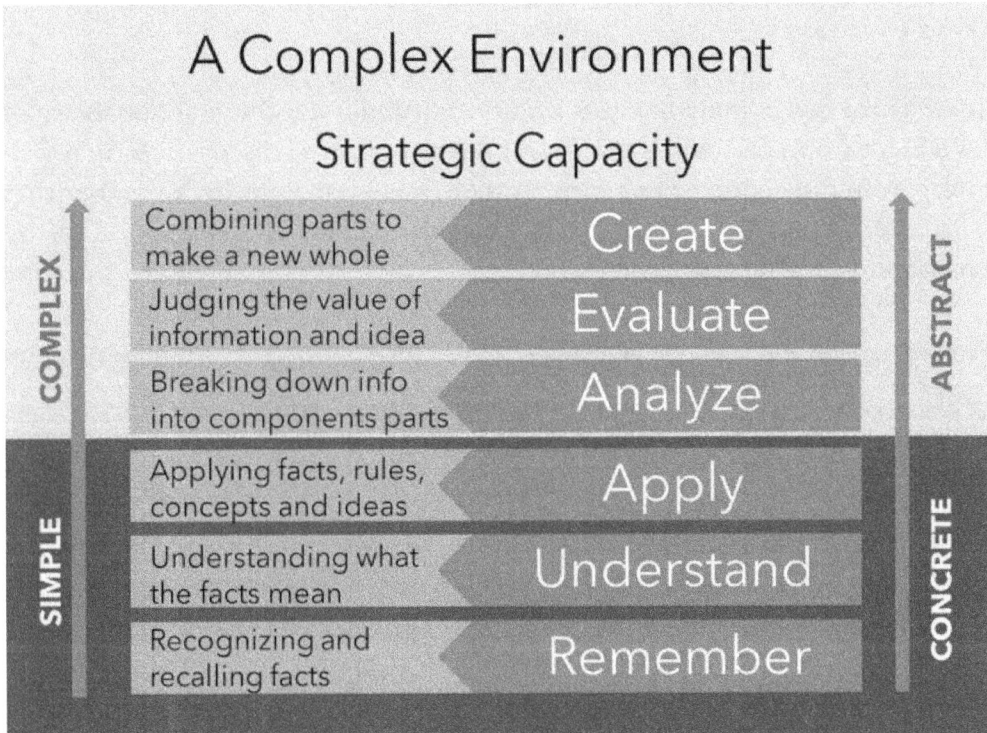

Image 1. Adapted from the Bloom Cognitive Taxonomy. © Integral Advantage®

Our ability to think in complexity and build strategic capacity resided in our ability to think in abstracts and approach complexity with curiosity, allowing nodes and data points to emerge through appreciative inquiry (See **Image 1**). This approach is optimal to avoid feeling overwhelmed when faced with complex systems, as gaining clarity can lead to a better, clear, and elegant strategic solution.

We need to analyze without paralyzing ourselves. We need to evaluate without complicating it, and ultimately, we must create new approaches to address complex issues in the context in which we operate. Indeed, those approaches may be elegant in their simplicity. In Chapters 8 and 9, we will explore the Entrusted Empowerment framework, which provides an example of an elegant and clear approach to a complex topic without complicating it. It is not about making the complex simple, it is about elegantly addressing the critical issues that are part of the complex system without being seduced by the simplistic answer we may find when we address the symptoms of the issues rather than the critical issue itself. Symptoms of a critical issue are comparable to the alluring singing voices of the Sirens faced by Ulysses.

To enhance our cognitive lenses and better understand the actionability of CADE, let's operationalize each component and then discuss how they can interplay in the context of an organization. It is important to remember that while we discuss them individually, they don't occur in isolation, and the compounding effect is non-linear.

THINKING POINT

Section Takeaways
CADE is a model encapsulating the contextualizable, amorphous, dynamic, elastic nature of complexity. It provides a framework for understanding and addressing complexity, promoting a mindset of inception, adaptability, resilience, and innovation.

The terms within CADE represent important aspects of complexity: Contextualizable stresses the influence of surrounding conditions; Amorphous underscores the unpredictable and evolving nature of complexity. Dynamic indicates the ever-changing nature of complex systems; Elastic signifies the inherent resilience and adaptability of such systems.

CADE offers a richer understanding of complexity that differs from the VUCA model (Volatility, Uncertainty, Complexity, Ambiguity) as CADE provides an actionable framework in one of the components of VUCA, the C for complexity. CADE is not sequential, and its components do not occur in isolation. The interplay of the elements is non-linear, forming a compounded effect.

Reflective Questions

How have you previously perceived complexity, and how does the CADE model alter this perspective?

Can you recall a situation where a simplistic or linear approach to a complex problem was ineffective? How would the CADE model have guided a different course of action?

Contextualization Prompt

Consider a complex challenge or situation currently present in your professional environment. Analyze this situation through the CADE lens. Identify how it is Contextualizable, Amorphous, Dynamic and Elastic. How can this deeper understanding of its complexity guide your strategy to manage and navigate this situation more effectively?

The C in CADE: Complexity is Contextualizable

As mentioned, the term contextualizable underscores the profound influence of surrounding conditions on understanding and interpreting complexity. In terms of leadership and organization, this could involve recognizing the unique influences, both internal and external, that impact their mission and operations. It's about understanding the demographic, economic, social, political, and technological factors affecting the industry and the organization itself.

The effects of trends highlighted in the Future of Jobs Report 2023, released by the World Economic Forum, and addressing the 2023-2027 timeframe, vary significantly across different sectors and countries. The report emphasizes that there is no 'one-size-fits-all' approach to address these changes. Each sector and country need to contextualize these trends, taking into consideration its unique labor market characteristics, technological readiness, and socio-economic conditions. For instance, high-income countries are dealing with tight labor markets, while low- and lower-middle-income countries are grappling with high unemployment levels.

Bearing this importance in mind, I have developed a dynamic and comprehensive framework - the **Core-Tangential-Peripheral (CTP) Awareness framework**. Inspired by the fluidity and interconnectedness reflected in the concept of Flow, the CTP model aids organizations and individuals in making sense of and navigating through the labyrinth of complexities inherent in their ever-shifting environment. The concept of Flow, proposed by Mihaly Csikszentmihalyi, a Hungarian-American psychologist, is relevant to the optimal experience when operating in complexity, as its tenet of the flow channel when skills and task are aligned is augmented by the CTP Awareness framework. The CTP Awareness framework helps us focus on those aspects that are tangibly relevant – the Core Awareness - without losing sight of those elements that may become relevant – Tangential and Peripheral Awareness, thus enabling us to contextualize the complexity of the context in which we operate.

The CTP Awareness framework comprises three concentric ellipsoids, each representing a distinct but interconnected sphere of awareness: Core Awareness, Tangential Awareness, and Peripheral Awareness (refer to **Image 1A**). The interplay among these spheres is designed to guide organizations and individuals through the labyrinth of complexities inherent in the rapidly changing world. This model proposes an active engagement with immediate concerns, a vigilant understanding of related factors that might pose significant implications, and an anticipatory observation of distant trends that could be disruptive or opportunistic.

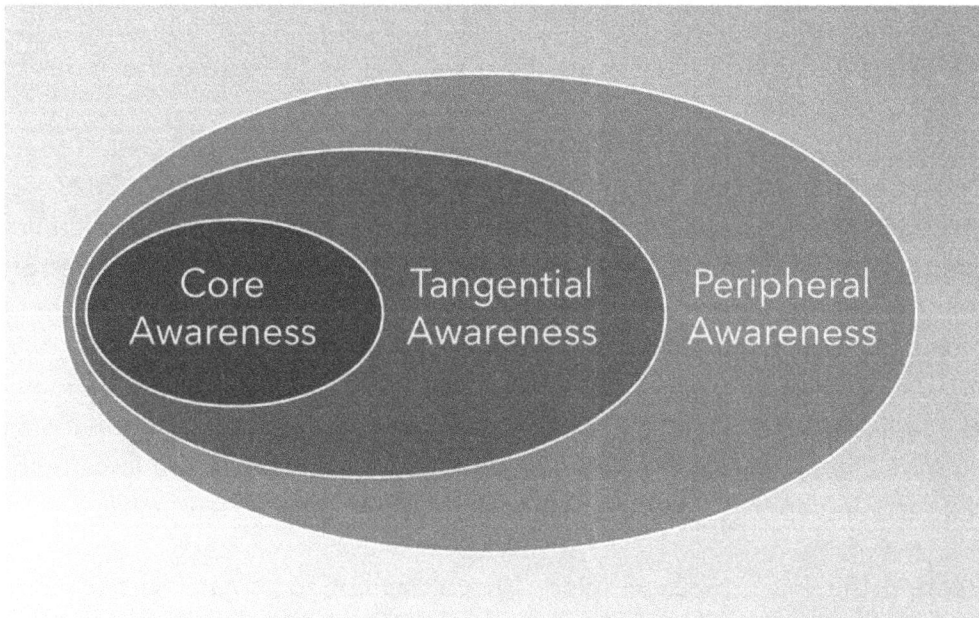

Image 1A. The CTP Awareness framework (Radi, 2022 - 2023) © Integral Advantage®

The Core-Tangential-Peripheral (CTP) Awareness framework is a strategic approach that balances focus and broad vision, ensuring organizations stay ahead of the curve by continually updating their understanding of the evolving environment. It provides the essential scaffolding for building agility and resilience, equipping entities to not only survive but thrive amidst uncertainty and complexity.

Core Awareness: This is the inner ellipsoid, the kernel of the framework I am proposing. It represents the issues and aspects of the environment that are most immediately relevant and pressing to an organization or individual. This includes the complexity of core business activities, main competitors, and key market trends. It's essentially what one needs to focus on daily. These are the factors allowing you to be a high performer. It embodies the immediate context within which an organization operates, underlining the idea that complexity is not an abstract concept but directly tied to the daily realities and challenges an organization faces.

Tangential Awareness: This is the second ellipsoid surrounding Core Awareness. It represents aspects of the environment that are not directly related to the immediate complexity of operations of the organization or individual but which can still have significant implications. These could include broader industry trends, peripheral competitors, societal changes, or emerging technologies. While not the primary focus, these elements are important to track and understand as they can eventually transition into Core Awareness without much warning. It symbolizes the related context that might not be immediately connected to an organization's operations, showing that complexity often extends beyond an organization's immediate environment and can be influenced by seemingly unrelated factors.

Peripheral Awareness: This is the third ellipsoid, encompassing both Core and Tangential Awareness. It represents the broadest view of the environment, including global trends, distant markets, unfamiliar industries, and so on. While these factors might seem far removed from the immediate concerns of the organization or individual, they represent potential sources of disruption or opportunity. These are also latent aspects or trends currently hidden or not obvious but could rise in importance with environmental or context shifts. This level requires a degree of foresight and anticipation to identify. They are areas to keep an eye on but not necessarily actively engaged with unless they start moving toward Tangential or Core Awareness. It signifies the broader, global context, illustrating the point that complexity is not confined to an organization's immediate and related environment but also extends to the wider world. This emphasizes the importance of anticipating and preparing for potential sources of disruption or opportunity.

The A in CADE: Complexity is Amorphous

Consider the ongoing evolution of the automobile industry. Once dominated by gasoline-powered vehicles, the industry is amid a shift towards sustainable and electric technologies. This change is not yet fully codified or universally accepted, reflecting the 'Amorphous' characteristic in the CADE model.

Similarly, personalized medicine, driven by advancements in genomics and bioinformatics, is transforming the healthcare landscape. This shift from a one-size-fits-all approach to individually tailored treatments based on unique genetic makeup and lifestyle factors is another instance of amorphous complexity. Ethical, social, and policy questions surrounding the use of personal genetic information add further layers of complexity and uncertainty.

Lastly, consider the profound impact of emerging technologies, such as artificial intelligence, augmented reality, and various social media platforms, on society. These technologies continually reshape interactions and influence politics, personal relationships, mental health, and culture in unforeseen ways. As new platforms emerge and user behavior changes, the "shape" of this social-technological system persistently shifts.

The amorphous nature of job markets is evident in the variety of emerging roles as presented in the Future of Jobs Report 2023, released by the World Economic Forum, and addressing the 2023-2027 timeframe. The top three roles expected to rise in demand include Data Analysts and Scientists, AI and Machine Learning Specialists, and Big Data Specialists. This illustrates the unpredictable and emergent nature of complexity in job markets, evolving in ways that may not have been anticipated a few years ago. Furthermore, the report's prediction that 40% of workers will require reskilling of six months or less and 94% of business leaders expect employees to pick up new skills on the job underscores the continuously evolving requirements in the labor market.

In the current debate regarding AI, the focus is often placed on the jobs that AI will destroy, but rarely do we talk about the value AI can assist us in creating. Is AI replacing work that was being done or opening the opportunity to address work that needed to be done but wasn't getting done?

In these "Amorphous" situations, widely varying perspectives can lead to polarization because of the absence of a consensus or standard. Understanding this aspect of complexity can help organizations or individuals navigate these issues more effectively. They can foster flexibility, promote open dialogue, and learn from differing viewpoints while acknowledging the absence of a clear or established path forward.

Organizations need to nurture an *Inception Mindset* to operationalize the "Amorphous" aspect of the CADE model. This mindset includes promoting curiosity, adaptability, and lifelong learning, coupled with the understanding that change is a constant. Staying informed about emerging trends, technologies, and societal changes can help organizations anticipate shifts and respond proactively and effectively.

THINKING POINT

Section Takeaways
Understanding and interpreting complexity requires contextualization, considering unique internal and external influences impacting an organization's operations and mission.

The Future of Jobs Report 2023 underscores the varying effects of trends across different sectors and countries, emphasizing the need for contextualization.

The Core-Tangential-Peripheral (CTP) Awareness framework, inspired by the concept of Flow, aids in navigating through complexities by focusing on aspects relevant now (Core Awareness) and those that may become relevant (Tangential and Peripheral Awareness).

Complexity is amorphous, constantly shifting and evolving, as seen in industries like automobile, healthcare, technology, and job markets. An *Inception Mindset* is vital to navigating these amorphous complexities.

Reflective Questions

How do you currently contextualize complexity in your organization or leadership role? Can you identify Core, Tangential, and Peripheral Awareness elements in your current strategy?

How do you perceive the amorphous nature of complexity? Can you identify examples in your field or sector? What steps can you take to foster an *Inception Mindset* within your organization to navigate amorphous complexity better?

Contextualization Prompt

Consider the changing trends in your industry. How can the CTP framework help you better understand and respond to these shifts? Consider how the three levels of awareness (Core, Tangential, and Peripheral) might look in your specific context. Reflect on the amorphous nature of complexity in your industry, job market, or organizational culture.

How can fostering an *Inception Mindset* help you navigate these ever-changing landscapes? Use these reflections to draft a strategy or proposal that accounts for both complexity's contextualizable and amorphous nature.

The D in CADE: Complexity is Dynamic

The dynamic nature of complexity means that it's ever-changing and often yields unpredictable outcomes. This dynamism comes from the countless interactions between numerous elements of complex systems, and it's accentuated by the non-linearity of these interactions. Understanding this aspect of complexity is crucial for the success of organizations, particularly in the current era of rapid change.

The Future of Jobs Report 2023, released by the World Economic Forum and addressing the 2023-2027 timeframe, shows that the job market is non-static and ever-changing. Several variables, including technological advancements, economic growth, supply shortages, and the need for sustainable practices, interact over time and shape the labor market. This interaction is not linear, with technology both creating and displacing jobs. The challenge lies in shifting from simplistic approaches to strategies that acknowledge and address the multi-dimensional nature of labor market changes.

One clear example of this dynamism is the rise of digital transformation in business. Organizations are forced to adapt to rapidly changing technology, customer expectations, and a shifting competitive landscape. The change is not just incremental; it often involves radical shifts in business models, operational processes, and customer interactions.

Top 10 skills on the rise	
Creative Thinking Type of skill: cognitive skill	**Systems Thinking** Type of skill: cognitive skill
Analytical Thinking Type of skill: cognitive skill	**AI and Big Data** Type of skill: technology skill
Technological Literacy Type of skill: technology skill	**Motivation and Self-Awareness** Type of skill: self-efficacy
Curiosity and Lifelong Learning Type of skill: self-efficacy	**Talent Management** Type of skill: management skill
Resilience, Flexibility, and Agility Type of skill: self-efficacy	**Service Orientation and Customer Service** Type of skill: engagement skill
Note: The skills judged to be increasing in importance most rapidly between 2023 and 2027	

Table 1. Source: World Economic Forum, Future of Jobs Report 2023.

Take, for example, the growing phenomenon of artificial intelligence (AI) and big data, a skill rapidly increasing in organizations' desirability among their workforces. See Table 1 for additional information on the "Top 10 skills on the rise," and predicted to be increasing in importance most rapidly between 2023 and 2027.

One clear example of this dynamism is the rise of digital transformation in business. Organizations are being forced to adapt to rapidly changing technology, changing customer expectations, and a shifting competitive landscape. The change is not just incremental; it often involves radical shifts in business models, operational processes, and customer interactions.

Additionally, consider how the rise of e-commerce has disrupted traditional retail. The rapid growth of online shopping platforms like Amazon or Alibaba has forced many brick-and-mortar retailers to fundamentally restructure their business models, including investing in digital platforms, restructuring supply chains, and overhauling customer service processes. It is not a simple "stop this, start that" approach but a multi-dimensional, ongoing process of adaptation to a continuously evolving landscape. Yet, giants like Amazon are not insulated from the very dynamics they have enjoyed, as the terrain is still shifting as demand and consumption is also evolving.

Unfortunately, many issues in communities around the world are approached with linear thinking, especially in cities and municipalities' local governments. The vocal few holding on to the past derail the future for the many. The "We have always done it this way" or "If it isn't broken, don't fix it" mantras are prime examples of the inability to recognize the dynamic nature of complexity. When multiple stakeholders are at play, the linear solution is a non-starter. The rise of short-term vacation rental platforms like Airbnb and VRBO has revolutionized the hospitality industry and brought significant economic, social, and environmental impacts to destination communities across the United States. However, due to the dynamic complexity of the issue, the solution is not as simple as allowing or prohibiting the practice.

Addressing these issues necessitates an understanding of the dynamic complexity involved. The multifaceted interactions between local economies, housing markets, tourism trends, and community well-being make a one-size-fits-all solution untenable. Simply banning these platforms could curtail economic opportunities and limit tourism growth, while unrestricted operations could exacerbate housing shortages and community disruptions.

In a dynamically complex system like this, every action can lead to ripple effects that create new patterns and challenges over time. Therefore, the solution lies in an adaptive, balanced approach that considers each community's distinct needs and contexts. Policymakers must engage with diverse stakeholders, including property owners, residents, businesses, and the platform's solutions that balance economic growth with community well-being and housing affordability.

Regulatory strategies could include licensing systems, taxes, and restrictions on the number of rental days or the type of properties that can be rented. However, these strategies must be regularly reassessed and adjusted based on changing conditions and impacts.

Another example can be found in the media industry, where the rise of streaming services has led to a significant shift in how content is produced, distributed, and consumed. Have you noticed in recent times the amount of content produced in South Korea that is available on Netflix? This shift has resulted in significant changes to business models, including moving to subscription models and developing original content. These changes have upended the traditional media landscape and created a new dynamic of competition and collaboration.

To operationalize the "Dynamic" aspect of the CADE model, leaders must foster an *Inception Mindset* and encourage their organizations to be learning-oriented. This involves embracing change as a constant, being willing to experiment and learn from failures, and continuously seeking to understand and adapt to the changing environment.

Moreover, leaders must move away from binary thinking and instead adopt a more holistic perspective that considers the multiple dimensions and interdependencies inherent in complex systems. This requires skills such as systems thinking, which involves understanding the relationships and interactions between parts of a system, and scenario planning, which involves anticipating different future states and planning for them.

By understanding and embracing the dynamic nature of complexity, organizations can be better equipped to navigate and thrive in today's fast-paced, uncertain world.

THINKING POINT

Section Takeaways

Dynamic complexity involves ever-changing, often unpredictable outcomes. This dynamism results from numerous interactions between elements of complex systems.

The job market is non-static and dynamic, influenced by variables like technological advancements, economic growth, supply shortages, and sustainable practices.

Organizational adaptation to changing technology, customer expectations, and a competitive landscape is a clear example of dynamic complexity.

Recognizing and addressing dynamic complexity is crucial for policymakers when regulating industries, like the hospitality sector, affected by platforms like Airbnb and VRBO.

Leaders must foster an *Inception Mindset* and learning orientation within their organizations to embrace the new elements of dynamic complexity.

Reflective Questions

How has your organization adapted to the dynamic nature of complexity, particularly in terms of technology and market changes?

Can you implement any strategies to better navigate dynamic complexity within your industry or field?

How can leaders within your organization foster an *Inception Mindset* to navigate dynamic complexity effectively?

Contextualization Prompt

Consider an industry or field you are familiar with. How has it shown signs of dynamic complexity in recent years? Reflect on the changes that have taken place and the adaptability required by individuals and organizations within that field.

The E in CADE: Complexity is Elastic

The idea of elasticity in complexity refers to the inherent resilience and adaptability of complex systems. It indicates the ability of these systems to stretch and adjust in response to changes and then revert or evolve when conditions allow. This elasticity is often reflected in the adaptability of individuals or groups within these systems.

Consider the way companies adapt to economic downturns as an example of this elasticity. During a recession or industry shift, businesses often must make tough decisions to survive, including cost-cutting measures, strategic pivots, or workforce restructuring. However, when economic conditions improve, these same companies may be able to rebound and even expand. For instance, during the 2008 economic crisis, many companies reduced their workforce and cut costs, but as conditions improved, they regained their footing and even grew.

A more recent example can be seen in how companies have adjusted to remote work due to the COVID-19 pandemic. Pre-pandemic, remote work was relatively uncommon in many industries. However, many businesses quickly adapted to the pandemic conditions required, leveraging digital tools and platforms to enable remote work. Despite the challenges, the shift to remote work has also led to several benefits, including cost savings, increased flexibility, and improved work-life balance for employees. At the time of this writing, the new work model emerging from the pandemic has not yet been codified, and the elastic tension between the various potential models, from hybrid work, going back to the office, to full remote work, is in full play. Whatever emerges will likely be contextual to individual organizations, and most certainly, it will not be "going back to what things were."

The elasticity or resilience of the job market is underscored by the Future of Jobs Report 2023, released by the World Economic Forum, and addressing the 2023-2027 timeframe, which finds that the "jobs of tomorrow" are increasing their share in the overall job opportunities from 7.8% to 8.1%. Despite significant displacement, the market shows an ability to create new roles and opportunities, reflecting the inherent elasticity of complexity.

Schools and universities have demonstrated elasticity in the education sector by transitioning from traditional in-person teaching to online or hybrid models in response to the pandemic. However, many institutions have been adapting for well over a decade prior to the pandemic, with some having recognized the elastic complexity in delivering quality education through the advent of remote asynchronous online education. This required flexibility and adaptability from educators, students, and administration to leverage the newfound capability of transitioning back to remote learning as contextually needed.

In contrast, we have seen how primary K12 education faced serious challenges with a remote approach during the pandemic, which required promptly returning to in-person teaching as conditions allowed. The experience of young individuals during those days will most certainly reflect on how they perceive the educational environment as they approach higher education.

To operationalize the "Elastic" aspect of the CADE model, leaders need to cultivate a culture of resilience and adaptability within their organizations. This involves encouraging flexibility, fostering a learning culture, and equipping people with the skills and tools they need to adapt to changing circumstances. Leaders must also anticipate and prepare for potential disruptions, developing contingency plans and maintaining a certain degree of organizational slack to respond to unexpected challenges.

Moreover, leaders should focus on building a resilient workforce, and promoting personal resilience skills such as emotional intelligence, stress management, and adaptability. By doing so, they can ensure their teams are equipped to handle the challenges of working within complex, ever-changing systems. Recognizing and harnessing the elasticity inherent in complex systems can enable organizations to survive, adapt, and thrive in the face of change, uncertainty, and disruption.

THINKING POINT

Section Takeaways

Elastic complexity refers to the resilience and adaptability of complex systems, showing their ability to adjust to changes and evolve.

Companies adapt to economic downturns, and the shift to remote work due to the COVID-19 pandemic are examples of elasticity in action.

The job market's ability to create new roles despite significant displacement reflects the inherent elasticity of complexity.

The transition from traditional teaching to online or hybrid models in response to the pandemic demonstrated elasticity in education.

Leaders need to cultivate a culture of resilience and adaptability to operationalize the "Elastic" aspect of the CADE model.

Reflective Questions

Can you identify moments where your organization demonstrated elasticity in the face of change or disruption?

How well is your organization currently equipped to adapt to unexpected changes?

What steps can be taken to increase the resilience and adaptability of your team or organization?

Contextualization Prompt

Think about the most significant change or disruption your organization has faced recently. How did it demonstrate elasticity in its response? What lessons were learned that can help the organization become even more resilient in the future?

Superimposition of CADE

When taken together, the superimposition of CADE, the organization should be seen as a fluid, adaptable entity that thrives in the face of complexity. It's about striking a balance between remaining grounded in the organization's mission and values while being adaptable and resilient enough to navigate the complex, ever-changing environment. Ultimately, the implementation of CADE will depend on the unique conditions of each organization and the creative, innovative, and cognitive capacity of its leaders.

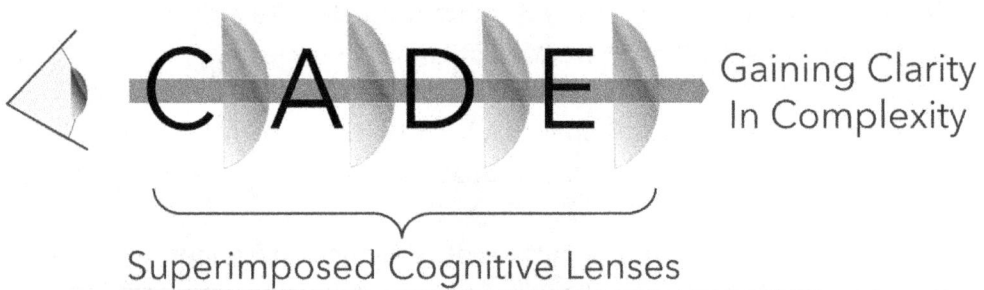

Image 2. The Superimposed CADE Model (Radi, 2020 - 2023) © Integral Advantage®

However, the CADE model functions as Superimposed Cognitive Lenses (See **Image 2**) and is actionable as it provides a methodology to gain clarity in complexity to operate at the optimal level. In summary, embracing the CADE model is about maintaining an *Inception Mindset*, staying curious, adaptable, and resilient in the face of complexity. It's about acknowledging and embracing the inherent complexity of our world and finding ways to thrive within it. To start the conversation, Consider your organization's unique circumstances and challenges. How might the CADE model be implemented to enhance your approach to complexity? Think about potential strategies and actions that could make a difference. By doing so, we gain clarity, enhance strategic capacity, and can ultimately drive organizational value creation.

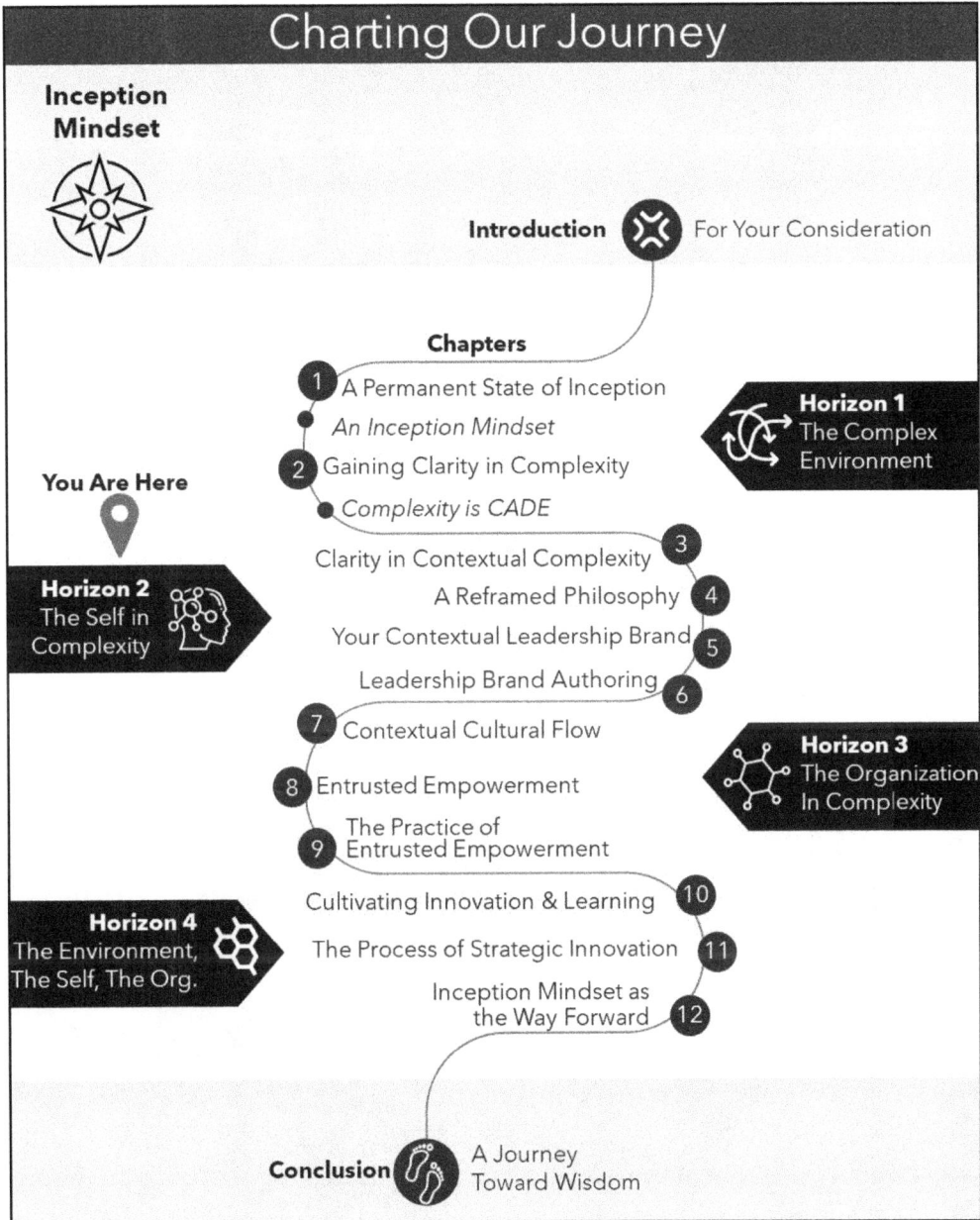

Charting Our Journey

Inception Mindset

Introduction For Your Consideration

Chapters

1 A Permanent State of Inception
   An Inception Mindset

Horizon 1
The Complex Environment

2 Gaining Clarity in Complexity
   Complexity is CADE

You Are Here

3 Clarity in Contextual Complexity
4 A Reframed Philosophy
5 Your Contextual Leadership Brand
6 Leadership Brand Authoring

Horizon 2
The Self in Complexity

7 Contextual Cultural Flow
8 Entrusted Empowerment
9 The Practice of Entrusted Empowerment

Horizon 3
The Organization In Complexity

10 Cultivating Innovation & Learning
11 The Process of Strategic Innovation
12 Inception Mindset as the Way Forward

Horizon 4
The Environment, The Self, The Org.

Conclusion A Journey Toward Wisdom

© 2023 Integral Advantage®, Inc.

PART II

HORIZON 2: THE SELF IN COMPLEXITY

Defining ourselves is the most challenging part of the never-ending journey into contextual complexity. To operate in complexity, we need to develop an **Inception Mindset** as we have seen in **Horizon 1**. To develop an *Inception Mindset*, we need to develop clarity about who we are. Effective leadership in such a dynamic environment requires a solid foundation of knowledge and skills to foster the ability to innovate, inspire, and adapt. Effective leadership in complex environments requires the development of a strong and distinct sense of self. **Horizon 2** examines aspects of self-authoring, the humanistic essence in meaning-making through the **Mindful Vortex,** leadership branding and its function in fostering self-awareness, authenticity, and personal growth, all relevant to develop an *Inception Mindset* to operate in contextual complexity.

Leadership branding is about creating and disseminating an identity that encapsulates a person's unique strengths, values, and vision. It promotes trust, credibility, and influence by shaping the perceptions, expectations, and behaviors of those we lead and interact with. A powerful leadership brand functions as a compass in a complex environment, allowing leaders to navigate the ever-changing landscape with a sense of purpose, direction, and resilience.

At the core of leadership branding is self-authoring, a lifelong process of introspection, reflection, and self-discovery that enables individuals to take charge of their personal narratives and shape their direction. Self-authoring enables leaders to delve deeply into their fundamental beliefs, values, and aspirations, aligning their actions with their genuine selves and nurturing a sense of coherence and continuity in their lives. This process assists leaders in establishing a solid foundation for their leadership brand, enhancing their adaptability and ability to flourish in complex situations. We will explore the significance of self-awareness as a prerequisite for effective leadership in complex environments, discussing multiple assessment instruments and techniques for obtaining insight into one's strengths, weaknesses, and behavioral tendencies.

CHAPTER 3

CLARITY IN CONTEXTUAL COMPLEXITY: SELF-AUTHORING

"Between stimulus and response there is a space.
In that space is our power to choose our response.
In our response lies our growth and our freedom."
— Viktor Frankl

Externalities and Self-Authoring

As we have explored the environment in **Horizon 1**, we need to appreciate the concept of externality and its implications for individuals, organizations, and the various layers of society. For those unfamiliar, externalities are those pesky little factors that exist outside of ourselves, wreaking havoc on our lives like a horde of mischievous gremlins. They infiltrate every corner of our existence, from families to organizations and from communities to global systems. Take families, for example. As the ever-wise author Jennifer Garvey Berger once said, "Parenting is in the complex domain." Well, thank you, Jennifer, for that earth-shattering revelation! Where were you in 2008 when my spouse and I naively thought, "Hey, let's have kids; we have run businesses. It'll be a piece of cake!"?

In all seriousness, in this context, I am defining externality as any entity or factor that exists outside of oneself. It is crucial to appreciate the interconnectedness and relationships that exist within and between different social systems while recognizing the individual as an autonomous being.

In a family, while each member has a unique identity and experiences, they are also part of a collective that requires adaptability, understanding, and alignment to maintain harmony. In this context, the family unit exists as a separate entity from the individual, even though it plays a significant role in shaping each member's identity and experiences.

Similarly, organizations can be considered externalities to their employees or leaders. Regardless of where an individual is on the organization's totem pole, they are part of a more extensive system that often operates independently of them. For instance, a leader may be at the strategic apex of a business unit, but they are still subject to the influences and constraints of the organization in its entirety. The concept of externality can be extended further to encompass the various layers of society, such as communities, local and national governments, and even global systems. Each layer represents an externality that interacts with and influences the other layers in complex and dynamic ways. So much for: "I am in charge here!"

Managerial and senior leaders can develop a more holistic perspective and make more informed choices when taking into consideration the broader context in which they operate by first gaining clarity about themselves through self-authoring. And I will go a step further and state that we cannot operate in complexity if we don't have clarity about who we are individually. There, I said it!

One crucial distinction must be understood in the journey of personal growth and development of an *Inception Mindset*: the difference between self-authoring and being authored by others. Self-authoring refers to taking charge of one's life and shaping one's identity, values, and beliefs based on personal reflection and experience. In contrast, being authored by others implies that an individual's identity, values, and beliefs are primarily influenced and shaped by external forces, such as family, culture, society, or other authority figures. At one point in our lives, we all were authored by forces external to the self.

The concept of self-authoring emphasizes the importance of cultivating self-awareness, introspection, and autonomy to lead a more authentic and fulfilling life. It encourages individuals to question, challenge, and ultimately define their values, beliefs, and life paths rather than merely accepting the expectations and norms imposed upon them by others. At times we are called to hold two truths at once. These factors enable us to be a product of our own expectations rather than a product of our circumstances.

In contrast, being authored by others can lead to a life characterized by conformity, dependence, and a lack of personal growth. Individuals are more likely to follow the paths laid out by external forces rather than pursue their passions and interests. In this chapter, we will explore how we can take control of the *Mindful Vortex* and shape our meaning-making process to be focused on our purpose. The overarching question is: **How do we respond to stimulus from externalities?**

There is a plethora of books and resources with respect to self-authoring, and I am providing a short synopsis of the books that from my perspective, stand out the most. In "The Road Less Traveled," M. Scott Peck delves into the nature of love, relationships, and personal growth, highlighting the significance of self-discipline, responsibility, and spiritual development in achieving a fulfilling life. By blending psychological insights with practical advice, Peck equips readers with the tools to surmount personal obstacles and cultivate healthier, more loving relationships. During the COVID-19 pandemic lockdown, I felt the need to revisit Viktor Frankl's "Man's Search for Meaning." It was part of a dialogue I was trying to have with my son, who was in middle school. I told him that he would read "The Diary of Ann Frank" and I would read "Man's Search for Meaning" to remind ourselves that as abrasive the lockdown was, we had it good, really good, as many people in the world were experiencing real suffering.   Viktor Frankl recounts the Holocaust survivor's experiences in Nazi concentration camps, where he developed his theory of logotherapy. In it, he asserted that the primary human drive is the quest for meaning and purpose. Frankl's work stands as a powerful testament to the resilience of the human spirit and the importance of pursuing a meaningful life. Another relevant piece of work is Brené Brown's "The Gifts of Imperfection," in which she investigates the concept of wholehearted living, emphasizing the importance of embracing vulnerability, imperfection, and authenticity. She offers practical strategies based on her research on shame, exposure, and resilience. Brown helps readers overcome self-doubt, perfectionism, and fear of judgment while cultivating self-compassion, courage, and connection. Then there is Robert Kegan's "In Over Our Heads: The Mental Demands of Modern Life," in which he analyzes the psychological challenges of modern life and the struggle individuals face in managing its complexities. In proposing a model of human development centered on the five stages of self-authorship, Kegan provides insights into how individuals, families, and institutions can support adult development and better cope with the challenges of contemporary life. Lastly, Paul Tillich's "The Courage to Be" examines the concept of courage within the framework of existentialism and the human condition. Tillich postulates that courage is a fundamental aspect of human existence and delves into the individual's pursuit of meaning, authenticity, and self-affirmation in the face of anxiety, despair, and uncertainty, offering a thought-provoking exploration of courage and its role in surmounting existential challenges.

The Mindful Vortex

"It is not necessary to react!" That was the mantra that the late Professor Wayne Strom, Ph.D., would remind his students in the President and Key Executive MBA at Pepperdine. Well, from my perspective, and as a good economist would say, "It depends." if you are in some Temple of Doom attempting to remove an artifact from a weight-sensitive ancient security system pedestal, by replacing said artifact with an equally weighted bag of something, and let's say for the sake of this discussion that you fail in your attempt, and a huge spherical boulder start chasing you, my humble recommendation is for you to promptly react and **run for your dear life**.

In this context, we are addressing the type of reactions often the root cause of outcomes we didn't intend to achieve. Over the past three years I have been exploring how to best illustrate the space between an event (stimulus) and our reaction to it (response) for the benefit of the participants in the leadership development course I teach and facilitate. That "space" that Viktor Frankl brought into our awareness in 1959 (See my interpretation in **Image 3**), as it is within this space that he claims we can consciously choose how we respond, ultimately affecting our personal growth and freedom. My curiosity has been driven to understanding and providing others with the ability to answer a question: **What takes place in that space in between stimulus and response when we operate in contextual complexity?**

Stimulus

The Space
(Power to
Choose)

Response
(Our Growth and
our Freedom)

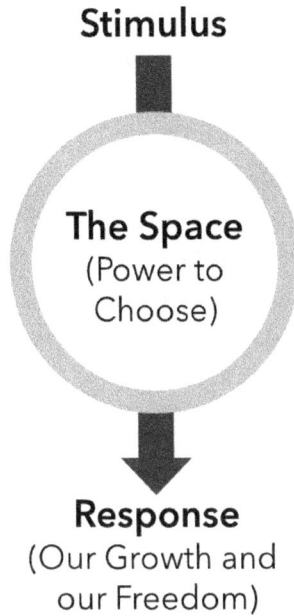

Image 3. Adapted from: Dr. Viktor Frankl, 1959

Metaphors and Similes

One of the realizations we can all agree on is that *"The Space"* is not quiet and reflective. As we develop and mature through our intentional choices, we appreciate the struggle in *"The Space."* The struggle is necessary for our growth and to make meaning of what we are experiencing. We can all recall a time when we may have lost sleep over something that happened in our lives, and today we realize how insignificant the event was. But at that time, we perceived it to be significant to us. There is a certain level of brain hardwiring that we need to overcome. Some meaning-making models illustrate how we need to make meaning by tapping in our iOS, which stands for **inner or internal** Operating System, a play on the internal Operating System that first came into the popular lingo in 2007 courtesy of Apple. Is it the iOS "the space?" Perhaps, but I will have to disclose that anything drawing parallels between humans and machines makes me quite uncomfortable because we cannot decode **The Human Experience** with the same lenses of technology, intelligent or otherwise. The first electronic digital computer, the Electronic Numerical Integrator and Computer (ENIAC), was introduced in 1946. It was developed by J. Presper Eckert and John W. Mauchly at the University of Pennsylvania. ENIAC was a massive machine that filled an entire room and used vacuum tubes to perform calculations. In contrast, the first civilization recorded in history emerged around 6,000 years ago. One of the earliest known civilizations is the Sumerians in Mesopotamia, present-day Iraq. The Sumerian civilization began about 4500 B.C. Mesopotamia is often called the "Cradle of Civilization" as it was the first region where urbanization, agriculture, and the development of complex social structures emerged. The Ancient Egyptians, who developed a civilization along the Nile River around 3100 B.C., were another early civilization. So, the human experience and our meaning-making process cannot be compared to our highest degree of knowledge at a point in time.

Before the advent of computers, brain processing and processes were often compared to other familiar systems. For example, in the 17th century, philosopher and mathematician René Descartes compared the brain to a hydraulic system, with the flow of fluids representing the flow of thoughts and sensations. This mechanical metaphor was consistent with the scientific understanding of the time. In the 19th century, the development of the telegraph and telephone led to new comparisons of the brain with these communication systems. Scientists and philosophers viewed the brain as a network of interconnected "wires" that transmitted signals, like how messages were sent through telegraph and telephone lines.

The invention of the computer in the mid-20th century provided a new and powerful metaphor for understanding brain processes. The brain is seen as an information-processing system, with neurons acting as switches and the flow of information being represented by electrical impulses. This comparison has been especially influential in developing cognitive science, which seeks to understand the brain through computational models and simulations. While these comparisons have helped simplify complex ideas and guide scientific inquiry, it is essential to recognize that they are only metaphors and not literal descriptions of how the brain works. The human brain is an incredibly complex and unique organ that cannot be fully understood through comparison or analogy. As our scientific understanding of the brain continues to evolve, new comparisons and metaphors may emerge, providing fresh insights and perspectives on the nature of human cognition and consciousness.

THINKING POINT

Section Takeaways

Externality refers to any entity or factor that exists outside oneself. It is present in all social systems and significantly influences individuals, organizations, and various societal layers. Recognizing the concept of externality helps appreciate the interconnectedness within and between different social systems and emphasizes the individual as an autonomous being.

Self-authoring is the practice of shaping one's identity, values, and beliefs based on personal reflection and experience instead of being authored by others, where external forces primarily shape these aspects. It is crucial for personal growth, authenticity, and fulfillment.

The Mindful Vortex represents the space between an event (stimulus) and our reaction to it (response). This space is where we can consciously choose our response, affecting our personal growth and freedom.

Reflective Questions

Reflect on the influence of externalities in your personal and professional life. How have they shaped your decisions and experiences?

Where do you see yourself in the spectrum between self-authoring and being authored by others? How has this position evolved, and how might it change in your way forward?

Consider a recent event that caused a significant reaction in you. Can you identify the elements at play within the 'Mindful Vortex'?

Contextualization Prompt

Identify a recent decision or action you've taken in response to an externality. Imagine you had taken a more self-authored approach. How might this have changed the outcome? Reflect on this experience and consider how you might apply a more self-authored approach to similar situations in the future.

No Struggle, No Wings

The struggle we experience in processing the stimuli of the environment is complex in human beings as we need to deal with those bothersome emotions, and the process of meaning-making is seldom linear. Back to our 17th-century friend René Descartes from France, we can appreciate how he viewed emotions (or "passions") as physiological reactions to external stimuli, mediated by the brain and the "animal spirits" (a concept related to vital fluids or gases) that flow through the nerves.

The term **"mediated by the brain"** is critical in what I crafted over the past couple of years and in my assessment, has relevance when it comes to leadership in contextual complexity. In the philosophical, literary work "The Passions of the Soul" (1649), Descartes argued that passions **are not** inherently harmful or disruptive to rational thought. Instead, they serve a vital function in human life by alerting us to important events, guiding our behavior, and motivating us to act. He believed that passions are essential for survival and well-being, as they help us recognize and respond to opportunities and threats in our environment.

So, are passion emotions and emotions passions? Just when it couldn't get more confusing. A very wise senior executive in a course I was co-facilitating said: "You cannot engineer emotions out of people." My friend Professor Dr. Kerns at Pepperdine often states that "the entire human being shows up for work." And those darn emotions are part of the human being showing up for work as they cannot be downloaded onto Alexa before leaving the house or moving to the workspace in the same house. Yet, there is rationality in emotions. During the writing process of my dissertation, I became familiar with the work of George Lakoff, an American cognitive linguist, philosopher, and professor emeritus at the University of California, Berkeley. As my dissertation topic was about the construct of narrative by leaders facing adversities, this quote from Dr. Lakoff hits the spot: "Emotions are an inescapable part of normal thought. Indeed, you cannot be rational without emotions. Without emotion, you would not know what to want since like and not-like would be meaningless to you." Well, there you have it! You can't be rational without emotions, and the struggle is real. I rest my case.

Illustrating the Mindful Vortex

I realized, and perhaps after you already did, that when operating in complexity, we are rarely impacted by a single stimulus. We are drinking from the proverbial firehose and often dealing with a myriad of stimuli rendering certain events more complex or heightening the perception of complexity. That is one of the aspects leading me to coin the term **Mindful Vortex**. These stimuli go through our mindful vortex with intensifying factors and mitigating factors. The key for a leader is the ability to remain in the mindful vortex before a response or action is taken for the two sides, intensifying factors, and mitigating factors, to resolve and find equilibrium. The leader may take an incremental approach instead of addressing a complex issue with a single decision. They see the outcome and return to meaning-making in the mindful vortex to craft the next step asking themselves, "What is the next optimal move in this context"? The outcome of this process may not be visible or manifest itself for some time. As you can see, once again, the *Inception Mindset* plays a considerable role in this context.

Allow me to elaborate. In a complex situation, leaders face stimuli likely to impact emotional and cognitive reactions processed within the mindful vortex. The interplay between **intensifying and mitigating factors** determines how the leader makes meaning of the situation and ultimately decides on a response or action (See **Image 4**).

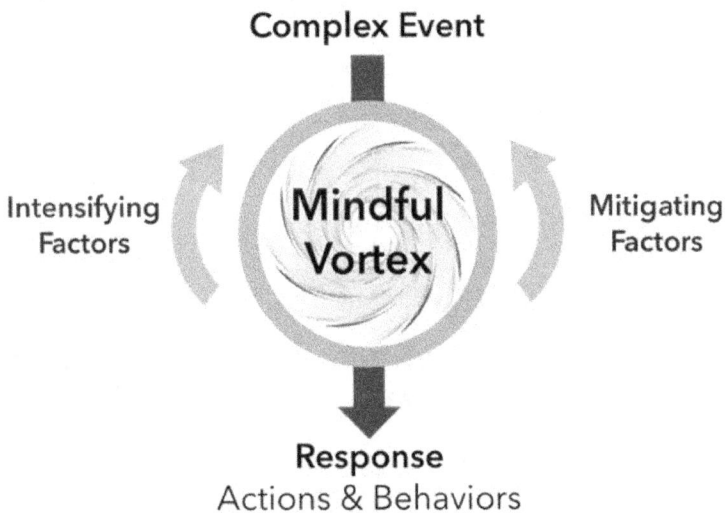

Complex Event

Intensifying Factors

Mindful Vortex

Mitigating Factors

Response
Actions & Behaviors

Image 4. Mindful Vortex: (Radi, 2020 – 2023) © Integral Advantage®

The ability to remain in the mindful vortex, allowing time for the intensifying and mitigating factors to **reach equilibrium**, is crucial for effective leadership. This process enables leaders to make more thoughtful and informed decisions rather than reacting impulsively or purely emotionally to challenging situations. I would further argue that the statement "all my decisions are made without emotions" is an illusion. We all have a limbic system, which is aroused when faced with adverse conditions. It is not by sitting around a fire and talking out our feelings that we will gain understanding. It is by recognizing that emotions play a role in our responses that will empower us. We do not have to dehumanize ourselves and others to show strength, courage, selflessness, and executive zest. The beloved Fred Rogers, known by the audiences as Mr. Rogers, said, "Anything that's human is mentionable, and anything that is mentionable can be more manageable. When we can talk about our feelings, they become less overwhelming, less upsetting, and less scary. The people we trust with that important talk can help us know that we are not alone." The more we gain clarity about ourselves, the more we gain clarity about others.

The Mindful Vortex is in That Space

In proposing a new conceptual framework centered around the mindful vortex, I emphasize the importance of balancing intensifying factors and mitigating factors during the meaning-making process, enabling leaders to make more informed and thoughtful decisions to increase their effectiveness over time. I argue that meaning-making occurs in the space Dr. Frankl taught us (See **Image 5**). Instead of envisioning an isolated place or "iOS" where meaning-making happens, thinking of the mindful vortex as the space where this process unfolds is more accurate.

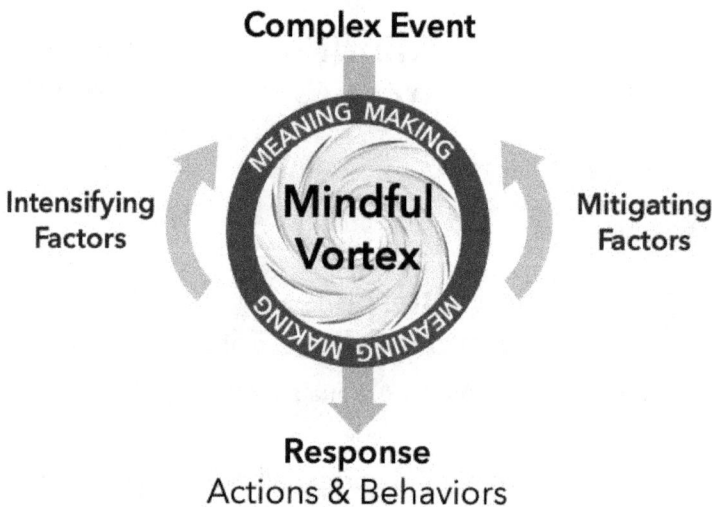

Complex Event

Intensifying Factors

MEANING MAKING

Mindful Vortex

MEANING MAKING

Mitigating Factors

Response
Actions & Behaviors

Image 5. Mindful Vortex: (Radi, 2020 – 2023) © Integral Advantage®

In the mindful vortex, individuals are constantly navigating the interplay between intensifiers and de-escalators, working to find equilibrium and make meaning of the situation. The mindful vortex represents a more dynamic and fluid concept of meaning-making that acknowledges the complexity of human emotions, thoughts, and experiences. It accounts for the fact that individuals must actively engage with both the intensifying and calming forces at play to arrive at a deeper understanding of the situation and make better contextual decisions (See **Image 6**).

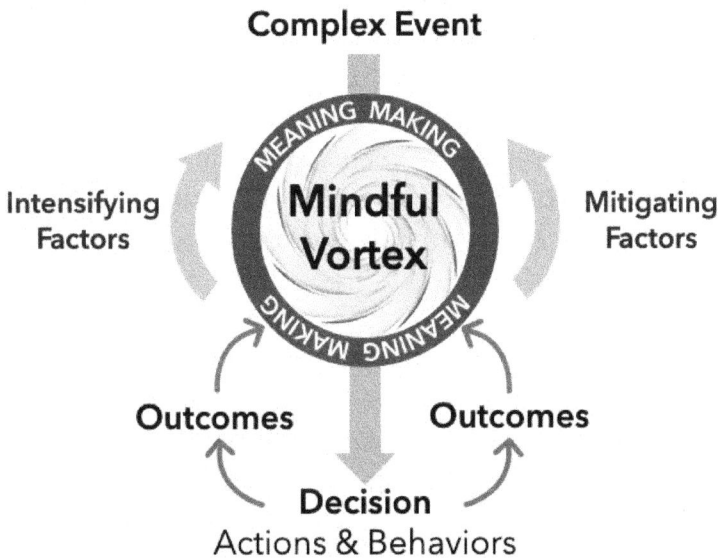

Image 6. Mindful Vortex: (Radi, 2020 – 2023) © Integral Advantage®

By recognizing that meaning-making occurs within the mindful vortex, we can develop strategies that account for the various factors influencing our emotions and thought processes, ultimately enhancing our ability to navigate complex or challenging situations more effectively. The onus is on us to make meaning of all that on the surface doesn't make sense.

While Frankl might not have used the term "mindful vortex," the principles and ideas from his work align with the model I have described. He would likely appreciate the emphasis on meaning-making, personal responsibility, and the dynamic interplay between intensifiers and mitigating factors within the mindful vortex. We will never know what his perspective would be. However, Viktor Frankl's work, particularly his "logotherapy" concept, aligns with many aspects of the mindful vortex model I have described. While Frankl might not have used the same terminology, the principles of his approach share similarities with the mindful vortex concept. For example, the search for meaning, in logotherapy, the primary motivational force for individuals is the search for meaning. This notion aligns with the idea of meaning-making as a central process within the mindful vortex. Another aspect is the importance of personal responsibility. Frankl stressed the importance of taking responsibility for one's thoughts, emotions, and actions. The mindful vortex model acknowledges the need for individuals to actively work on finding a balance between **Intensifying Factors** and **Mitigating Factors**, which also involves taking responsibility for one's emotional and cognitive responses. Finally, is the role of suffering and struggle. No struggle, no wings. Here, Frankl believed that suffering and struggle are essential aspects of human existence and can provide opportunities for personal growth. The mindful vortex model incorporates the idea that navigating the tension between **Intensifying Factors** and **Mitigating Factors** can be a struggle but ultimately leads to personal development and better decision-making.

This model is highly relevant for leaders operating in increasingly complex environments. It becomes even more important in such contexts, as leaders' challenges and uncertainties tend to be more dynamic and multifaceted. Leaders often encounter rapidly changing circumstances, multiple stakeholder perspectives, and ambiguous information in complex environments. The mindful vortex model provides a framework for leaders to navigate these challenges effectively:

1. **Encouraging** self-awareness and reflection enables leaders to recognize their biases, emotions, and cognitive distortions.

2. **Promoting** the development and use of emotional intelligence skills, character strengths, and mindfulness practices serves as mitigating factors in the face of complexity.

3. **Supporting** an incremental problem-solving approach allows leaders to adjust and adapt their strategies based on evolving circumstances and feedback from their actions.

4. **Reinforcing** the importance of patience and openness to learning, as the outcomes of the meaning-making process may not be immediately apparent in complex situations.

By mastering the mindful vortex model, leaders can enhance their ability to understand and navigate the complexities of their environments, ultimately making more effective and strategic decisions.

THINKING POINT

Section Takeaways:

The struggle of processing stimuli from our environment is crucial to our survival and well-being, serving to alert us to important events and motivating us to act. Emotions are an inescapable part of rational thought and decision-making.

The Mindful Vortex conceptualizes the interplay between intensifying and mitigating factors in our decision-making process. It encourages a more thoughtful, patient, and open approach to complex situations. Principles from Viktor Frankl's logotherapy align with the Mindful Vortex model, emphasizing meaning-making, personal responsibility, and the role of struggle in personal growth.

The Mindful Vortex model provides a framework for leaders to navigate complexities more effectively, emphasizing self-awareness, emotional intelligence, an incremental problem-solving approach, and openness to learning.

Reflective Questions:

How does your understanding of the role of emotions in decision-making change after reading this section?

How can the concept of the Mindful Vortex be applied to a recent complex situation you've encountered?

How can you incorporate self-awareness, emotional intelligence, an incremental problem-solving approach, and openness to learning into your leadership?

What's In Your Mindful Vortex?

"What's in your wallet?" Samuel L. Jackson asks in a credit card commercial. In this section, we will take a close look at what the **Intensifying Factors**, those elements intensifying the vortex and the **Mitigating Factors**, those elements de-escalating the intensity of the vortex, are in general, and in the next section, we will explore how you can identify those factors in a way that are true to you as an autonomous individual with agency and willpower.

When we look at the mindful vortex framework, we see that intensifying factors, such as social threats (SCARF model), cognitive distortions, and emotional triggers, can heighten emotional reactions and cognitive biases. Conversely, mitigating factors, including character strengths, emotional intelligence skills, and mindfulness practices, help to de-escalate emotional intensity and promote balance.

The following table provides an overview of some key Intensifying Factors and Mitigating Factors, and after that, I provide an overview of each, to help you recognize and explore their influence on your mindful vortex processes. Keep in mind that this list is not exhaustive, and these factors may vary between individuals. Everyone's experience will be unique, and engaging in self-discovery and self-reflection is essential to gain deeper insight into your own Intensifying and Mitigating Factors. In the next section, we will look at some techniques for discovering and mastering intensifying and mitigating factors, and we will take a deep dive into Chater 4, 5, and 6 to empower you to pursue your self-authoring journey. Hence, see this as a reflective table (See **Table 2**) to consider.

Intensifying Factors	Mitigating Factors
SCARF Model (Social Threats)	**Character Strengths**
Cognitive Distortions	**Emotional Intelligence Skills**
Emotional Triggers	**Mindfulness Practices**
Implicit Biases	**Resilience**
Reactive Fears	**Empathy and Compassion**
Negative Past Experiences	**Self-Awareness and Reflection**
Social and Cultural Influences	**Social Support and Connection**
Misplaced Loyalties	**Purpose and Vision**

Table 2. Mindful Vortex: (Radi, 2021 – 2023) © Integral Advantage®

Intensifying Factors

The following is a summary of the definitions of crucial Intensifying Factors listed in the table:

SCARF Model (Social Threats) - Developed by Dr. David Rock, the SCARF Model represents five domains of human social experience (Status, Certainty, Autonomy, Relatedness, and Fairness) that can evoke strong emotional reactions when threatened. To discover your SCARF sensitivities, you can access the free self-assessments provided by the NeuroLeadership Institute, which will help you identify your reactions in each domain. Understanding your SCARF profile can offer insight into the factors most likely to intensify your emotional responses in the mindful vortex.

Cognitive Distortions are irrational thought patterns that can negatively influence our emotions, behavior, and decision-making. Identifying and challenging these distortions through techniques such as cognitive-behavioral therapy can help individuals reduce their impact on emotional processes.

Emotional Triggers are specific situations, events, or stimuli that provoke intense emotional reactions. Recognizing and understanding one's emotional triggers can help individuals manage their responses more effectively in the mindful vortex.

Implicit Biases are deeply ingrained attitudes or beliefs that influence our decision-making and behavior, often without our awareness. To identify and mitigate implicit biases, individuals can self-reflect and seek feedback from others.

Reactive Fears concern anxiety and stress experienced by individuals when perceiving potential threats or risks, often related to a fear of failure or loss. Addressing these reactive fears can involve:

- Developing a growth mindset.
- Learning from setbacks.
- Encouraging a culture of experimentation and innovation within organizations.

Negative Past Experiences are previous encounters or situations that have left a lasting emotional impact on an individual, potentially shaping their perceptions and reactions in the present. Reflecting on and learning from these experiences can help individuals minimize their influence on emotional processes.

Social and Cultural Influences are external factors, such as societal norms, cultural values, and group dynamics, that can shape an individual's emotional reactions and decision-making. Increasing awareness of these influences and challenging assumptions can help individuals manage their emotions more effectively within the mindful vortex.

Misplaced Loyalties - This factor refers to individuals' potential emotional attachment to specific values, beliefs, or relationships that no longer serve their best interests. Recognizing and addressing misplaced loyalties can help individuals minimize the impact of these attachments on their emotional processes.

Mitigating Factors

The following is a summary of the definitions of crucial Mitigating Factors listed in the table:

Character Strengths - These are positive traits or qualities that contribute to a person's overall well-being and effectiveness. The VIA Institute on Character offers a free assessment to help individuals identify and develop their unique character strengths, which can help buffer against emotional turbulence in the mindful vortex.

Emotional Intelligence Skills - The ability to recognize, understand, and manage our own emotions and the emotions of others effectively. Developing emotional intelligence skills, such as self-regulation, empathy, and social awareness, can help individuals navigate emotional challenges more effectively within the mindful vortex.

Mindfulness practices include meditation, deep breathing, and yoga that promote present-moment awareness and nonjudgmental acceptance of thoughts and emotions. Incorporating mindfulness practices into daily life can help individuals manage their emotional processes and maintain balance within the mindful vortex. A word about yoga. My wife likes to point out that what I do is not yoga. My response is always the same: "At least I am doing it!"

Resilience is adapting and recovering from adversity, stress, or setbacks. Building resilience involves:

- Developing coping strategies.
- Fostering a growth mindset.
- Learning from challenging experiences can help individuals navigate the mindful vortex more effectively.

Empathy and Compassion refer to the ability to understand and share the feelings of others and to respond with care and support. Cultivating empathy and compassion can help individuals better manage their emotional reactions and foster more positive interactions within the mindful vortex.

Self-Awareness and Reflection involve regularly examining one's thoughts, emotions, and behaviors to gain insight and understanding. Self-awareness and reflection can help individuals identify patterns in their emotional processes and make more informed choices within the mindful vortex.

Social Support and Connection are relationships and networks that provide emotional, informational, and instrumental support. Strong social connections can help buffer against stress and promote emotional well-being, enabling individuals to navigate the mindful vortex more effectively.

Purpose and Vision - A clear sense of direction and meaning in life can provide motivation and inspiration in the face of emotional challenges. Developing a strong sense of purpose and vision can help individuals stay grounded and focused within the mindful vortex.

Discovering and Mastering

You can use the following techniques to clarify your unique Intensifying Factors and Mitigating Factors. These steps will serve as a starting point for understanding how these factors come into play in your life, helping you find balance and effectively navigate the mindful vortex.

Self-reflection.

- Set aside regular time for introspection and journaling.
- Ask yourself questions about the situations in which you tend to experience strong emotional reactions and identify the underlying factors contributing to these emotions.
- Pay attention to patterns in your thoughts, feelings, and behaviors to help pinpoint your Intensifying and Mitigating Factors.

Mindfulness meditation. Practice mindfulness meditation to cultivate present-moment awareness and nonjudgmental acceptance of your thoughts and emotions. This approach can help you objectively observe and understand your emotional processes and identify the factors that influence them.

Seek feedback from others. Ask trusted friends, family members, or colleagues about your emotional reactions and coping strategies. Their feedback can provide valuable insights into your Intensifying and Mitigating Factors.

Misplaced Loyalties

I want to take a moment to touch upon one aspect that seems to be a recuring theme when I conduct my seminars and workshops: "I have been loyal. How could they do that?" Rather than using the "Well, life is not fair, toughen up buttercup," let me offer some advice, as I am self-advising. Do not be discouraged if someone in your life, personal or professional, has taken your loyalty for granted and turned it into an opportunity to belittle you with their unwarranted and endless criticism. Do not regret all you have done to show your dedication, reverence, and appreciation. Please do not feel ashamed for being willing to take a bullet **for** them, but rest assured that you do not have to take a bullet **from** them. How they may have treated you says more about where they are in their life than anything about you. Some individuals fake their wisdom, but the "fake it until you become it" will eventually crumble around them, leaving sorrow and desolation. Let them work through it; their burden of self-doubt, arrogance, mistrust, and paranoia is not for you to carry. The gift they were once upon a time may have turned into an unsustainable and unbearable cost. Let it go. Instead, rejoice in your humanity, empathy, kindness, generosity, and ability to care for others. Rejoice in what makes you - you. No one can take away your identity; no one can steal or duplicate who you are. Yes, the realization of your misplaced loyalty came like a bucket of cold icy water, but rude awakenings have a divine purpose. They redirect us toward what is meaningful to us, what we want to do for others and with others. Those moments bring clarity. **These are inception points.** New beginnings bring new opportunities to engage with people that will hear, value and respect you. Build the playground where others like you want to come and play, and then keep transforming that playground with them. Be the lighthouse and let your light shine, and those who can see the light will.

THINKING POINT

Section Takeaways

The mindful vortex framework is influenced by intensifying factors, which heighten emotional reactions and cognitive biases, and mitigating factors that de-escalate emotional intensity and promote balance.

Intensifying factors include social threats, cognitive distortions, emotional triggers, implicit biases, reactive fears, negative past experiences, social and cultural influences, and misplaced loyalties. Mitigating factors include character strengths, emotional intelligence skills, mindfulness practices, resilience, empathy and compassion, self-awareness and reflection, social support and connection, and purpose and vision.

It's important to regularly examine and understand our intensifying and mitigating factors through self-reflection, mindfulness meditation, and feedback from others. Misplaced loyalties can be emotionally challenging, but it's essential to let go of the burden and rejoice in one's humanity and empathy.

Reflective Questions

Which intensifying factors do you identify with the most, and how do they influence your emotional reactions?

Can you name some of your own mitigating factors? How do they help in diffusing your emotional intensity?

How often do you engage in self-reflection and mindfulness practices to gain insights into your emotions and reactions?

Contextualization Prompt

Reflect on a recent emotional reaction you've had in a personal or professional setting. Can you identify the intensifying factors that might have heightened your emotional reaction in that situation? What mitigating factors were available to you or could you have employed to de-escalate your emotional intensity?

Neuroscience in Leadership: Authentic Engagement

The expression "Fake it until you make it" has been a recurring figure of speech in self-help and motivational circles for many years. Often, it is used as a thong-in-cheek expression when someone expresses their lack of experience. The expression's origin usually depends on who you ask. Some argue that Simon & Garfunkel's "Fakin' It," released in 1968, is what started it all: "And I know I'm fakin' it, I'm not really makin' it." Whatever the origin, there are substantive leadership implications as the expression promotes inauthenticity and adversely affects individuals and those around them. We have seen many instances where executives have taken "Fakin' It" literally and a few steps too far with disastrous consequences for organizations, the community, and society. Am I exaggerating? How about those "easy and accurate" blood tests that only needed a drop of blood as an example?

The mindset that we can replace acquiring competency through mindful learning with a "winging our way to competency" mentality encourages individuals to present a false image of themselves in the context in which they operate. Rather than embracing their true selves and working to improve their weaknesses by leveraging their strengths, they are misguided in pretending they already have the desired qualities.

This attitude often triggers the Dunning-Kruger effect, a cognitive bias where people with low abilities in a particular domain overestimate their performance and skills. This effect can occur because individuals with limited skills and knowledge cannot often recognize their shortcomings, leading to an inflated sense of self-confidence. The Dunning-Kruger effect has important implications for personal and professional development, highlighting the need for self-awareness and a growth mindset.

Why is the "Fake it Until" a critical issue? Because in a time where authenticity is vital to leaders operating in complexity, inauthenticity can be detrimental to an individual's sense of self-worth. When people pretend to be something they're not, it can also be challenging to maintain this façade, leading to anxiety and stress. Another problem with the "Fake it Until" mindset is that it can lead to a lack of growth and development.

When individuals focus on pretending to have qualities rather than working to develop them, they miss out on the opportunity to learn and grow. By concentrating on appearing confident and capable, individuals may miss the chance to develop the core competencies they need to succeed in their careers and can have adverse effects on those around them. When individuals present a false image of themselves, they can deceive others and create false expectations. To use the words of Santiago Ramón y Cajal, the renowned father of neuroscience, I am arguing that they are "sculpting" such mindset in their brains, leading to disappointment, mistrust, and damaging relationships. Furthermore, when those in executive positions pretend to be something they're not, they can create a toxic work environment where everyone is trying to present a false image, leading to feelings of anxiety and competition. Literally, they model the way, and not in a constructive fashion.

Choosing Curiosity

While curiosity may "kill the cat," it is essential in learning and developing leadership competencies. Authentically engaging with our dynamic environment and the people that operate in our context is critical in entering a space of meaning-making when seeking clarity in complexity. This is also fundamental in developing an *Inception Mindset*. This mindset recognizes that value creation and growth come from embracing our authentic selves and working to improve our weaknesses by leveraging our strengths and enrolling the help of others. Being vulnerable and openly acknowledging our challenges creates a sense of authenticity and builds trust with others. Furthermore, engaging in activities that align with our values and character strengths makes us more likely to experience fulfillment.

This mindset also promotes growth and development by encouraging individuals to focus on building their core competencies. Rather than pretending to have qualities they don't possess, individuals are encouraged to identify their weaknesses and work to improve them, leading to a deeper understanding of oneself and can help individuals build the skills and expertise they need to succeed in their careers and life. Authentically engaging allows us to express our genuine curiosity toward other individuals' experiences, skills, knowledge, and perspectives. Socrates celebrated his limited knowledge by depicting his learning as a white dot on a large black slate.

When was the last time we nodded our heads when something was said in a meeting, and we didn't know what it meant but felt we needed to show we knew? An acronym, a financial or technical figure, or a place? Yes, perhaps it wasn't a big deal, and we "googled" later, but at that moment, we denied our curiosity and the opportunity for the other party to share their expertise. By being vulnerable and engaging in activities aligned with our values and character strengths, we are more likely to experience happiness, success, and fulfillment. Brené Brown, a renowned researcher and speaker on vulnerability, courage, and shame, defines vulnerability as "uncertainty, risk, and emotional exposure." According to Brown, vulnerability is the cornerstone of authentic relationships, allowing individuals to connect with others on a deeper, more meaningful level.

When individuals are willing to share their concerns, insecurities, and emotions with others, they build trust and create a sense of belonging. Furthermore, when individuals feel they can be their authentic selves with others, they experience a greater understanding of self-acceptance and self-worth.

Leveraging Neuroplasticity

Authentic Engagement is the mindset we ought to adopt to "sculpt" our brains, as suggested by Santiago Ramón y Cajal (1852–1934), who observed before the advent of MRI and CAT Scans the ability of the brain to generate new neuro patterns because of nontraumatic events. Neuroplasticity is the brain's ability to adapt and change in response to new experiences, learning, and development. It is a critical component of leadership and character development, allowing individuals to develop new skills and behaviors, overcome limitations, and grow in various ways.

Neuroplasticity refers to the brain's ability to reorganize itself in response to new experiences, and it plays a critical role in enabling individuals to learn and develop new competencies. For leaders who authentically engage with others to learn and grow, neuroplasticity can facilitate acquiring and refining new skills and developing more effective communication and collaboration strategies.

Neuroplasticity facilitates leadership development by strengthening neural connections that underpin social interactions. When leaders engage with others, they are exposed to various experiences and perspectives that challenge their assumptions and expand their understanding of the world. This exposure can lead to the development of new neural connections, which can help leaders communicate more effectively, collaborate more productively, and build more resilient relationships. I often tell the participants in my workshops and seminars that all development is incremental and that neuroplasticity facilitates leadership development through deliberate practice. This approach involves breaking down complex skills into smaller, more manageable components and then practicing those components systematically over time.

THINKING POINT

Section Takeaways:

"Fake it until you make it" attitude can lead to detrimental consequences, as it promotes inauthenticity and prevents growth and self-development. The Dunning-Kruger effect is a cognitive bias where people with limited abilities overestimate their skills, leading to an inflated sense of self-confidence and hindering personal growth.

Curiosity is vital for self-improvement, authentic engagement, and leadership growth. It is a doorway to vulnerability, which allows for genuine connections and building trust. Authentic engagement encourages individuals to embrace their true selves and work towards developing their weaknesses, leading to a deeper understanding of oneself and a greater sense of self-worth.

Leveraging neuroplasticity, the ability of the brain to adapt and change, can be instrumental in leadership and character development. It enables individuals to acquire new skills, overcome limitations, and grow personally and professionally.

Reflective Questions:

Can you recall a time when curiosity led to a significant learning experience or a shift in your perspective?

How has authentic engagement helped you build trust and meaningful relationships in your personal and professional life?

Can you think of an instance where neuroplasticity played a role in your learning or development of a new skill?

Contextualization Prompt:

In your work or personal life, think of a situation where you felt the need to "fake it." Reflect on how it affected your relationship with others and your sense of self-worth. Now imagine how this situation could have been different if you had chosen to authentically engage instead. How might this shift in attitude have influenced your learning, personal growth, and the quality of your relationships? As you consider this, think about how understanding and leveraging the concept of neuroplasticity might impact your future learning and development.

CHAPTER 4

A REFRAMED PHILOSOPHY

" Be yourself; everyone else is already taken." — Oscar Wilde

As we explored in Chapter 3, leaders can strengthen the neural connections associated with specific competencies, such as active listening, strategic thinking, and emotional intelligence by engaging in deliberate practice. Over time, these strengthened neural connections can develop more efficient and effective brain circuits that support the targeted competencies. This is made possible by neuroplasticity which facilitates leadership development by cultivating a growth mindset. This mindset involves embracing challenges, persisting in the face of setbacks, and seeking feedback and learning opportunities. By adopting a growth mindset, leaders can foster the neural plasticity necessary to develop new competencies and overcome limitations that may have previously held them back.

Neuroplasticity provides a powerful mechanism for leaders who authentically engage with others to learn and develop competencies. By building new neural connections, engaging in deliberate practice, and cultivating a growth mindset, leaders can strengthen their social, cognitive, and emotional capabilities and become more effective and resilient. In this chapter, we will explore a methodology to increase the intentional sculpting of our brain, and we will then embark upon a journey that will end **Horizon 2** with the authoring of our leadership brand.

The Zing–Zap Approach

How do you sculpt a masterpiece in marble? You remove everything that is not the form you want to achieve and then you polish the stone. As a bridge to our exploration in Chapter 3, and a way forward into the realm of Leadership Branding, I am introducing you to another framework I have developed and used in leadership development for a few years: the ZING-ZAP approach (See **Image 7**). In this framework, I argue that through the intentional increase of our self-awareness, we become more attuned to those elements we internalize and may have become implicit biases re-sulting in undesired responses. As we become more self-aware, we tend to feel more ZINGS.

The ZING-ZAP approach is an empowering framework that enables indi-viduals to actively address undesired responses to stimuli by harnessing the power of self-awareness and neuroplasticity. By increasing self-aware-ness, individuals can become more attuned to their internalized elements, such as implicit biases, which may result in undesired responses. When a person experiences a ZING, a moment of awareness about their implicit bias, or reaction to externalities or behaviors they want to change, they can act through the ZAP process at the moment. This means not putting it out for another time to deal with. It is the equivalent of picking up the can instead of kicking it down the alley.

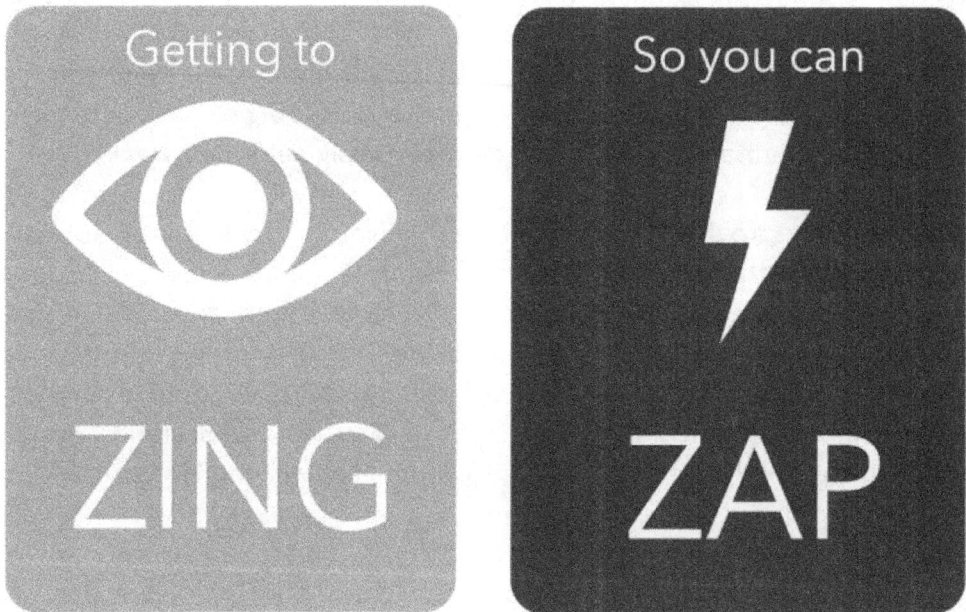

Image 7. The Zing–Zap Approach: (Radi, 2018 – 2023) © Integral Advantage®

"Why should I care"? The ZING-ZAP approach is relevant for leaders as they navigate the complexities of their personal and professional lives. Like everyone else, leaders are subject to Intensifying Factors that can lead to undesired responses or behaviors. By engaging in the ZING-ZAP process, leaders can enhance their leadership capabilities and effectively manage their challenges by intentionally focusing on self-awareness and engaging in the ZAP process, to foster a growth mindset, develop more effective behaviors, and ultimately drive better outcomes for themselves, their teams, and their organizations.

Zapping: Self-Coaching Techniques

The essence of the Zing-Zap approach is acting in the moment we sense the Zing. It is an "in the moment" approach. At its center are self-coaching techniques. Over the years I simmered those techniques down to **four** that I now recommend as clients reported them to be the most useful and effective, and these techniques can and should be done "in the Zinging moment."

1. **Annotating.** Writing down thoughts, emotions, and experiences can help individuals gain clarity, process emotions, and identify patterns in their thinking and behavior. Best if you have a pad available. Our brains love it when we handwrite. Otherwise, annotate on your phone. Have an app like Notes, or Google keep and annotate some keywords. All this assumes you are stationary or not the driver in a vehicle, of course.

2. **Self-coaching questions.** Asking yourself thought-provoking questions to help reveal insights and promote self-awareness by zinging perceptions. Examples may include.

- Is what I sense indeed what is taking place?
- What thoughts or beliefs are contributing to my reaction?
- How did my response align with my values?
- What could I have done differently in this situation?
- Do I really believe that…?
- Am I reading the dynamics for what they are?

The key is to ask yourself questions that are relevant to the specific conditions you are experiencing.

3. **Visualization.** Imagining yourself in various scenarios or facing challenges can help individuals rehearse and refine their responses,

fostering greater emotional resilience and adaptability. For example, you can see yourself as a third party looking at the situation you are experiencing to hold a different perspective.

4. **Seeking other perspectives.** Asking someone to describe what they see in a situation in which you are feeling the ZING is another technique. The key here is to calmly ask other individuals questions that are not leading in nature. In other words, is not asking "Do you see what I see" but asking "What do you see?"

By incorporating these self-coaching techniques into our daily lives, we can work towards greater self-awareness, emotional regulation, and personal growth, ultimately becoming more effective in our personal and professional lives.

Deepening Our Understanding

As mentioned in the previous chapter, we will now take a deeper dive into building our understanding of what takes place in the Mindful Vortex and begin to master our ability to operate effectively in contextual complexity. It is not Jedi stuff. It is about opening the aperture and moving the camera to a place where we can have a reframed perspective. I used to ask my undergrad students some twenty years ago, "Who is photographer in this class" to leverage that person's experience to explain how to reframe a perspective. One hand from time to time would go up in the air. Today, we are all photographers as we have a cell phone in our pocket with the imaging power that we never thought would be possible. We know that as we move our devices we see a scenery, an object, or a loved one, from a reframed perspective. Strong on the perspectives that we built in Horizon 1 and Chapter 3 of this book, we are now going to explore methods and techniques to strengthen our understanding of self-authoring and increase our ability to manage ourselves in the Mindful Vortex by authoring, curating, and deploying our Leadership Branding.

Defining Leadership Branding

To understand leadership branding, we need first to understand **what is not.** In 1966, Peter Drucker wrote the following: "Every knowledge worker in the modern organization is an 'executive' if, by virtue of his/her; position or knowledge, he/she is responsible for a contribution that materially affects the capacity of the organization to perform and to obtain results." Drucker had developed foresight about a future state of knowledge and the role that it would play in executing tasks. We use the title 'executive' to define an organization's position, which is seen as a point of arrival in careers. Money, prestige, power, you name it, comes from the positioning on the totem pole. We often fall into the trap of celebrating the 'rock star executive' with little attention to how results are attained. We look at the attire, watches, and shoes and call that a brand. We often don't pay attention if the 'rock star executive' has a brain and never mind a heart.

We have come to use efficiency and effectiveness as interchangeable terms when the reality is that they often reside on the opposite side of the spectrum. To effectively influence and inspire others, one must first understand what sets them apart as a leader and then articulate and regularly deploy those qualities. This idea extends beyond formal roles to include the traits, beliefs, and actions that make a person a leader. By developing a compelling leadership brand, individuals can gain insight into their own capabilities and development areas while also gaining respect and support from their network.

A Reframed Philosophy

The concept of individual branding came to my awareness about twenty years ago while I was having lunch with a client. As part of that discussion was the possibility of licensing our trademarked name, Radi Design, to be used on an upscale segment of their consumer electronics offering. They say, "You know, just like Pininfarina or Porche Design, you design, we make them and sell them." Interesting, I thought. Risky but interesting. But then, the conversation got more interesting as the concept of individual branding was brought up. I was not familiar with the concept. As my professional life at the time was focused on consumer product strategy, my mental model was focused on designing and branding products and services, but branding people? Well, that was not on my radar until that meeting, and Tom Peters's work entered my life.

Since then, I have been fascinated by the concept. However, it wasn't until some ten years later, as I was working on my Ph.D. between 2012 and 2015, that I started to dedicate time and energy to research the subject and better understand it to develop a leadership branding philosophy and comprehensive methodology to enable leaders and emerging leaders to assess, develop and congruently deploy their Leadership Brand in the context in which they operate. In contrast, Peters, in his article "The Brand Called You" (Fast Company, 1997), and Montoya and Vandehey, in their book "The Brand Called You" (McGraw-Hill, 2002), do focus primarily on personal branding for career success. My leadership branding philosophy goes beyond that, addressing the broader implications of a leader's behavior on multiple levels. It doesn't categorize or compare individuals as each leader and emerging leader operates in unique contexts with unique dynamics. My research has brought me to identify leadership brand dimensions that can be measured quantitatively and qualitatively through a focus group-inspired perspective. Everyone is unique, so it is their brand.

Further, my philosophy centers on the importance of self-awareness, self-discovery, and the unique characteristics that define an individual's leadership brand. Building upon the foundation of spirituality, science, and the self, I have identified nine fundamental characteristics that inform an individual's Leadership Brand profile. This holistic approach differentiates my philosophy from other notable personal branding books, such as "Reinventing You" by Dorie Clark, which emphasizes the importance of redefining and reinventing one's personal brand to adapt to changing career and life goals. "Crush It!" by Gary Vaynerchuk, focuses on using passion and personal branding to succeed in the digital age. The author discusses the power of social media and online platforms to create a unique personal brand that resonates with audiences and drives success. And "You Are a Brand!" by Catherine Kaputa offers a step-by-step approach to personal branding for business success, highlighting the importance of self-promotion and marketing one's unique skills and qualities to achieve career goals.

While these books offer valuable insights into personal branding, my philosophy stands out in its focus on leadership branding, which encompasses the development of a unique leadership identity and the practical impact of leadership actions on individuals and organizations. I emphasize the broader implications of a leader's behavior on multiple levels, offering a more comprehensive perspective on leadership development.

My Leadership Effectiveness waterfall definition further solidifies the distinctiveness of my philosophy. This definition highlights the cascading effect of a leader's actions, attitudes, and behaviors on their organization and the people they lead. In essence, my approach emphasizes the importance of understanding the unique characteristics that shape an individual's leadership brand while also recognizing their leadership's ripple effect on the world around them.

When contrasted with other personal branding literature, my philosophy delves deeper into the realm of leadership and its effects on various aspects of life, such as personal growth, relationships, professional value generation, and the ability to effect change. By focusing on the nine fundamental characteristics of a leadership brand, my approach offers readers a more comprehensive and practical understanding of what it takes to be an effective leader.

My leadership branding philosophy distinguishes itself by focusing on a comprehensive understanding of leadership, emphasizing the nine fundamental characteristics of an individual's Leadership Brand profile, and recognizing the cascading impact of a leader's behavior on multiple levels. This holistic approach to leadership development sets it apart from other personal branding literature, providing readers with a more profound and actionable understanding of what it takes to become an exceptional leader.

THINKING POINT

Section Takeaways

Leadership branding goes beyond the surface-level attributes often associated with successful individuals, such as attire or prestige. It centers on the unique traits, beliefs, and actions that set a leader apart and effectively influence and inspire others.

Leadership branding isn't a new concept, but it is increasingly important in the context of knowledge work and organizational performance. As such, it extends beyond personal branding for career success, focusing instead on the broader implications of a leader's behavior on multiple levels.

The author's philosophy on leadership branding incorporates self-awareness, self-discovery, and the unique characteristics that define an individual's leadership brand. It offers a holistic perspective on leadership development that acknowledges the cascading impact of a leader's actions on their environment.

Reflective Questions

How have you previously understood leadership branding? How does this new perspective challenge or enhance your existing perceptions?

Do you agree that leadership branding extends beyond personal branding for career success? Why or why not?

How do you view the nine fundamental characteristics of a leadership brand outlined in the author's philosophy? Can you relate them to your own leadership behavior or that of leaders you admire?

Contextualization Prompt

Think about leaders you admire, whether they are public figures, colleagues, or people in your personal life. Reflect on their unique traits, beliefs, and actions that set them apart and make them effective leaders. What aspects of their leadership would you incorporate into your own Leadership Brand? Consider how you can apply the author's philosophy of leadership branding in your own life and career.

The Nexus

We must explore Nexus to understand the leadership brand's role in grasping the imperative of self-authoring in achieving clarity in contextual complexity. The Nexus framework conceptually represents interconnectedness between Your Leadership Brand, Emotional Intelligence, and Clarity in Complexity (See Image 8).

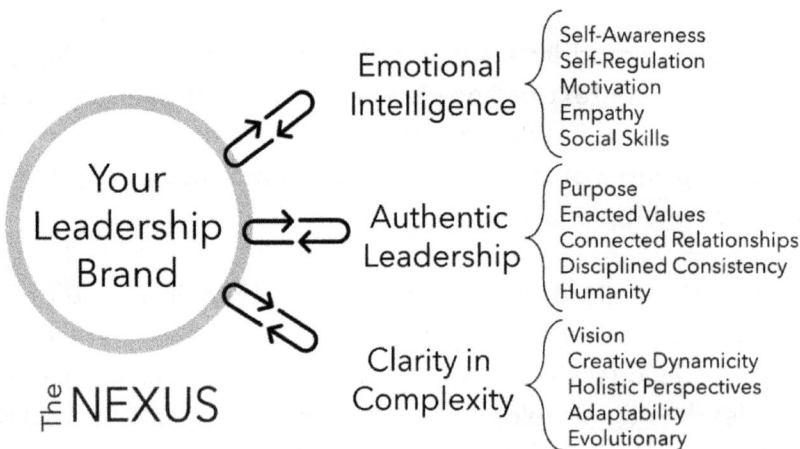

Image 8. Leadership Brand: The Nexus (Radi, 2015 – 2023) © Integral Advantage®

Emotional Intelligence (EI)

In essence, Emotional Intelligence (EI) refers to the ability to recognize, understand, and manage our emotions and the emotions of others. It is a critical skill for effective communication, relationship-building, and decision-making. Renowned psychologist Daniel Goleman brought the concept of EI to be mainstream with two books, Emotional Intelligence: Why It Can Matter More Than IQ and Working with Emotional Intelligence. These are the five key components of EI:

Self-Awareness: This is the ability to recognize and understand our emotions, strengths, weaknesses, and triggers. Self-aware individuals are in tune with their emotional states and can identify how their emotions affect their thoughts and behaviors.

Self-Regulation: This involves effectively managing our emotions and impulses, allowing us to respond appropriately to various situations. Self-regulation includes skills such as self-control, adaptability, and emotional resilience.

Motivation: This component is about being driven by an intrinsic passion for personal growth and achievement rather than external factors like money or status. Motivated individuals are goal-oriented and persistent, even when faced with challenges.

Empathy: Empathy refers to the ability to understand and share the feelings of others. It involves attuning to others' emotional states, recognizing their perspectives, and responding compassionately to their needs.

Social Skills: These skills are necessary to build and maintain healthy relationships with others. Socially skilled individuals can effectively communicate, collaborate, and navigate social situations. Critical social skills include active listening, conflict resolution, and persuasion.

Authentic Leadership

Authentic Leadership is a leadership approach that emphasizes self-awareness, transparency, ethical behavior, and openness to feedback. It is characterized by leaders who are genuine, self-aware, and true to their values and beliefs. While there are several definitions of Authentic Leadership, I favor some modifications I made; the components of Authentic Leadership, as proposed by authors Mary Crossan, Jeffrey Gandz, and Gerard Seijts, include

Purpose: Authentic leaders clearly understand their mission and vision, which drives their actions and decision-making processes. They can inspire and motivate others by effectively communicating the meaning behind their actions.

Enacted Values: (originally Values): Authentic leaders consistently demonstrate their values and principles through behavior. They are true to their beliefs, even in challenging situations, and their actions align with their stated values. By adding "enacted," I emphasize that authentic leaders hold values and actively demonstrate them through their behavior. This distinction is important because it separates leaders who merely claim to have values and seldom exhibit them from those who consistently live by them.

Connected Relationships (originally Relationships): Authentic leaders foster strong relationships built on trust, respect, and open communication. They actively engage with others, listen to feedback, and support the growth and development of their team members. By adding "connected," I am highlighting the depth and quality of the relationships authentic leaders do foster. Connected relationships are built on trust, respect, and open communication, demonstrating that authentic leaders are actively engaged and invested in fostering strong connections with others.

Disciplined Consistency (originally Consistency): Authentic leaders demonstrate consistency in their behavior and decision-making processes. By adding "disciplined," I reinforce the intentional and persistent nature of authentic leaders' behavior and decision-making processes. This aspect illustrates that authentic leaders work diligently to maintain trust and credibility with their followers by remaining consistent in their actions and decisions.

Humanity: Authentic leaders exhibit humility, empathy, and compassion, recognizing the importance of treating others with kindness and understanding. All I have to add to this one is, as Confucius stated, "To become a leader, you must first become a human being."

Clarity in Complexity

The third element in the Nexus framework I have proposed captures the essential interrelationship Clarity in Complexity. As we have seen in Chapter 2, the superimposed cognitive lenses of the CADE model enable us to gain clarity in complexity. Attaining clarity in complexity is vital for leaders to navigate the challenges and contexts of our time and for the Self to operate in complexity there are five components that I have identified:

Vision: A clear vision provides direction and purpose for leaders, allowing them to set meaningful goals and chart a course toward achieving them. Leaders can inspire and motivate their teams by having a compelling vision, fostering a sense of unity and commitment towards shared objectives. Often leaders who operate captive units in large organizations must develop a vision (theirs) within a vision (the organization).

Creative Dynamicity: In an ever-changing world, leaders need to be creative and dynamic in their approach to problem-solving and decision-making. Creative dynamicity involves exploring new ideas, embracing innovation, and being open to novel approaches to challenges. This skill enables leaders to stay ahead of the curve and adapt to the rapidly changing business landscape.

Holistic Perspectives: Leaders need to consider various aspects of a situation and understand the broader context in which they operate. A holistic perspective encourages leaders to consider the interconnectedness of different elements and consider multiple viewpoints, leading to more informed decisions and better overall outcomes.

Adaptability: As the world around us evolves, so must leaders. Adaptability is the ability to adjust to new circumstances, learn from experiences, and respond effectively to change. Adaptable leaders can pivot when needed, ensuring they remain effective despite shifting challenges and opportunities.

Evolutionary: An evolutionary mindset involves continuous personal and professional growth and development. Leaders who embrace an evolutionary approach are committed to learning, improving, and refining their skills and understanding. This ongoing development enables leaders to stay relevant, respond to new challenges, and lead their organizations more effectively.

THINKING POINT

Section Takeaways:

The Nexus framework conceptually represents the interconnectedness between Leadership Branding, Emotional Intelligence (EI), and Clarity in Complexity, all of which are essential for effective leadership.

Emotional Intelligence refers to the ability to recognize, understand, and manage our own emotions and those of others. It involves five key components: self-awareness, self-regulation, motivation, empathy, and social skills.

Authentic Leadership is characterized by self-awareness, transparency, ethical behavior, and openness to feedback. It includes the aspects of purpose, enacted values, connected relationships, disciplined consistency, and humanity.

Clarity in Complexity is vital for leaders to navigate the challenges and contexts of our time effectively. Five components are identified for operating in complexity: vision, creative dynamicity, holistic perspectives, adaptability, and an evolutionary mindset.

Reflective Questions:

How do you see the interconnectedness between your Leadership Brand, Emotional Intelligence, and ability to have Clarity in Complexity?

Reflect on your Emotional Intelligence. How well do you recognize and manage your emotions? How well do you understand and manage the emotions of others?

Consider the components of Authentic Leadership: purpose, enacted values, connected relationships, disciplined consistency, and humanity. Which of these components do you feel you demonstrate well, and where could you improve?

Contextualization Prompt:
Consider a recent leadership challenge you faced. How did your Leadership Brand come into play? What role did Emotional Intelligence play in addressing this challenge? How did Clarity in Complexity help you navigate the situation? Reflect on the interplay of these three elements in your leadership behavior and consider how you might further develop in each area to become a more effective leader.

You Are Unique. Your Brand is Unique.

My ethical holding is to recognize everyone as an autonomous human being, with the agency and faculty to make choices. To begin our self-authoring journey toward developing our leadership brand statement, we need to introspectively reflect on these three rules I have established:

Rule 1. It is about your leadership brand, but it is not about you.

Rule 2. It is not about appearances, as a brand transcends the package.

Rule 3. Leadership Branding is about making and fulfilling a promise.

In leadership branding, embracing the idea that "You Are Unique. Your Brand is Unique " requires understanding the three interrelated aspects of human existence: Spirituality, Science, and Self. These aspects collectively highlight the uniqueness of each individual and form the foundation of a distinctive leadership brand.

Spirituality. Throughout history, various spiritual and religious doctrines have almost universally emphasized that every human possesses a unique soul or essence. In Christianity, for instance, the Bible states that God created each person in His image (Genesis 1:27), indicating that each individual possesses a divine essence distinct from all others. Hinduism and Buddhism also teach the concept of Atman and Anatman, respectively, which refer to an individual's transcendent inner personality or individuality. In Islamic teachings, the Quran emphasizes the uniqueness of each individual by stating that God created humans with distinct features, colors, and languages (Quran 30:22). Moreover, the concept of Fitrah, or inherent human nature, suggests that every individual is born with a unique disposition and spiritual development potential. In Jewish teachings, the Talmud instructs each individual to declare, "For my sake, the world was created" (Mishnah Sanhedrin 4:5), emphasizing each individual's significance and unique role. Many indigenous spiritual traditions worldwide celebrate the interconnectedness of all living things and each individual's distinct role in preserving the natural world's equilibrium. In Taoism, Wu Wei, or effortless action, teaches individuals to accept their unique character and exist in harmony with the natural flow of life. By comprehending and aligning with their inherent essence, Taoist leaders can establish a leadership brand that is genuine, adaptable, and in sync with life's ever-changing circumstances. So, across most gradients of spirituality, we are considered unique.

Science. Well, here is where science did play catch up. In 1953, James Watson and Francis Crick's discovery of DNA revealed the genetic blueprint underlying each individual's unique characteristics, traits, and predispositions. This revolutionary discovery demonstrated that, except for identical twins, no two individuals share the same genetic composition. Another scientific area relevant to individual uniqueness is the field of epigenetics, which is the study of what Allis, Jenuwein, & Reinberg define as heritable variations in gene expression that do not involve changes to the DNA sequence. This scientific field considers various factors, such as lifestyle choices and environmental factors, influence epigenetic modifications, resulting in distinct gene expression patterns for each individual. I include epigenetics in this discussion because this concept illustrates how identical siblings with the same genetic makeup can have distinctive traits and behaviors due to gene expression patterns. So, even twins are not the same!

Then there is uniqueness in our brains and neuro patterns. As previously discussed, neuroplasticity aids us in understanding that each individual's brain develops uniquely.

This development often responds to an individual's life experiences, contributing to their unique cognitive abilities, emotions, and behaviors. Last but not least, in more recent times, we are starting to hear more about the human microbiome, which according to an article by the National Institute of Health, comprises trillions of microorganisms living in and on the human body (I would add rent-free!). They play a vital role in many aspects of human health, such as digestion, immunity, and mental health. These advancements in science are bringing personalized medicine to center stage, which entices tailoring medical treatments to the unique genetic composition and health profile. This approach acknowledges and emphasizes the significance of understanding individual differences to optimize healthcare outcomes. So, science agrees with spirituality: you are labeled unique. I made my case.

The Self. At certain points in life, we become aware of our uniqueness and the factors that set us apart. Do you have a memory of becoming aware of your uniqueness? A sense of self-awareness enables you to sense and cultivate your unique identity, values, and beliefs, enhancing your overall sense of self. For instance, Carl Rogers, a renowned humanistic psychologist, emphasized the significance of self-actualization in pursuing personal development and self-discovery. Self-actualization refers to the journey of recognizing and realizing one's potential. Everyone's life experiences, such as upbringing, education, relationships, and occupation, influence their perspectives and contribute to their sense of self. Hence, everyone's experiences result in a distinctive worldview and approach to problem-solving, decision-making, and interpersonal interactions.

If we juxtapose this perspective with cognitive patterns, we better understand how individuals think, perceive, and process information. We can appreciate the difference in cognitive methods, including analytical, intuitive, and creative thinking. These factors contribute to the diversity of individuals' approaches and perspectives. Everyone's unique combination of cognitive styles molds their self-concept and influences how they approach challenges and opportunities.

Appreciating the interconnected aspects of Spirituality, Science, and Self constitute the pillars upholding how I developed my concept of uniqueness in leadership branding. By delving into their spiritual essence, recognizing their genetic individuality, and fostering self-awareness, leaders can create and congruently enact a unique leadership brand that resonates with their core values and strengths, effectively guiding and inspiring their teams and organizations. Embracing this uniqueness also fosters a culture of authenticity, inclusivity, and individuality, allowing diverse ideas and perspectives to thrive and contribute to the organization's success.

How Do We Manifest the Self?

Robert Burns (1759 – 1796), a Scottish poet and lyricist, stated, "I wish for a power to give us this gift: Being able to see ourselves the way other people see us." Essentially, this quote speaks to the congruency between how we see ourselves and others' perceptions. We need to define who these individuals are in the context in which we operate. It is not about making everyone else happy. A little story here may explain my perspective. In 2022, after a long and contentious process concerning a controversial project in La Quinta, CA, the matter was finally in front of the City Council, of which, at that time, I was a member. At the closing of the public testimony, The Mayor recognized me to speak first as part of the deliberation process. Throughout the entire saga, I have been very vocal in protecting the developer's right to due process as enshrined in the Fifth and Fourteenth Amendments of the U.S. Constitution. It is to be noted that people have given their lives to gain and protect those rights. As disappointing as it may be, taking a few dozen nasty and insulting calls and emails is not heroic; it is just the bare minimum that someone can do to ensure due process. In my deliberation, I explained the framework I used to make my decision and why I was unable to vote in favor of the project. The project was eventually voted down. I knew I had disappointed many who favored the project—individuals who had supported me over the years and whom I greatly respected.

As the rumors and innuendos were still flying the following day, I received an email from a landowner near the proposed project's site who favored the demised project. In that email, he explained how he disagreed with my decision but understood the dynamics that brought me to it. He closed the short email by expressing appreciation for my integrity and years of service. In the following days, I heard much of the same from others. In essence, our actions result in others experiencing our leadership brand. And this aspect is the central tenet of how I propose the methodology to develop and congruently deploy a leadership brand (See Image 9).

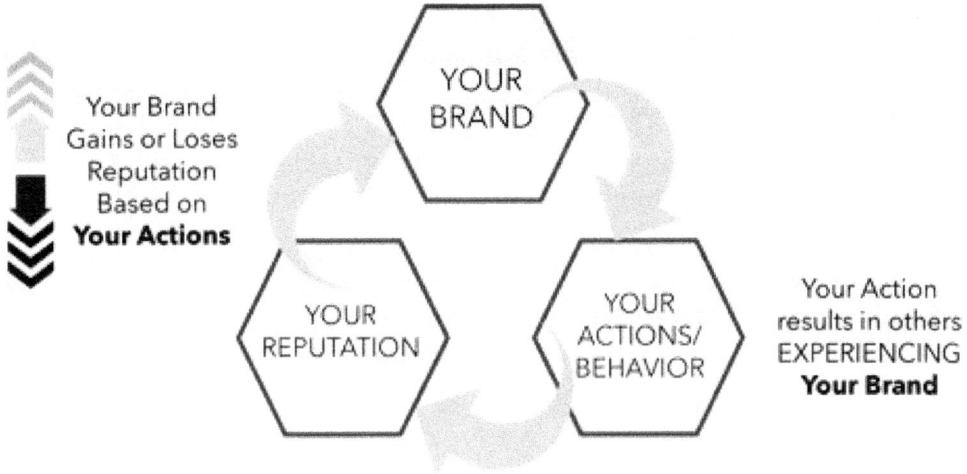

Image 9. Leadership Brand Deployment (Radi, 2015 - 2023) © Integral Advantage®

Henry Ford stated, "You can't build a reputation on what you are going to do." As the Leadership Brand Deployment Framework shows, others experience our leadership brand through our actions and behavior, which in turn impacts our reputation, and our leadership brand gains or loses reputation based on our actions. This can be a virtuous cycle or a vicious cycle. Knowing or unknowingly, you already have a leadership brand, but the question is intentionally developed, and are you in charge of deploying it and curating it for the context in which you operate?

THINKING POINT

Section Takeaways

Leadership branding is rooted in the inherent uniqueness of individuals, encompassing their spiritual essence, genetic individuality, and sense of self.

Understanding and aligning with one's inherent essence can lead to the creation of a genuine and adaptable leadership brand that resonates with core values and strengths.

Our actions and behavior shape how others experience our leadership brand. This relationship, in turn, impacts our reputation, which feeds back into our leadership brand in a continuous cycle. Intentional development and deployment of a leadership brand can ensure it remains relevant and effective in the context in which it operates.

Reflective Questions

How do you perceive your uniqueness in terms of spirituality, science, and self?

Can you recall a time when your actions and behavior noticeably impacted the perception of your leadership brand?

In what ways can you intentionally develop and deploy your leadership brand to ensure it remains relevant in your operating context?

What steps can you take to align your leadership brand with your core values and strengths?

Contextualization Prompt

Reflect on a time when your perception of your leadership brand didn't align with the perception of others. What were the circumstances? What insights did you gain from the experience? How did you adapt your leadership brand to better align with your desired reputation? What was the impact of these changes on your leadership effectiveness?

CHAPTER 5

YOUR CONTEXTUAL LEADERSHIP BRAND

"When I look around, I always learn something, and that is, to always be yourself and to express yourself. To have faith in yourself. Do not go out and look for a successful personality and duplicate him." — Bruce Lee

There is a saying. If a person says you have a tail, well, that person is crazy. If two people tell you have a tail, well, that is most certainly a conspiracy. If three people tell you have a tail; you need to turn and glance. To be effective, leaders must develop self-awareness and gain clarity about how they show up in the environmental context in which they operate. This is a critical aspect in leadership branding as two individuals operating in two different contexts cannot be compared.

The Integral Advantage® Encompass Assessment

In this chapter, I will periodically refer to the Integral Advantage® Encompass to enhance the illustration and explanation of several fundamental concepts. I want to make clear that for you to gain the benefit of the concepts illustrated in this chapter, you don't have to invest financial resources to take the assessment. While the assessment is effective in providing a clear perspective with a relatively minor effort from you and those you chose to evaluate you, it will not do the work for you once you are aware of your results. In this chapter, I will provide you with all you need to self-assess, reflect and for you to generate ideas on how to involve others. Yes, it takes more time than if you take the assessment, but before its introduction, we used to do it "old school" if you wish. I just don't want you to feel obligated or pressured into taking the assessment. Is there a right way to learn? Yes! How you prefer to learn and process new concepts is the right way!

I developed the Integral Advantage® Encompass as a solution to empower leaders and emerging leaders to evaluate their leadership brand holistically and create a developmental way forward aimed at deploying a well-defined and articulated leadership brand, congruent with their purpose, identity, and context in which they operate. More information about the assessment is available at IntegralAdvantage.com.

Integral Advantage® Encompass doesn't categorize or compare individuals, as each operates in unique contexts with unique dynamics. Each assessment measures the leadership brand dimensions quantitatively and qualitatively via a focus group perspective. Everyone is unique, so it is their brand.

The Integral Advantage® Encompass utilizes a mixed method of quantitative and qualitative proprietary researched psychometric questions in survey format, requiring twenty minutes from self and evaluators to complete. It assesses five encompassing dimensions:

Dimension	Methodology
Leadership Brand Profile	via 9 researched sub-dimensions.
Leadership Brand Attributes	via the researched qualitative questions.
Leadership Effectiveness	via the proprietary waterfall definition.
Leadership Presence	via 3 researched sub-dimensions.
Leadership Brand Calibration	via qualitative feedback for development.

Table 3. The Leadership Brand Dimensions (Radi, 2015 - 2023) © Integral Advantage®

Let's delve into all five dimensions and savor the ideas for introspective reflection and self-assessment, developmental planning, seeking feedback, and gain clarity about the interplay of the dimensions and subdimension of a leadership brand.

Dimension 1: The Leadership Brand Profile Dimension

My research has established nine (9) fundamental characteristics informing an individual Leadership Brand Profile. With introspective reflection prompts, the developmental plan, and the resources provided, you are well-equipped to embark on a journey toward cultivating the nine (9) fundamental characteristics of a leadership brand profile. It is an opportunity to open the aperture and intentionally explore and strive for continuous growth and self-improvement.

Image 10. The Leadership Brand Profile Dimension (Radi, 2015 - 2023) © Integral Advantage®

FUNDAMENTAL CHARACTERISTIC 1: TRUSTWORTHINESS

The congruency between message and actions informs Trustworthiness, the ability to foster confidence in followers, maximize the benefit to all those involved, and sustain trusting and value-driven relationships.

Introspective Reflection and Self-Assessment:

The following prompts are provided for your introspective reflection on Trustworthiness:

1. In what situations have I demonstrated congruency between my words and actions?

2. Have I encountered instances where my actions may not have aligned with my stated values?

3. How have I worked to build trust among my followers or team members?

4. What actions have I taken to ensure that my decision-making process is transparent and benefits all parties?

Developmental Plan for Trustworthiness:

Enhance self-awareness: With your core values and principles in mind, reflect on how they align with your actions and decision-making processes. Consider seeking feedback from others to identify areas for improvement.

Communicate openly and transparently: Keep your team informed about your intentions, goals, and progress. This transparency fosters trust and demonstrates your commitment to staying aligned with your values.

Be consistent: Show consistency in your words, actions, and decisions, reflecting your commitment to your values and the well-being of your team or organization.

Encourage feedback: Create an environment where feedback is welcomed and valued. This practice will help you identify areas for improvement and demonstrate your commitment to continuous growth.

Embodiments of Trustworthiness

A few diverse examples of high Trustworthiness can be appreciated in these individuals. Howard Schultz, the former CEO of Starbucks, is known for his trustworthiness and consistent alignment with the company's values. Under his leadership, Starbucks became recognized for its commitment to ethical sourcing, environmental stewardship, and employee well-being. Schultz's dedication to these values has been evident in his actions and decisions, earning him the respect and trust of employees and customers. Nelson Mandela's unwavering commitment to his values, even during his 27 years in prison, earned him the trust of his followers and former adversaries. His actions consistently aligned with his words, and he led South Africa through immense change with integrity and compassion. As the former CEO of PepsiCo, Indra Nooyi demonstrated trustworthiness by focusing on sustainable growth and promoting healthier products. Her actions consistently aligned with her message of creating a more sustainable future, earning her the trust and respect of her team and industry peers.

FUNDAMENTAL CHARACTERISTIC 2: PERFORMANCE

Performance is informed by the propensity to provide high performance, the commitment to collective strategic performance, consistency in delivery, and the ability to address performance barriers.

Introspective Reflection and Self-Assessment:

The following prompts are provided for your introspective reflection on Performance:

1. Can I recall instances where I have delivered on my promises and consistently met or exceeded expectations?

2. How do I handle situations where I or my team face performance barriers?

3. How do I demonstrate commitment to the organization's strategic goals and direction?

4. How do I ensure my unit operates at its highest potential and achieves optimal results?

Developmental Plan for Performance:

Set clear expectations: Communicate your expectations and goals to your team, ensuring they understand the standards required for High Performance.

Foster a culture of accountability: Encourage your team members to take ownership of their tasks and be responsible for their performance.

Address performance barriers: Identify and address any obstacles or barriers that may hinder your team's performance, be it lacking resources, inadequate training, or interpersonal conflicts.

Continuously assess and adjust: Regularly review your team's performance against set goals and adjust to maintain alignment with the organization's strategic direction.

Embodiments of Performance

A few diverse examples of high performance can be appreciated in these individuals. Sheryl Sandberg, COO of Facebook and founder of LeanIn. Org, has consistently demonstrated commitment to performance in both the for-profit and non-profit sectors. As COO, she has helped scale Facebook's operations and revenue while her non-profit organization empowers women to achieve their ambitions. Nuria I. Fernandez. She is the Administrator of the Federal Transit Administration (FTA), a division of the United States Department of Transportation (DOT). She was confirmed by the U.S. Senate on June 10, 2021. As a result of her focus on performance, Fernandez has earned the respect and trust of her employees and the public. She is seen as a leader who can deliver results and who is committed to making public transportation a more reliable and efficient option for all Americans. Richard Dickson, the President and Chief Operating Officer of Mattel, a leading global toy company. He is known for setting high standards and for holding himself and his team accountable. He is also a strong communicator who is able to clearly articulate his vision for Mattel. He is constantly looking for ways to improve Mattel's business and its products. He is also a strong advocate for innovation and creativity.

FUNDAMENTAL CHARACTERISTIC 3: SATISFACTION

Satisfaction is informed by the perception of leadership quality and related satisfaction, the ability to care for others' sense of overall satisfaction, exemplary leadership behavior, and a sense of robust reliability.

Introspective Reflection and Self-Assessment:

The following prompts are provided for your introspective reflection on Satisfaction:

1. How do I perceive my leadership quality and its impact on the satisfaction of those I lead?

2. How do I demonstrate care and concern for my team members' job satisfaction?

3. Can I think of instances where I have been a dependable leader?

4. How do my leadership behaviors inspire others to emulate me?

Developmental Plan for Satisfaction:

Lead by example: Demonstrate the behaviors and values that you expect from your team, setting a positive example for them to follow.

Communicate and engage: Regularly communicate with your team members, ensuring they feel heard, valued, and included in the decision-making process.

Support your team's development: Identify opportunities for growth and development for your team members and provide the necessary resources and support.

Be dependable and consistent: Cultivate a reputation for reliability by consistently following through on your commitments and delivering on your promises.

Embodiments of Satisfaction

A few diverse examples of high satisfaction can be appreciated in these individuals. Tony Hsieh, the late CEO of Zappos, was known for his focus on customer and employee satisfaction, creating a unique company culture that prioritized happiness and personal growth. His leadership behavior emphasized servant leadership and empowerment. Stephan Winkelmann is the current CEO of Automobili Lamborghini, an Italian luxury sports car manufacturer. He is a highly respected leader who is known for his ability to create a positive and productive work environment. His employees are consistently satisfied with their jobs and their work-life balance. Malala Yousafzai, a human rights activist, and the youngest Nobel Prize laureate has inspired millions with her leadership in advocating for education and gender equality. Her courage, resilience, and dedication to her cause have contributed to her ability to create satisfaction and impact in the lives of others. Jacinda Ardern, the Prime Minister of New Zealand, has been praised for her compassionate and empathetic leadership behavior. She has effectively navigated crises, such as the Christchurch Mosque shootings and the COVID-19 pandemic, with a focus on the well-being and satisfaction of her country's citizens.

FUNDAMENTAL CHARACTERISTIC 4: EXPERIENCE

Experience is informed by how others experience interpersonal and professional interactions, consistency in these experiences, overall affiliative approach, and prioritization of collective recognition over self.

Introspective Reflection and Self-Assessment:

The following prompts are provided for your introspective reflection on Experience:

1. How do others feel when they interact with me, both professionally and personally?

2. Am I consistent in the way I behave and interact with others?

3. Do I prioritize collective recognition over my achievements?

4. How would I describe my overall approach to leadership, and is it affiliative?

Developmental Plan for Experience:

Build strong interpersonal skills: Enhance your communication, listening, and empathy skills to foster positive experiences for those around you.

Cultivate consistency: Develop consistent behavior patterns that reflect your values and build trust among your team members.

Foster a team-centric environment: Encourage collaboration and prioritize the success and recognition of the team.

Be approachable and authentic: Create an environment where your team feels comfortable sharing their thoughts and ideas and engage in open and transparent communication.

Embodiments of Experience

A few diverse examples of high satisfaction can be appreciated in these individuals. Richard Branson, the founder of the Virgin Group, is known for his open and approachable leadership behavior. He consistently prioritizes the experience of his employees, often engaging with them and taking their feedback into account when making decisions. Ellen Johnson Sirleaf, the former President of Liberia and Nobel Peace Prize laureate, led her country through a rebuilding period after years of civil war. Her focus on unity and collaboration fostered a positive experience for her fellow citizens and helped create a more stable and prosperous nation. Brene Brown, a research professor, author, and speaker, is known for her work on vulnerability and empathy. Her authentic and empathetic approach to leadership has inspired many to create environments where people feel safe to express themselves and learn from their experiences.

FUNDAMENTAL CHARACTERISTIC 5: ELICITING LOYALTY

Eliciting Loyalty is informed by the ability to reciprocate loyalty, foster functional and healthy relationships, appropriate warmth and compassion, and an overall sense of emotional safety.

Introspective Reflection and Self-Assessment:

The following prompts are provided for your introspective reflection on Eliciting Loyalty:

1. Do I consistently reciprocate loyalty to those who are loyal to me?

2. Am I adept at fostering functional and healthy relationships within my team or organization?

3. Do I demonstrate appropriate warmth and compassion in my interactions with others?

4. Do my team members feel psychologically safe and supported under my leadership?

Developmental Plan for Eliciting Loyalty:

Be genuine in your loyalty: Demonstrate consistent loyalty to your team members by supporting them, advocating for their growth, and acknowledging their contributions.

Create a positive work environment: Foster a culture of trust, open communication, and collaboration that helps nurture healthy and functional relationships.

Demonstrate empathy and compassion: Show understanding, care, and support for your team members, recognizing their unique challenges and needs.

Develop emotional intelligence: Enhance your self-awareness, self-regulation, motivation, empathy, and social skills to create a sense of emotional safety for your team members.

Embodiments of Eliciting Loyalty

A few diverse examples high in eliciting loyalty can be appreciated in these individuals. Herb Kelleher, the late co-founder and CEO of Southwest Airlines was known for his unwavering loyalty to his employees. He created a supportive work environment prioritizing employee satisfaction, and his genuine care for his team members resulted in a highly loyal workforce. Alan Mulally, the former CEO of Ford Motor Company, was known for turning the company around by creating a culture of collaboration, open communication, and trust. His genuine interest in the well-being of his employees and his ability to make sense of emotional safety within the organization contributed to high employee loyalty. Satya Nadella, CEO of Microsoft, has been praised for his ability to foster a culture of empathy, collaboration, and growth. By focusing on the well-being of his employees and demonstrating genuine loyalty, he has earned the respect and allegiance of his team members. Annie Young-Scrivner is the Chief Executive Officer of Wella Company. She is a charismatic and inspiring leader who is able to build strong relationships with her employees and customers. She is also known for her ability to motivate and inspire others to achieve their goals.

FUNDAMENTAL CHARACTERISTIC 6: APPROACHABILITY

Approachability is informed by the ability to provide desirable interaction, remain approachable, and be a calming influence in adversities while developing and maintaining a deep connection with others.

Introspective Reflection and Self-Assessment:

The following prompts are provided for your introspective reflection on Approachability:

1. How do I perceive my level of approachability in my professional interactions?

2. How accessible and available do I make myself to your team members?

3. What strategies do I employ to create a calm and composed atmosphere during challenging situations?

4. How do I build and maintain deep, meaningful connections with others?

Developmental Plan for Approachability:

Cultivate openness: Encourage open communication, be receptive to feedback, and actively listen to others to establish a more approachable demeanor.

Demonstrate empathy and understanding: Show genuine care and concern for your team members' well-being, validating their feelings and experiences.

Build emotional intelligence: Enhance your self-awareness, empathy, and social skills to foster deeper connections and maintain approachability.

Develop resilience and composure: Practice stress management techniques and model calm, composed behavior during adversities to inspire confidence and maintain approachability.

Embodiments of Approachability

A few diverse examples of high approachability can be appreciated in these individuals. Once again, Sir Richard Branson, founder of Virgin Group, is known for his approachable and charismatic leadership behavior. He maintains an open-door policy and encourages communication at all levels of the organization, fostering a positive environment where team members feel comfortable and supported. Melinda Gates, philanthropist, and co-founder of the Bill and Melinda Gates Foundation has demonstrated her approachability through her work in global health and development. She consistently engages with beneficiaries, listens to their stories, and values their experiences, making her a relatable and approachable leader. Aung San Suu Kyi, Burmese politician, and Nobel Peace Prize laureate is admired for her approachable and compassionate leadership behavior. She has always remained accessible to her followers and provided a calming presence amidst political turmoil, encouraging open dialogue and understanding.

FUNDAMENTAL CHARACTERISTIC 7: MINDFULNESS

Mindfulness is informed by overall self-awareness, willingness to be held accountable, mindfulness in examining assumptions, ability to own up to mistakes while retaining the desire to learn from them, awareness of self-composure, and constant search for meaning.

Introspective Reflection and Self-Assessment:

The following prompts are provided for your introspective reflection on Mindfulness:

How do I demonstrate accountability and ownership of my actions in professional relationships?

How do I handle mistakes and what steps do I take to learn from them?

How effective am I in examining my assumptions before making decisions?

How do I maintain composure under pressure and stressful situations?

What practices do I engage in to search for meaning and purpose in my work?

Developmental Plan for Mindfulness:

Foster self-awareness: Engage in regular self-reflection and seek feedback to increase your understanding of your strengths, weaknesses, and areas for growth.

Embrace accountability: Take responsibility for your actions, decisions, and their outcomes, and hold yourself accountable for your performance.

Challenge assumptions: Develop critical thinking skills and actively question assumptions to make well-informed, unbiased decisions.

Learn from mistakes: View mistakes as opportunities for growth, and actively seek to learn and improve from them.

Practice composure: Develop strategies to manage stress and maintain composure under pressure, such as mindfulness meditation or deep breathing exercises.

Search for meaning: Engage in activities that foster personal growth, explore your values, and align your work with a greater sense of purpose.

Embodiments of Mindfulness

A few diverse examples of high mindfulness can be appreciated in these individuals. Ruth Bader Ginsburg, former Associate Justice of the United States Supreme Court, was renowned for her composure, careful examination of assumptions, and unwavering search for meaning in her work. She remained steadfast in her commitment to justice and equality throughout her career. Oprah Winfrey, a media mogul and philanthropist exemplifies mindfulness through her ability to connect with others, focus on self-improvement, and commit to living a purpose-driven life. She has used her platform to promote self-awareness and personal growth for millions worldwide. Tim Cook, CEO of Apple, has demonstrated mindfulness in his leadership by fostering a culture of accountability, humility, and learning from mistakes. He consistently emphasizes the importance of self-awareness, examining assumptions, and finding meaning in one's work.

FUNDAMENTAL CHARACTERISTIC 8: AUTHENTICITY

Authenticity is informed by overall authenticity through the ability to exhibit integrity, purposeful articulation in addressing controversial issues, selfless courage in taking actions, and consistency in remaining true to self.

Introspective Reflection and Self-Assessment:

The following prompts are provided for your introspective reflection on Authenticity:

1. How transparent and genuine am I in your interactions with others?

2. How do I demonstrate integrity in my leadership and decision-making?

3. How do I address controversial issues and communicate my thoughts directly?

4. In what ways do I exhibit selfless courage when acting?

5. How do I maintain consistency in being true to myself and pointing out the "elephant in the room"?

Developmental Plan for Authenticity:

Foster transparency: Be open, honest, and genuine in your interactions and communication with others.

Uphold integrity: Act in accordance with your values and principles and be consistent in your words and actions.

Address controversial issues: Develop the skill of articulating your thoughts and opinions directly while maintaining respect for others' perspectives.

Demonstrate selfless courage: Be willing to take risks and make difficult decisions for the greater good, even when it requires personal sacrifice.

Stay true to yourself: Continuously engage in self-reflection and maintain consistency in your values, beliefs, and actions, even in the face of adversity.

Embodiments of Authenticity

A few diverse examples of high authenticity can be appreciated in these individuals. Maya Angelou, the celebrated poet and civil rights activist, was known for her unwavering authenticity, addressing controversial issues, and standing up for what she believed in even when it was difficult. José Andrés, a world-renowned chef, and philanthropist, displays authenticity in his leadership by consistently exhibiting integrity, addressing social issues, and using his platform to create positive change through his non-profit, World Central Kitchen. Desmond Tutu, the South African Archbishop, and social rights activist, demonstrated authenticity throughout his life by fearlessly addressing controversial issues, maintaining his principles in the face of adversity, and inspiring others through his selfless courage. Mindy Grossman, former CEO of WW International (formerly Weight Watchers), is known for her genuine and down-to-earth personality. She is also a strong advocate for women's empowerment and has been open about her own experiences as a woman in business. This authenticity has helped her to connect with her employees and customers on a personal level. Last but not least is Patagonia's founder, Yvon Chouinard, who exemplifies authenticity in his leadership by remaining true to his environmental sustainability and social responsibility values, even when it meant making unconventional business decisions or challenging the status quo.

FUNDAMENTAL CHARACTERISTIC 9: PERSPECTIVE

Perspective is informed by systems awareness through the ability to appreciate stakeholders' perspectives, redesign systems to achieve optimal performance, hold a long-term and sustainable horizon, and remain aware of the interplay of functions, processes, and programs in systems.

Introspective Reflection and Self-Assessment:

The following prompts are provided for your introspective reflection on Perspective:

1. How well do I appreciate the perspectives of all relevant stakeholders in my organization or system?

2. Am I open to redesigning systems to achieve optimal performance?

3. How much do I focus on the long-term sustainability of my organization?

4. How effectively do I bring valuable foresight for improvements that benefit all stakeholders?

5. In what ways are you concerned with streamlining functions, processes, and programs for optimal organizational performance?

Developmental Plan for Perspective:

Cultivate empathy: Actively listen to and appreciate the perspectives of diverse stakeholders to understand their needs and concerns better.

Embrace change: Be open to redesigning systems and processes when necessary to achieve optimal performance and adapt to evolving circumstances.

Focus on long-term sustainability: Keep your organization's long-term health and success in mind when making decisions and prioritize sustainable practices.

Develop foresight: Engage in strategic thinking and planning to anticipate future challenges and opportunities and make well-informed decisions that benefit all stakeholders.

Streamline functions, processes, and programs: Continuously evaluate and optimize organizational functions, processes, and programs to ensure efficiency and effectiveness.

Embodiments of Perspective

A few diverse examples of high perspective can be appreciated in these individuals. Ray Dalio, the founder of Bridgewater Associates, consistently applies his unique perspective and systems thinking approach to investment management, focusing on long-term sustainability and the needs of diverse stakeholders. Dr. Jane Goodall, a renowned primatologist and conservationist, demonstrates perspective by considering the interplay between humans, animals, and the environment and promoting sustainable practices that benefit all stakeholders. Pat Egan, President & CEO of See's Candy has a strong understanding core business and the candy industry as a whole. He also has a deep understanding of the needs of See's Candies' customers and employees. This understanding allows him to make decisions that are in the best interests of the company and its stakeholders. He is not just focused on the short-term profits of See's Candies, but also on its long-term sustainability. He is also aware of the interplay of functions, processes, and programs in the company's system.

DIMENSION 2: LEADERSHIP BRAND ATTRIBUTES

Understanding leadership attributes is crucial for individuals striving to be effective leaders. By recognizing and embracing our unique qualities and characteristics, we can harness our strengths, address weaknesses, and develop leadership behavior capable of positively impacting our teams and organizations. Research has shown that understanding leadership attributes is essential for various reasons. However, there are five that are salient. The first is Self-awareness, a key element of emotional intelligence. Understanding our leadership attributes gives us a more profound sense of our strengths, weaknesses, and emotional triggers. This self-awareness allows us to manage our emotions, adapt our behavior, and make better decisions. The second is personalizing leadership development. When we approach development focusing on strengthening our unique qualities and addressing areas, we intentionally enhance our effectiveness. The third is our impact on team performance. When we are aware of our attributes, we can better align our leadership behavior with the needs of our team by adapting our approach to motivate, engage, and empower our team members, leading to improved performance and productivity. The fourth is a sense of authenticity. When we are genuine, self-aware, and true to our values, we are more authentic and enhance our capacity to foster trust and credibility within our team and organization. The fifth is another critical aspect, and it involves enhancing communication. When we understand our leadership attributes, we can better tailor our communication approach to different audiences, enhancing our ability to influence, inspire, and engage with others, ultimately fostering stronger relationships and more effective collaborations.

creativity
helpful
surprising
honesty

lazy
relaxed
avoiding

-X

focused
fun
reliable

Self Evaluation

Your Evaluators

Smart Leader
Brave Too-Nice-X
Helpful
Confidence-X
Patient
Reality
Community
Reluctant-to-Lead-X
Calm
Joy
Lazy-X
Happy Analytical
Attitude
Honest
Ideal
Discouraging-X
Enthusiasm
Empathy
Humor Fairness
Ambition

Image 11. Leadership Brand Attributes Dimension (Radi, 2015 - 2023) © Integral Advantage®

Brand Attributes: Discovering and Developing Your Unique Attributes

Now that we have explored how leadership brand attributes represent the distinctive qualities and characteristics that set you apart as a leader, we need to dive deeper into how to discover and develop these unique attributes. Suppose you have taken the Integral Advantage® Encompass (See **Image 11**). In that case, you clearly understand your leadership brand attributes, as the report would show a comparison between your perception and the perception of others.

However, as mentioned earlier, before the release of the Integral Advantage® Encompass, we were doing it "Old School." In this section, I will show you how to explore leadership brand attributes in three steps: Listen, Retain, and Fine Tune (See **Image 12**).

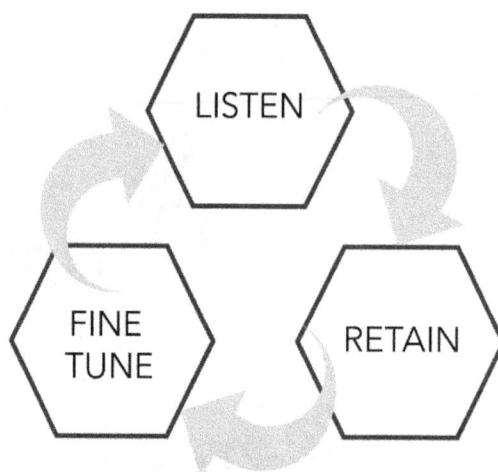

Image 12. Discovering Leadership Brand Attributes (Radi, 2015, 2018) © Integral Advantage®

By identifying these attributes, you can better understand your leadership strengths and areas for growth. helps you discover your unique leadership brand attributes through others feedback.

Listen: The Art of Listening

The first step in discovering unique brand attributes is leveraging the art of listening to gain insights. By evaluating the information, you receive through this process, you can better understand your leadership behavior and its impact on others. Here are some avenues to explore when seeking to discover your brand attributes:

Formal Feedback. Seek performance reviews, 360-degree assessments, or structured feedback sessions from your supervisors, peers, and subordinates. These formal channels can provide valuable insights into your strengths, weaknesses, and leadership effectiveness.

Casual Conversations. Engage in informal discussions with colleagues, team members, and mentors to better understand how you're perceived. By fostering open and honest conversations, you may discover unexpected attributes of your leadership.

"Throw Away" Comments. Pay attention to seemingly insignificant remarks made by others in passing, as they can offer clues about your brand attributes. These offhand comments reflect how others see you and reveal aspects of your leadership you may not have considered.

Formal & Informal Settings. Gather feedback from different settings, such as meetings, presentations, social events, and one-on-one interactions. By observing and analyzing your behavior in various contexts, you can better understand your leadership attributes and their impact on others.

RETAIN: RETAINING AND ANALYZING DISCOVERED ATTRIBUTES

Once you've gathered feedback on your brand attributes, retaining and analyzing this information is crucial, even if you need clarification on its significance. As you review the feedback, consider the following aspects to gain a deeper understanding of your leadership brand:

Perceptions: Remember that the feedback you receive reflects how others perceive you, which may not always align with your self-image. Be open to understanding these perceptions and use them as a basis for self-reflection and improvement.

Assumptions: People often form assumptions based on their experiences and interactions with you. Recognize that some of these assumptions may be inaccurate or incomplete but still offer valuable insights into how others perceive you.

Accuracy: Identify feedback that accurately captures your leadership attributes and strengths. This information can help you build on your existing capabilities, enhance leadership effectiveness, and further develop your unique brand.

Inaccuracy: Be aware of the feedback that may be inaccurate or misrepresent your valid leadership attributes. Use these instances as opportunities for clarification, self-reflection, and growth. Understand the context in which the inaccuracy arose and explore ways to address misconceptions.

Introspective Reflection and Self-Assessment:

Reflect on the feedback collected and consider the following prompts for introspective reflection on your Leadership Brand Attributes:

1. What are the words or phrases most frequently used by evaluators to describe you?

2. Which aspects of my leadership do others admire the most?

3. What character attributes are consistently associated with me?

4. What leadership weaknesses have been identified by others?

5. How do evaluators define their relationship with me, and how does that make them feel?

6. What emotions do others experience when they interact with me or disagree with me?

7. What do evaluators find inspiring about me?

8. Which specific sense or trait do evaluators admire in me?

9. What leadership strengths have been highlighted by others?

Fine Tune: Ideas for Fine-Tuning Your Leadership Brand Attributes

Embrace your strengths: Recognize and leverage your unique leadership strengths to enhance your effectiveness as a leader.

Address your weaknesses: Identify areas for improvement and actively work to develop skills and competencies to overcome your leadership weaknesses.

Enhance your relationships: Foster positive relationships with others by understanding their emotions and experiences when interacting with you and adjust your communication style accordingly.

Cultivate inspiration: Reflect on what inspires others about you and continue to develop those attributes to motivate and encourage those around you.

Embrace feedback: Regularly seek feedback from others to gain insight into your leadership brand attributes and make necessary adjustments to your leadership.

DIMENSION 3: LEADERSHIP EFFECTIVENESS. A WATERFALL DEFINITION

First, I should preface that there are many leadership effectiveness definitions. I have not developed this original waterfall definition, drawn from literature and empirical data, to counter any other definitions but to leverage over thirty years in the tranches and craft a holistic definition that can be measured. However, some definitions, part of 360 assessments available on the market, are heavily geared towards follower/employee satisfaction. I find that curious and allow me to illustrate. Let's say that I come to work for you, and as time goes by, I turn in late work, and you let it slide. I turn in shoddy work, and you fix it before sending it out. I leave early to attend all kinds of private events and come in late the next day. At some point, I received a survey asking if I was satisfied with your leadership. Satisfied? I am ecstatic!

But are you effective as a leader?

My waterfall definition provides a comprehensive and aspirational view of effective leadership. It emphasizes the importance of several key characteristics and behaviors essential for leaders to succeed in today's complex and dynamic environments.

One of the strengths of this definition is that it provides a clear and compelling vision of what effective leadership looks like. It highlights the importance of leadership behaviors that promote alignment, engagement, empowerment, and sustainability in organizations. The definition also recognizes the importance of context by emphasizing the need to operate in complexity and engage with a broad range of stakeholders.

Northouse (2018) provides a comprehensive overview of various leadership theories, models, and approaches in his book "Leadership: Theory and Practice." He discusses the trait, skills, and situational approaches to leadership, among others. While these approaches focus on different aspects of leadership, they all aim to understand the factors that contribute to effective leadership. In contrast, my waterfall definition offers a more holistic perspective, encompassing various dimensions of leadership and examining how they interact and build upon each other to create effective leadership.

Collins (2001) explores the factors that enable organizations to achieve sustained greatness in his book "Good to Great." His framework for organizational success includes Level 5 leadership, which emphasizes a combination of personal humility and professional will. Although not explicitly mentioned in the waterfall definition, the qualities of Level 5 leaders can be considered part of the broader range of attributes and actions that contribute to leadership effectiveness in the model I propose.

Kouzes and Posner (2017) present the Five Practices of Exemplary Leadership model in their book "The Leadership Challenge." The practices include Model the Way, Inspire a Shared Vision, Challenge the Process, Enable Others to Act, and Encourage the Heart. These practices focus on leaders' actions to be practical rather than solely on their attributes. The waterfall definition I propose shares a similar focus on combining personal attributes and activities that contribute to leadership effectiveness while emphasizing the interplay of various leadership dimensions. While all of the sources discussed indeed present a different model than my waterfall definition for leadership effectiveness, they offer valuable insights and complementary concepts that can be used to further develop and refine this unique approach, so I am bringing them to your attention.

ROBERT RADI'S WATERFALL DEFINITION

An **individual outward mindset** consistently and congruently contributing to the conditions needed for organizational alignment and optimal performance...

...**through the fundamental characteristics** of exemplary conduct, cohesive strategic clarity, selfless courage, enlightened confidence, compassionate composure, perspectives' inclusiveness, integrated commitment, talent appreciation, and actionable foresight...

...**for the purpose of** connecting, inspiring, aligning resources and performance accountability, maximizing organizational discretionary energy, engaging and empowering, sustaining broad stakeholders' satisfaction, and achieving optimal and rewarding results while operating in complexity.

However, like anyone enjoying research, I must find potential limitations in my work. I will recognize that it may be difficult for some leaders to fully embody all the characteristics and behaviors described. Effective leadership is a complex and multifaceted concept, and balancing the many demands and expectations of leadership in practice can be challenging. Additionally, some of the characteristics described in the definition may be more important in specific contexts or for certain organizations. They may not be universally applicable, so you will need to be the judge of that and focus on those characteristics that are most relevant in the context you operate.

Nevertheless, while it may not be easy to fully embody all these characteristics and behaviors in practice, they provide a valuable guide for leaders seeking to improve their effectiveness and positively impact their organizations and stakeholders. Aspirations help challenge our self-limiting beliefs and attitudes. This Leadership Effectiveness Waterfall definition is constructed to be measured via the Integral Advantage® Encompass, and you can use it as a source for introspective reflection to ponder on your contextual Leadership Effectiveness.

DIMENSION 4: LEADERSHIP PRESENCE

Leadership presence is an essential aspect of being an effective leader. It goes beyond simply having a commanding presence or being an influential figure. Instead, it's about inspiring, engaging, and connecting with others while maintaining self-awareness and authenticity. My research, drawn from literature and empirical data, shows the leadership presence dimension comprises three equally important components: **Awareness, Communication, and Energy.**

Various authors have sought to define and explore the components that contribute to an individual's ability to exude a sense of presence, influence, and charisma. This short literature review briefly analyzes three notable works in this domain and compares their frameworks to the one I proposed.

In "The Power of Presence," Kristi Hedges offers a practical approach to developing a strong leadership presence. She identifies four key components: intention, individuality, inclusion, and inspiration. While there is some overlap with my framework, particularly in terms of awareness and communication, Hedges' focus on inclusion and inspiration as essential aspects of presence distinguishes her approach. Sylvia Ann Hewlett's "Executive Presence" explores the concept through three main components: gravitas, communication, and appearance. Gravitas, the core of her framework, encompasses confidence, decisiveness, and emotional intelligence. Communication and appearance align with the author's focus on communication and energy (including non-verbal cues). However, Hewlett's framework emphasizes the importance of appearance in shaping perceptions of presence. Amy Jen Su and Muriel Maignan Wilkins' book "Own the Room" introduces a concept called "signature voice," which consists of five core elements: character, substance, style, emotional intelligence, and adaptability. While these elements align with aspects of my framework, particularly awareness and communication, Su and Wilkins' approach is more focused on the development of a unique and authentic voice as the key to mastering leadership presence.

I do recommend all these books as they were beneficial to me in drafting a leadership presence framework as it is constructed to be measured via the Integral Advantage® Encompass. Each component, **Awareness, Communication, and Energy,** has distinct aspects that contribute to a well-rounded leadership presence. In this section, I will define each component and some salient questions for your introspective reflection and self-assessment.

Awareness

Awareness is the foundation of leadership presence. Understanding your strengths, weaknesses, and values ultimately helps you develop confidence, perspective, and clarity.

> **Confidence:** Awareness of what you bring to the table allows you to act with self-assurance and make informed decisions.
>
> - What are my strengths and weaknesses as a leader?
> - How do I leverage my strengths and address my weaknesses?
>
> **Perspective:** Knowing the roles and responsibilities associated with your position enables you to act appropriately and align your actions with the organization's goals.
>
> - What are the roles and responsibilities associated with my position?
> - How do I effectively align my actions with the organization's goals?
>
> **Clarity:** Understanding your values and staying true to them helps you navigate complex situations while maintaining integrity and authenticity.
>
> - What are my core values, and how do they influence my leadership behavior?
> - How do I stay true to my values in challenging situations?

Communication

Effective communication is crucial for establishing and maintaining a leadership presence. It encompasses the ability to persuade, advocate, and connect with others in meaningful ways.

Persuasion: Framing dialogues effectively and using the right language and tone can help you inspire and motivate others to act.

- How do I frame dialogues effectively and motivate others to act?
- What language and tone do I use to inspire and persuade others?

Advocacy: Practicing advocacy involves championing ideas, projects, or people, and demonstrating your commitment and passion for the cause.

- How do I champion ideas, projects, or people?
- How do I demonstrate my commitment and passion for the cause?

Connecting: Engaging with your audience by actively listening, empathizing, and responding to their needs, and fostering strong relationships and trust.

- How do I practice my active listening, empathy, and response skills to connect with others?
- What steps do I take to foster strong relationships and build trust with my team?

Energy

Energy plays a significant role in leadership presence. It involves the conscious use of non-verbal cues, energy management, and making your presence known to create a positive and lasting impact.

Non-Verbal: Being aware of your body language, facial expressions, and gestures can help you communicate more effectively and display confidence and authority.

- *Am I aware of my body language, facial expressions, and gestures when communicating with others?*
- *In what ways can I adjust my non-verbal cues to convey confidence and authority?*

Use of Energy: Managing your energy levels and using them to set the tone in your organization can inspire others and create a positive atmosphere.

- *How can I effectively manage my energy levels to set a positive tone within my organization?*
- *What strategies can I use to re-energize myself and maintain focus during challenging times?*

Presence: Making your presence known involves showing up, being present, and actively participating in conversations and decision-making processes. It demonstrates your commitment to the organization and its success.

- *How do I make my presence known and actively participate in conversations and decision-making processes?*
- *What steps can I take to show my commitment to the organization and its success?*

In essence, cultivating leadership presence requires a balance of self-awareness, effective communication, and energy management. By developing these components and their respective aspects, leaders can create a strong and authentic presence that positively impacts their teams, organizations, and communities.

DIMENSION 5: LEADERSHIP BRAND CALIBRATION

Leadership Brand Calibration is a critical dimension in the overall development of a leadership brand, drawing its foundation from strategic thinking and management. Drawing from the concepts in strategy, I propose a leadership calibration framework, where individuals can make informed decisions on how to adjust their leadership approach based on feedback and their current situation.

I first became aware of this strategic approach in 2010, while working on my MBA, from the renowned book Blue Ocean Strategy, a business framework that encourages organizations to create new market spaces and differentiate themselves from competitors. In it, the authors W. Chan Kim and Renée Mauborgne introduce a tool called the "Eliminate-Reduce-Raise-Create Grid" (ERRC Grid) to help companies shift from competing in existing markets (red oceans) to creating new, uncontested markets (blue oceans). This got me thinking.

Like the Leadership Brand Calibration dimension, the Blue Ocean Strategy model emphasizes the need for continuous innovation and adaptation in response to changing market conditions. In conjunction with concepts from Baumeister & Finkel's Advanced social psychology, Blustein's The Oxford Handbook of the Psychology of Working and Bono's Lateral Thinking: Creativity step by step, I assessed the usefulness in crafting the Leadership Brand Calibration, which in the Integral Advantage® Encompass is populated by the self and others qualitative feedback.

This dimension emphasizes the importance of continuous growth, adaptability, and self-awareness in becoming an effective leader. The calibration process consists of four main elements (See Image 13).

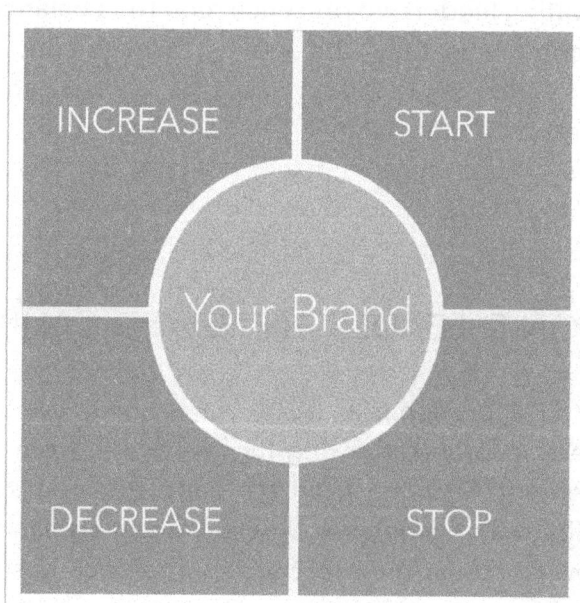

Image 13. Leadership Brand Calibration (Radi, 2015 - 2023) © Integral Advantage®

Decrease: Identifying areas where the leader needs to do less of something. For instance, a leader might realize that they need to reduce micromanagement to empower their team members and foster a more collaborative work environment.

Increase: Recognizing aspects of their leadership that need to be amplified or done more frequently. An example might be increasing active listening and empathetic communication to better understand and support their team.

Stop: Determining which behaviors or practices should be abandoned altogether, as they may be counterproductive or harmful to the team or organization. For example, a leader may decide to stop making decisions unilaterally and instead involve their team in the decision-making process.

Start: Identifying new behaviors or practices that leaders should adopt to enhance their effectiveness. For instance, a leader might start setting aside regular one-on-one time with each team member to provide personalized guidance and support.

By incorporating feedback from others, leaders can gain valuable insights into their strengths and weaknesses, allowing them to calibrate their leadership approach accordingly. This feedback can be gathered through formal evaluations, informal conversations, or observations of how their actions affect their team and organization.

CHAPTER 6

LEADERSHIP BRAND AUTHORING

"Life's most persistent and urgent question is:
'What are you doing for others?'" – Martin Luther King, Jr.

The journey to becoming an exceptional leader begins with self-discovery and introspection to bring us into a space of self-authoring. All leadership growth is incremental, and to visualize it, let's think about the Fibonacci sequence that has captured people's imagination throughout history due to its unique properties and applications in nature, art, and architecture. Often referred to as the Golden Spiral, the Fibonacci sequence starts with 0 and 1, and each subsequent number is the sum of the two preceding ones (0, 1, 1, 2, 3, 5, 8, 13...). The nautilus shell is often used as a symbol for the Golden Spiral, a logarithmic spiral that grows outward while maintaining its shape. This spiral is closely related to the Golden ratio, as the growth factor of the spiral is equal to the Golden ratio (approximately 1.618). The nautilus shell is an excellent visual for leadership development and personal and professional growth. In the context of personal growth, the Fibonacci sequence can be visualized as a series of expanding squares, beginning with a 1 by 1 square. This growth pattern mirrors personal development's incremental, compounding nature, where small steps eventually lead to significant progress. Similarly, the Golden ratio reminds us of the harmony and balance we strive to achieve in our lives as we continually grow and adapt in our leadership journey.

In this chapter, we will explore the process of Leadership Brand Authoring, which is designed to help you integrate the insights gained from the Integral Advantage® Encompass or the self-assessment and introspective reflection across the five Leadership Branding dimensions facilitated in Chapter 5: Leadership Brand Profile, Leadership Brand Attributes, Leadership Effectiveness, Leadership Presence, and Leadership Brand Calibration.

For the entirety of the content in this chapter, "We will go old school!" **Pen and paper.** As Mueller and Oppenheimer title of their article: "The Pen

Is Mightier Than the Keyboard." Writing by hand is important because it engages the brain differently than typing, leading to improved retention, creativity, and self-awareness. Handwriting allows for a slower pace, encourages mindfulness, and fosters a personal connection with the content. This more profound engagement with the material can enhance personal growth and development.

To start, you must review the five dimensions' most salient aspects and their corresponding components. Write down your key takeaways and observations, reflecting on how these aspects interconnect and contribute to your leadership behavior.

Next, craft a short integrative narrative in the present tense and the first person. This narrative should encompass your ideal leadership brand, incorporating the positive aspects of each dimension, even if you are not yet fully embodying them. By visualizing your desired leadership brand in this way, you will create a powerful mental image that can guide your future growth and development.

As you work through this process, remain open to seeking feedback and be willing to adapt your approach as you learn and grow. By embracing the principles of Leadership Brand Authoring, you will be well-equipped to navigate the complex world of leadership and make a meaningful impact on those around you.

Leadership Brand Profile
Leadership Presence
Leadership Brand Calibration
Leadership Brand Attributes
Leadership Effectiveness

Integrate

Image 14. Leadership Dimensions Integration (Radi, 2015 - 2023) © Integral Advantage®

In this chapter section, I will guide you through a streamlined but methodical process to craft your Leadership Brand Statement. This statement captures your unique leadership qualities, purpose, vision, and values, a powerful reminder of your leadership identity. The process involves four key steps: defining the Value Proposition, exploring personal Values, clarifying your Purpose and Vision, and discovering Strengths through the SCARF and VIA assessments.

The Value Proposition

If you are in marketing or have taken marketing classes, you are familiar with the various methodologies used to craft a unique value proposition for products and services. As I embarked on the journey to develop a method for individuals to craft, curate, and deploy a leadership brand, I knew that the individual value proposition would be part of the process. However, I didn't deem any techniques I learned in marketing to be viable. There is a simple reason for my determination. **People are not products, and they are not services. They are human.**

With this perspective in mind, I developed a methodology for individuals to establish their value proposition, which requires them to answer two questions and combine them into a single statement.

The two questions are: *How do I bring value? What value do I bring?*

Here's an explanation of my methodology and a step-by-step guide on how to use it:

"How do I bring value?" To answer this question, individuals should focus on their unique skills, abilities, or qualities that enable them to add value. These aspects include leadership, problem-solving, creativity, communication, and technical skills. They should also consider personal characteristics that set them apart, like a strong work ethic, adaptability, or a positive attitude.

"What value do I bring?" To answer this question, individuals should identify the specific benefits or results that their skills, abilities, or qualities can produce. These aspects might involve increasing efficiency, generating revenue, improving team morale, or creating innovative solutions. The key here is to quantify or qualify the impact of their unique contribution whenever possible.

Integrate the Two. Once individuals have answered both questions, they should combine their responses into a single statement that clearly and concisely communicates their value proposition. This statement should emphasize the unique way they bring value and the specific benefits they provide.

For example, if someone is a skilled software engineer who excels at optimizing code for faster performance, their value proposition might be:

> *"I bring value as a software engineer by leveraging my deep understanding of code optimization techniques to improve system performance, ultimately saving time and resources for the company."*

By following this methodology, individuals can effectively communicate their unique value proposition to potential employers, clients, or collaborators, helping them stand out in a competitive marketplace.

As another example, here is **my value proposition**:

"I use my multifaceted experience to help individuals and organizations achieve growth, foster alignment, and perform in dynamic and complex environments."

In closing, a well-defined value proposition is helpful in gaining and preserving clarity about the value we bring in the context in which we operate, and it needs to be revisited periodically. We need to ask ourselves if the statement is still representative of how we create value, and furthermore, we need to ask if that value is still relevant.

Remember: Write down your Value Proposition and any thought you have at the margin. Pen and paper. Old school eye-hand coordination is needed in writing.

The Self: Your Values

One of the fundamentals in leadership, and frankly in life, is identifying our values. Their importance is undeniable, yet we see the practice and process of assessing an individual's values simmer down to picking a set of values from a list or set of cards. This oversimplified approach is prevalent in leadership development workshops and is done for efficiency. My best experience in identifying my values was with Dr. Wayne Strom as we attended his Effective Executive Workshop at Pepperdine as part of our PKE MBA program kick-off. He sent all nineteen of us, grown men and women, outside with a pen and a piece of paper with instructions to walk around the Malibu campus, reflect on our values, and write down the top five. It was a meaningful experience, and when we returned to the workshop room, he put us through the process of giving up one value at a time until we remained with one. It was excruciatingly painful, yet I never forgot that the top value I was left with was **integrity**. The value I was carrying became clearer and crystalized in my mindset. So, I would recommend you do the same. Go to a place meaningful to you with a piece of paper and a pencil, and do the following four steps:

Reflect on your past experiences: Think about the moments when you felt the most fulfilled, proud, or satisfied. What values were present during those times? Conversely, consider the times when you felt most frustrated or upset. What values were absent or compromised in those situations?

List your values: Make a comprehensive list of values that resonate with you and create your own based on your reflections. The self knows. Let it emerge into your consciousness.

Prioritize your values: Narrow down your list to the values that are most important to you. Prioritize these values by ranking them or selecting your top five core values. This approach will help you focus on the values that truly define you.

Evaluate alignment: Assess the alignment between your values and your current life or work situation. Are you living and working in accordance with your values? Identify areas where you may need to make changes or adjustments to align your actions with your values.

Once you are done with the four steps, consciously integrate your values into your everyday actions, decisions, and relationships. Use your values as a guide for decision-making and goal-setting to ensure you align with what matters most.

Remember: Write down your Values and thoughts at the margin: Pen and paper. Old-school eye-hand coordination is needed in writing.

The Self: Purpose and Vision

Purpose and vision are two essential components of effective leadership, but it's important to distinguish between the two. Purpose serves as a general heading, a guiding principle that provides direction and keeps us focused on our ultimate goals. It is abstract in nature, leaving room for interpretation and adaptation as circumstances change. Think of it as the North Star, guiding us on our journey even though we may never actually reach it.

On the other hand, vision is a specific destination, a vivid picture of the desired and optimal future. It's concrete and tangible, providing a clear and compelling image of what value will be created. To illustrate this distinction, the purpose of NASA at its inception was "advancing mankind's ability to explore the heavens," which conveys a noble and inspiring mission without specifying the exact steps to be taken. In contrast, a vision would be "a man on the moon by the end of the '60s," by John F. Kennedy, providing a clear and ambitious goal to work towards. Well, that was a vision and one that came to fruition. By the way, part of that vision was safely returning that man to earth. An example of effectiveness over efficiency!

Clarifying Your Purpose

Clarifying one's purpose is essential to personal and professional growth, as it helps individuals make informed decisions, set priorities, and maintain motivation. A clear sense of purpose provides direction and meaning to one's life and work, allowing them to be more effective, resilient, and fulfilled. To help you strengthen your understanding of your purpose, we have combined several vital sources and developed a set of questions that focus on identity, values, strengths, passions, relationships, legacy, and resource allocation.

The idea of clarifying purpose is deeply rooted in the works of various scholars and authors. Kegan's work on self-authorship emphasizes the importance of understanding one's identity in shaping one's life (Kegan, 1994). Similarly, Christensen et al. (2012) explored resource allocation and aligning one's life choices with their core values. Warren (2002) delved into the significance of a purpose-driven life in the context of spiritual development. By integrating these works and adapting their insights, we present a set of questions to help you clarify your purpose.

The Five Essential Questions

What aspects of your identity are most important to you and why? (Inspired by Robert Kegan's work on self-authorship)

What are your core values, and how do they guide your decisions and actions? (Inspired by Clayton Christensen's work on resource allocation)

What are your unique strengths and passions, and how can you leverage them to contribute positively to others? (Adapted from Rick Warren's Purpose Driven Life)

Who do you most want to impact positively, and why are these relationships important?

How do you envision your legacy, and how can you allocate your resources (time, energy, skills, etc.) to create the most significant positive impact on the world?

Write down your Purpose. Pen and paper. Old school eye-hand coordination is needed in writing.

IKIGAI: A Few Words

Ikigai is a Japanese concept that refers to the reason for being, the purpose that gives meaning and fulfillment to one's life. It is often portrayed as the intersection of four elements: what you love, what you are good at, what the world needs, and what you can be paid for. By finding your Ikigai, you can achieve a sense of balance, happiness, and purpose in life.

The Ikigai concept has gained popularity in the Western world as people increasingly seek meaning and purpose. It encourages individuals to reflect on their passions, strengths, and values and how they can align with their career and personal goals.

A highly recommended book on this topic is "Ikigai: The Japanese Secret to a Long and Happy Life" by Héctor García and Francesc Miralles. The book delves into the concept of Ikigai and shares insights from centenarians living in Okinawa, Japan, known for their longevity and happiness. The authors provide practical advice and tips on discovering your Ikigai, cultivating mindfulness, and incorporating healthy habits into your daily routine to lead a more fulfilling and purpose-driven life.

Clarifying Your Vision

To develop a clear vision, thinking about your long-term goals and aspirations is essential. A vision helps guide you through the journey of personal growth and achievement, providing direction and motivation to keep moving forward.

A vision is a specific destination or a mental picture of your desired future. Creating a compelling vision that aligns with your values, purpose, and passions is essential. Here are some questions that can help you clarify your vision:

1. What are your most important long-term goals?

2. How do you envision your life in five years? In ten years?

3. What aspects of your life are most important (career, relationships, personal growth, etc.)?

4. What legacy do you want to leave behind?

5. What key milestones must you achieve along the way to realize your vision?

By reflecting on these questions, you can better understand your aspirations and create a clear vision that will guide your actions and decisions. This vision will be a powerful source of motivation and inspiration, helping you stay focused and committed to your goals.

Remember that your vision should be flexible and adaptive, as your circumstances, interests, and priorities may change over time. Regularly revisiting and refining your vision will ensure it remains relevant and aligned with your evolving personal and professional growth.

Developing a solid vision is an essential step in becoming an effective leader. A clear vision can inspire others and help you align your team's efforts toward a shared goal. By defining and communicating your vision, you can create a sense of purpose, direction, and cohesion within your organization. Yes, once again. Write it down, pen and paper.

The Strength Within

In chapter 3, I suggested that you'd consider taking two self-assessments. Now, I would strongly recommend that you complete the two free assessments before completing the next steps. As a reminder, the **SCARF Model** was developed by Dr. David Rock, the SCARF Model represents five domains of human social experience (Status, Certainty, Autonomy, Relatedness, and Fairness) that can evoke strong emotional responses. To discover your SCARF sensitivities, you can access the free self-assessments provided by the NeuroLeadership Institute, which will help you identify your reactions in each domain. You can self-assess your **Character Strengths** at the VIA Institute on Character, which offers a free assessment to help individuals identify and develop their unique character strengths.

Crossing the Threshold

Leadership finds its roots in the Indo-European word Leith, which means "to cross a threshold" and, more specifically, "to cross a threshold or die." Not necessarily a physical death, but a significant loss. It is more detrimental to avoid crossing the threshold than to face uncertainty on the other side.

a. Reflect upon a recent situation in your professional or personal life when your presence was critical in crossing that threshold, a time when if you were not involved, the outcome would have likely not been as optimal. Indeed, you can take credit for your role in achieving your desired result. Think about the context surrounding the events.

b. Think about the behaviors you exhibited and the response of others. How did your character strengths were manifested? How did challenges turn into opportunities? Prepare a short 2 to 3-minute (maximum) narrative to share with others in your professional environment. It is important you deliver this narrative, if not comfortable doing it at work, deliver it to a friend, or family member.

c. Remember, the magnitude of what was achieved doesn't need to be monumental but relevant to you and those you enabled to cross that threshold.

Your Leadership Brand Statement

Now that you have completed reflecting on your leadership brand components through various dimensions and exercises, you are prepared to craft your brand statement. This statement is a distillation (see image) of all your work so far, capturing the essence of your leadership in a single, powerful declaration. It is an intentional statement; and while it is advisable for you to share with trusted advisors, you don't to do so unless you want. The key is your intention to enact your statement.

Remember the three rules from **Chapter 4**:

Rule 1. It is about your leadership brand, but it is not about you.
Rule 2. It is not about appearances, as a brand transcends the package.
Rule 3. Leadership Branding is about making and fulfilling a promise.

While the exact wording may not be the primary focus, you must approach this exercise with a strong intention to enact and embody the principles and values captured in your statement. This leadership brand statement will serve as a guiding compass, driving your actions and decisions as you continue to evolve and develop as effective and authentic leaders.

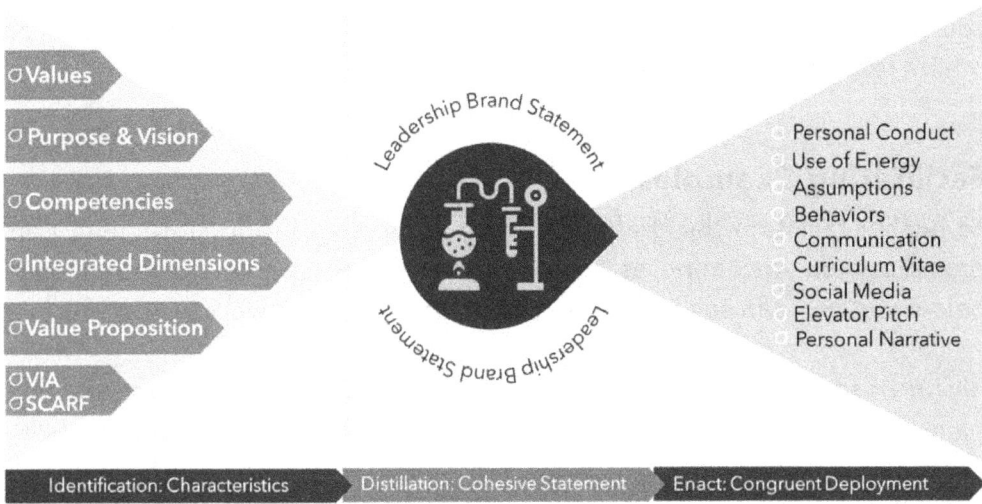

Image 15. Leadership Dimensions Integration (Radi, 2015 - 2023) © Integral Advantage®

The Construct of the Statement

In order to create a comprehensive and authentic Leadership Brand Statement, it is recommended that you follow this construct:

> Begin with: "My purpose is…"
>
> Continue with (in your preferred order):
>
> Integrate your VALUES and VALUE Proposition
>
> Integrate your top VIA Character Strength and top SCARF dimension.
>
> Integrate your Brand Attributes, Deep Belief, and Symbology

Allow your thoughts to flow naturally in a stream of consciousness as you craft your Leadership Brand Statement. This process encourages self-expression and fosters a deep connection with your inner leadership identity. By incorporating these elements, your statement will be a genuine reflection of your unique leadership behaviors, strengths, and aspirations.

This is not a one and done, you will likely need to craft several drafts to fine tune your leadership brand statement. Keep all of them. You will also need to keep it in your consciousness by revisiting it at least once a week. By continually reflecting on and evolving your Leadership Brand Statement, you can continue to grow and develop as a leader, ensuring your impact on others remains positive and significant.

Facilitating Examples

To further facilitate the drafting of your leadership brand statement, I am providing you with mine as an example. You can see it text format here below and you can see the construct on the image as well.

My purpose is to have a positive impact on others to the best of my abilities. I am the community I serve, and I must lead irrespective of personal recognition or consequences. I believe I must use my time on earth effectively and efficiently to pursue excellence, learn, and teach. I must help others achieve what I am not able to achieve. I value empathy as strength, integrity as a way of life, kindness as a driving force, compassion as the currency of justice, and inclusivity as the catalyst to collective growth.

In my Lord I trust.   *Last edited: 11/19/2020*

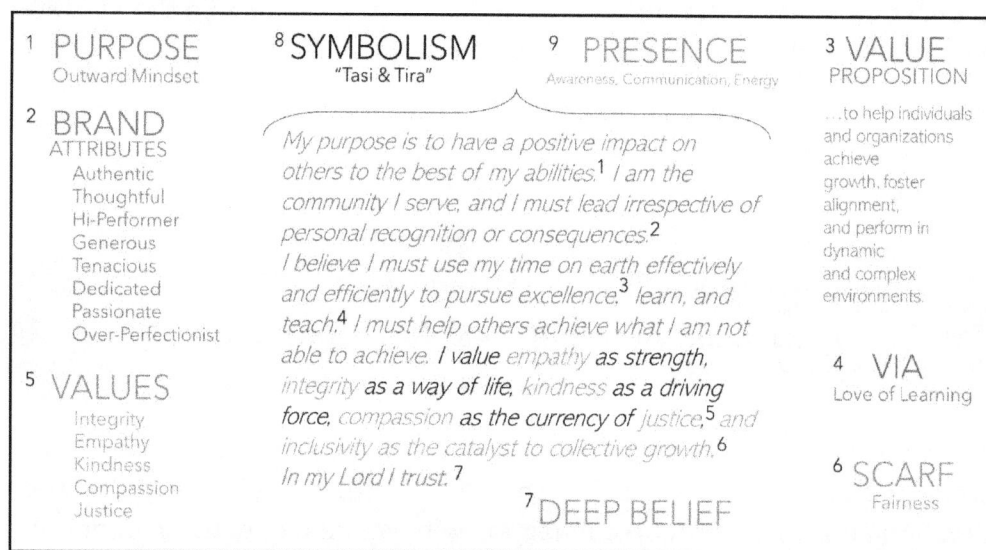

Image 16. Leadership Brand Statement Construct (Radi, 2015 - 2023) © Integral Advantage®

I would like to point out that the Leadership Brand Statement Construct is offered to you as a suggestion, to support you in authoring your Leadership Brand Statement that best resonated with you. I have used this methodology with hundreds of individuals, so I am proposing it to you as a facilitating framework.

I would like to say a few words about symbolism, as we didn't delve into it. Symbolism can be a word, a motto, a phrase, or even an image that resonates with you, or recall something, someone, or an experience in your life. In my case, the "Tasi & Tira" motto is meaningful as it was the motto of the Mountain Artillery in North Italy. That was the motto of our group. While most corps in the military have inspirational mottos written in Latin, our group motto was written in the Venetian dialect, "Tasi & Tira" which means "Shut up and Keep Moving Forward." At times it helps me when I need a boost of resiliency and grit.

This is another example from a client shared with permission:

My purpose is to inspire and empower others to realize their full potential and make a difference in the world. I value courage, resilience, adaptability, collaboration, and lifelong learning. I believe that everyone has unique talents and strengths that can be harnessed to create positive change. I am dedicated to cultivating an environment where individuals feel supported and encouraged to take risks and innovate. I leverage creativity and perseverance to help my team and foster autonomy and relatedness. In my actions, I embody a spirit of optimism and determination, pushing boundaries to achieve greatness together. I strive to be a role model for ethical leadership, consistently demonstrating compassion, humility, and a genuine desire to make a positive impact on the lives of others.

Now is your turn. Yes, once again. Write it down, pen and paper.

Enact: Congruent Deployment

In this chapter, we have explored the process of creating a leadership brand statement that reflects your values, purpose, vision, strengths, and unique attributes. Now, it's time to bring that statement to life by enacting your leadership brand in various aspects of your personal and professional life.

In January of 2022, after struggling with the issue for a couple of months, I concluded that to be congruent with my leadership brand, I needed to stay true to my principles and as stated during my campaign in 2014, complete my second term in office, and refrain from seeking re-election. It was a difficult decision, as one part of me wanted to serve a third term, but ultimately my principles regarding self-governing societies did prevail. As I was drafting my statement to be released to the local media and social media, I found guidance in my leadership brand statement.

In this context, "congruent deployment" refers to the act of implementing and practicing one's Leadership Brand in a manner that is consistent and aligned with their values, purpose, vision, and leadership brand statement. It involves making choices, taking actions, and communicating in ways that are in harmony with one's leadership principles and objectives. Congruent deployment helps to reinforce credibility, trustworthiness, and authenticity in a leader's personal and professional life. **It is about "doing the words."**

Here are some recommendations to help you embody and communicate your brand effectively:

Personal Conduct: Ensure your actions and decisions align with your values, purpose, and brand statement. Be a role model for the behaviors you wish to see in others and demonstrate consistency in your conduct.

Use of Energy: Be mindful of how you channel your energy and allocate your time. Focus on activities and initiatives that are in line with your leadership brand and contribute to your long-term vision.

Assumptions: Examine the underlying assumptions that guide your actions and decisions. Ensure that they are consistent with your values and leadership brand.

Behaviors: Adopt behaviors that reflect your brand statement and consistently demonstrate your commitment to your values, purpose, and vision.

Communication: Develop a clear and consistent communication style that resonates with your target audience and effectively conveys your leadership brand. Be mindful of both verbal and non-verbal cues.

Social Media: Utilize social media platforms to amplify your leadership brand and engage with your audience. Share content that is relevant to your values, purpose, and vision, and interact with your followers in a manner that reflects your brand.

Elevator Pitch: Craft a concise and compelling elevator pitch that summarizes your leadership brand statement. This pitch can be used in networking situations, job interviews, or other opportunities to showcase your unique value proposition.

Personal Narrative: Share your personal narrative, including your leadership journey, the challenges you have faced, and the lessons you have learned. This storytelling approach can help make your leadership brand more relatable and authentic.

In conclusion, developing a strong leadership brand is an ongoing process that requires self-reflection, intentionality, and consistent effort. By enacting your leadership brand through personal conduct, use of energy, assumptions, behaviors, communication, social media, elevator pitch, and personal narrative, you can create a powerful and lasting impact on the people you lead and serve.

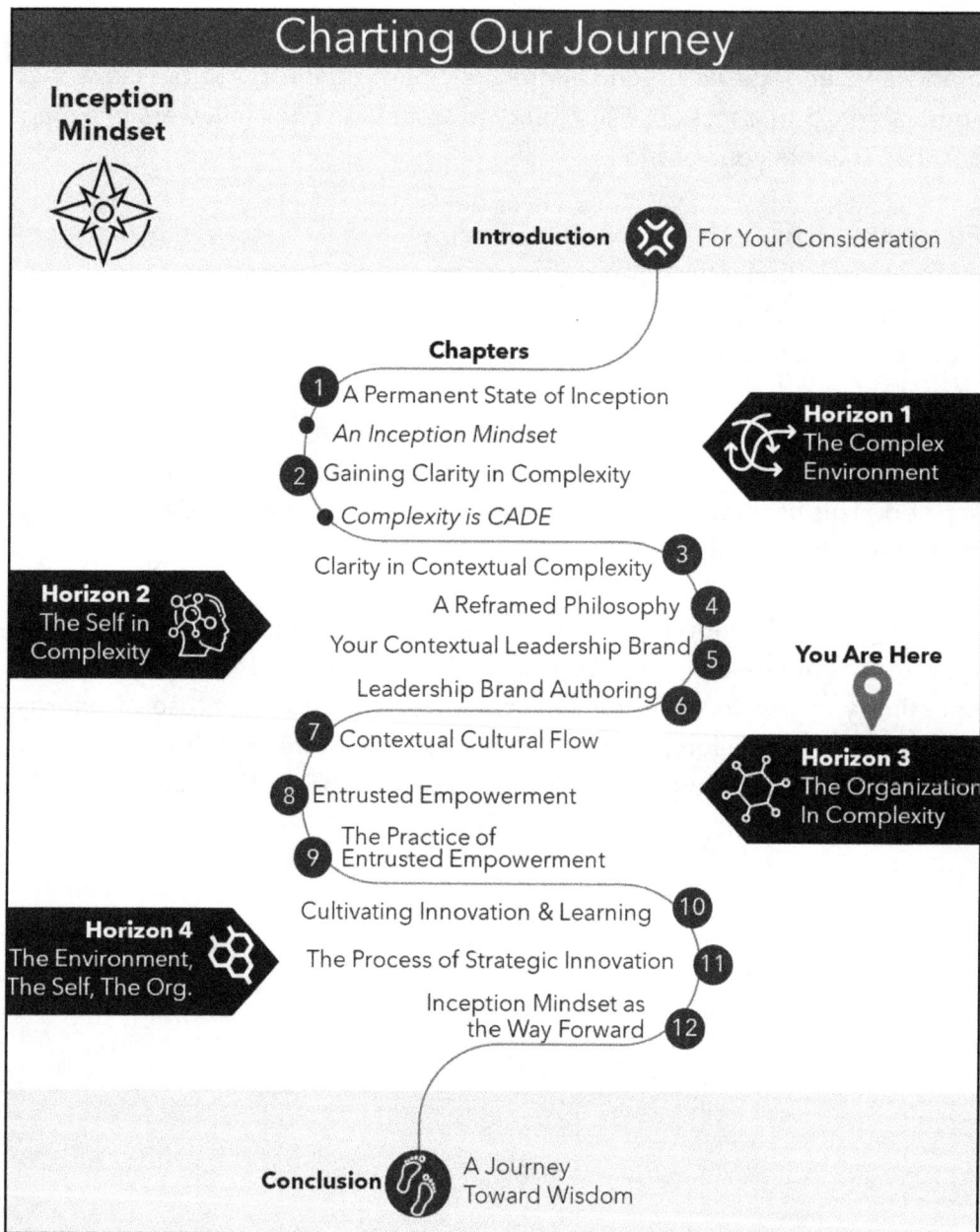

Charting Our Journey

Inception Mindset

Introduction — For Your Consideration

Chapters

1. A Permanent State of Inception
   An Inception Mindset
2. Gaining Clarity in Complexity
   Complexity is CADE

Horizon 1
The Complex Environment

3. Clarity in Contextual Complexity
4. A Reframed Philosophy
5. Your Contextual Leadership Brand
6. Leadership Brand Authoring

Horizon 2
The Self in Complexity

You Are Here

7. Contextual Cultural Flow
8. Entrusted Empowerment
9. The Practice of Entrusted Empowerment

Horizon 3
The Organization In Complexity

10. Cultivating Innovation & Learning
11. The Process of Strategic Innovation
12. Inception Mindset as the Way Forward

Horizon 4
The Environment, The Self, The Org.

Conclusion — A Journey Toward Wisdom

© 2023 Integral Advantage®, Inc.

PART III

HORIZON 3: THE ORGANIZATION IN COMPLEXITY

The concept of organizational culture in its modern sense can be traced back to the 1970s and 1980s. Although elements of the idea have been present in management thinking since the 1950s, researchers like Edgar Schein and William Ouchi gave it a specific focus and definition. Edgar Schein, in particular, is often credited with being one of the first to formalize the concept of organizational culture. He started writing about the topic in the late 1970s and early 1980s with his book "Organizational Culture and Leadership" first published in 1985. William Ouchi's 1981 book "Theory Z: How American Business Can Meet the Japanese Challenge" also significantly brought organizational culture to the forefront of management thinking.

However, it's important to note that these ideas did not emerge in a vacuum. Concepts like "corporate culture" and "organizational climate" had been part of the business lexicon for some time, and the work of Schein, Ouchi, and others built on this existing foundation. This is like how we know what we know since realizing that we don't get to eat all the mushrooms. A function of time is necessary for concepts to emerge and find their way into the mainstream. That is one of the reasons I don't get discouraged when I come up with a framework or methodology if it doesn't resonate immediately with individuals or organizations with whom I share those conceptual frameworks. Sometimes it is about returning to the drawing board, some other times, the recycling basket seems appropriate, but there are times that we need to clarify the message and remain steadfast.

In this Horizon, we will delve into the mainstream concepts of organizational culture and gain a wider perspective by opening the aperture and strengthening the lenses with what I define as Contextual Cultural Flow. We will then bridge into an actionable framework I have been developing and curating since 2015, for which I coined Entrusted Empowerment as its essential term. We will look deeply at the framework's diagnostic and actionable intervention benefits and the survey (n=552) conducted in April

2023, providing a better understanding of the correlations between the dimensions, interplay nodes, and some of the projected outcomes, representing another step in developing a methodology to support leaders and organizations in building strategic capacity and gain clarity in complexity.

CHAPTER 7

CONTEXTUAL CULTURAL FLOW

"Come to the edge," he said.
"We can't, we're afraid!" they responded.
"Come to the edge," he said.
"We can't, We will fall!" they responded.
"Come to the edge," he said. And so they came.
And he pushed them. And they flew."
— *Guillaume Apollinaire*

As we have seen, the concept of organizational culture appeared in the 1950s but found its way into the mainstream in the 1980s. Over the past 20 years, culture has become an inescapable aspect of organizational development across all sectors and industries for good reasons. We have seen a growing appreciation for organizational culture's pivotal role in shaping value creation. A wide range of scholarly and practical work has underscored the importance of a healthy, adaptive culture in fostering an environment where employees want to work and choose to stay and grow. There is much agreement on the importance of culture, but there are divergences of perspectives when it comes to organizational culture change. As always, the significance and popularization of a concept give life to a segment of "consulting angels" that, for a fee, will sort it all out for us. In this case, the "culture fixers," "culture mavens," or "culture curators" just take the name culture and slap an adjective next to it and let's get going. The proverbial question in the context of complexity is salient: What came first, the chicken or the egg? Do we change the culture to change things, or do we change things to change the culture? Regarding changing culture and culture climate in organizations, I belong to "the school" of Jay W. Lorsch and Emily McTague: You can't fix culture. More about this later in this Horizon.

The Optimally Ideal

Let's delve into some of the most influential works in this domain. We will also examine real-world examples of companies that have excelled in fostering the conditions for what have been considered robust cultures.

One of the most influential texts on this subject in recent years is Daniel Coyle's "The Culture Code: The Secrets of Highly Successful Groups." Coyle explores the dynamics behind some of the world's most successful organizations, distilling their success into three skills. The first is creating safety, which engenders trust, the bedrock of any successful group. The second is sharing vulnerability, which cultivates a sense of shared risk and fosters innovation. The final skill is establishing a purpose which aligns with individual and group goals. Kim S. Cameron and Robert E. Quinn's seminal work, "Diagnosing and Changing Organizational Culture," provides a methodology for managers and leaders to evaluate and transform their organization's culture. Using the Competing Values Framework, the authors identify the aspects of culture that need to change to enhance performance. Over the years, I found this framework practical and readily applicable when seeking clarity. I am a fan of Cameron & Quinn and often find myself spontaneously referencing them during my facilitations.

Southwest Airlines provides an illustrative example of Cameron and Quinn's principles in action. The airline's emphasis on teamwork, employee empowerment, and mutual respect is well-known. It has maintained a high-performance culture by ensuring these values permeate every level of the organization. Southwest's consistent profitability and high customer satisfaction ratings testify to the effectiveness of this approach.

Despite being published more than 15 years ago, "Corporate Culture and Performance" by John P. Kotter and James L. Heskett continues to influence our understanding of organizational culture significantly. Kotter and Heskett argue that adaptive cultures, characterized by leadership at all levels, yield better results than nonadaptive cultures. Their book refers to how Netflix's culture exemplifies this adaptive nature. Its well-known culture deck explicitly states, "We are a team, not a family," emphasizing performance over job security. Netflix encourages its employees to act in the company's best interests, rewarding high performers and letting go of underperformers. This adaptive culture has underpinned Netflix's success as a global streaming powerhouse. While I am not privy to where Netflix falls in 2023 in the framing proposed by

Kotter and Heskett, the elements they captured in their work are worthy of being brought into our awareness as we explore Horizon 3.

Is Edgar H. Shein the father of organizational culture? The Godfather? The Popularization Guru? Let's say that Edgar H. Shein is Edgar H. Shein, one of the most influential thinkers in history. When I learned that he had passed away in January 2023, it was a moment for reflection and gratitude for his life work. Edgar H. Schein's "Organizational Culture and Leadership" has stood the test of time, with its insights into the interaction between culture and leadership remaining as relevant as ever. Schein posits a reciprocal relationship in which leaders shape culture, which, in turn, molds future leaders. Apple, under the leadership of Steve Jobs and later Tim Cook, serves as a striking example of Schein's theory. Jobs' innovative vision and drive became ingrained in Apple's culture, shaping the company's trajectory and future leaders, including Cook.

Finally, Patrick Lencioni's "The Advantage: Why Organizational Health Trumps Everything Else in Business" makes a compelling case for the importance of an organization's health in determining its success. Lencioni argues that an organization with minimal politics, confusion, high morale, high productivity, and low turnover among good employees will consistently outperform its competitors. Costco is a shining example of Lencioni's principles with its above-industry-average wages, focus on employee satisfaction and wellness, and consequent low turnover rate. Costco's commitment to employee welfare has earned it a reputation as a desirable workplace and translated into a fiercely loyal workforce and customer base, contributing significantly to its sustained value creation. My wife and I have been members at Costco for over 15 years, and we greatly enjoy observing the flow when walking through the aisle and noticing the care in providing value to the members.

In addition to these influential books, the Harvard Business Review has published numerous articles highlighting the importance of organizational culture. Boris Groysberg, Jeremiah Lee, Jesse Price, and J. Yo-Jud Cheng's "The Leader's Guide to Corporate Culture" is a standout piece, demonstrating how leaders can shape and harness their organization's culture. They suggest that executives can nudge their culture toward desired behaviors by understanding the existing culture, envisioning a new culture, and making the necessary interventions. The case of Microsoft's cultural transformation under CEO Satya Nadella's leadership exemplifies this. Nadella inherited his predecessor's highly competitive, siloed culture, inhibiting the company's growth. His vision was for a culture of collaboration and learning, shifting from a "know-it-all" to a "learn-it-all" culture. By repeatedly reinforcing this message and embodying these values, Nadella succeeded in nudging Microsoft's culture toward his vision, revitalizing the tech giant's innovative spirit.

As the works of Coyle, Cameron and Quinn, Kotter and Heskett, Schein, and Lencioni demonstrate, creating a culture where people want to work, where they choose to stay, and where they can grow is not only possible but also a key determinant of long-term value creation by organizations operating in increasing complexity.

THINKING POINT

Section Takeaways

Organizational culture is fundamental in understanding how organizations function, evolve, and create value. It became a mainstream idea in the 1980s and has continued influencing organizational development and strategy.

Influential works by authors like Coyle, Cameron & Quinn, Kotter & Heskett, Schein, and Lencioni provide valuable insights into the dynamics of successful organizational cultures.

Organizations like Southwest Airlines, Netflix, Apple, and Costco demonstrate the successful application of these insights, reflecting how a positive, adaptive culture can drive performance and innovation.

Reflective Questions

How do the various definitions and approaches to a culture presented in this section resonate with your organizational experiences?

Can you identify instances where an organization's culture either supported or hindered its strategy and performance?

How does the idea of changing things to change the culture, rather than directly attempting to change it, align with your understanding and experience?

Contextualization Prompt

Consider an organization you are familiar with. How would you diagnose its culture using the insights from the authors discussed in this segment? What elements of its culture support its strategy and performance, and what elements might need to change? What challenges might affect such a change, and how could they be addressed?

Let's Call It Culture

Over the years, I have sat through some of the most exciting conversations about organizational culture. Some were constructive, some were thought-provoking, some were bizarre, and some were simply unsophisticated to the point of being painful. One aspect that piques my curiosity, and I find it interesting, is how often we try to define culture by a set of predetermined characteristics and build a hierarchy of the essential elements in organizational culture, often without the context of the environment in which the organization operates. Culture is this, and culture is that!

One of the most thought-provoking exchanges I can recall occurred as a student sitting in the classroom in 2011 during my PKE MBA's Strategy Module. The conversation went into the realm of organizational culture. The professor, Dr. Motamedi, got a bit irritated and claimed that without a degree in anthropology, talking about culture in organizations is useless and can even be detrimental. As the pushback from other executive students escalated, the back and forth reached some emotional boiling point. It got real. As things calmed down, I offered a "solution" to find a mid-ground and said, "What about if we refer to culture as **internal organizational dynamics**?" Dr. Motamedi, not totally convinced, replied: **"That is better."**

If it was better or not, I cannot say, but that thought-provoking exchange was fundamental for me to open the aperture about the challenge of defining something as intangible and multifaceted as culture. Opening the aperture and using a multitude of lenses emphasizes the ever-changing interactions, relationships, and behaviors within an organization rather than a fixed, predefined set of values or attributes.

While the term "internal organizational dynamics" is indeed used in academic and business literature, it is not typically used as a direct synonym for organizational culture, as I used it to "broker the peace."

Based on some publications, organizational culture is a component of internal organizational dynamics. The latter term is broader and encompasses a range of factors that influence the inner workings of an organization. Internal organizational dynamics often refer to organizational interactions and behaviors, including leadership behaviors and communication patterns, decision-making processes, conflict resolution mechanisms, power structures, and organizational culture.

So, by all means, let's call it culture! At least the term gives us a common language.

In this context, Dr. Motamedi's point of view could be seen as a call for a a more nuanced understanding of the nature of organizations. Rather than seeing culture as a fixed entity, it may be more beneficial to consider it a dynamic, evolving process. He also had a very interesting experience that supported his perspective, and it concerned one of his clients, a hospital in the Los Angeles area, hiring him to "fix the culture of the nursing staff to address the conflict with the doctors" just to discover trough empirical evidence that culture was not the culprit. The solution he provided had nothing to do with culture. More about culture not being the culprit later as we bridge into Entrusted Empowerment.

Another aspect that I do find curious is how many individuals misunderstood or misconstrued a quote by Peter Drucker. This significant quote has been reduced to a social media meme: "Culture eats Strategy for Breakfast." Many I heard speaking over the years claim that the intent is to focus on the culture of the organization and that strategy is not that important or not necessary. Indeed, this quote has been widely misinterpreted. Many have misconstrued it as a proclamation that culture is superior to strategy or that strategy is less important. This is far from Drucker's actual intention.

Organizations most need a strategy to operate in complexity. Drucker emphasized the undeniable influence of culture on the execution of a strategy. In essence, he was saying that even the most meticulously crafted strategy could fail if it is not aligned with the organization's culture. A strategy worth the paper is written on is constructed on robust external first and internal second meticulous analyses. Notice that I use the term strategy, not a strategic plan, and I speak of strategy, not "the strategy."

A component of the internal analysis is appropriately assessing the organization's culture. A strategy crafted without complete internal and external analyses is meaningless. Attempting to implement a strategy that doesn't take internal organizational dynamics, let's call it culture, will not be eaten for breakfast. It will be devoured at once.

It is, therefore, crucial to recognize that culture and strategy are not mutually exclusive or hierarchical. Instead, they are interdependent. A successful organization understands and harnesses the interplay between these two crucial elements.

A strategy without consideration of the organization's culture is destined for failure because it does not consider the behaviors, beliefs, and values driving the organization. On the other hand, a strong culture without a well-defined strategy lacks direction and focus, inhibiting the organization's ability to achieve its goals effectively.

Therefore, it's not about culture versus strategy but how culture and strategy can harmonize. A well-conceived strategy considers and leverages the organization's unique cultural dynamics to achieve its objectives. It's about aligning what the organization wants to achieve (its vision through strategy) and how it behaves and operates (its culture).

Contextual Cultural Flow

When it comes to the Four Horizons and gaining clarity in complexity, I prefer to conceptualize the integration of all the perspectives we discussed as Contextual Cultural Flow to better encapsulate the complexity and the fluidity of the relationships, patterns, and structures within an organization, making it a more suitable term for describing how organizations operate in the COMPLEXITY CADE -, Contextualizable, Amorphous, Dynamic and Elastic we discussed in Horizon 1, as the term aligns well with the concept of Contextual Cultural Flow, which acknowledges that organizations are not static entities but dynamic, evolving systems that need to adapt to the changing complexities of their environment.

This shift in perspective from "culture" to "Contextual Cultural Flow" might be a crucial step towards more effectively navigating the complexities of today's landscape. It is a way to strengthen our lenses rather than replace them. It encourages us to get a larger view of organizations as complex adaptive systems where the interactions and relationships between individuals and teams are just as meaningful, if not more so, than predefined cultural values or norms.

In the subsequent sections, we will delve deeper into the concept of Contextual Cultural Flow and how it forms the foundation for Entrusted Empowerment, allowing organizations to adapt, evolve, and thrive in the face of increasing complexity.

Organizations strive to establish and maintain a thriving culture that propels them toward achieving their Contextual Cultural Flow. This represents a state where they can adeptly navigate and adapt to the ever-changing landscapes of business and societal demands. An organization's culture, fundamentally, is the shared embodiment of its values, beliefs, and behaviors. It's an invisible yet palpable force that shapes how individuals and teams operate, make decisions, and interact internally and externally.

But how does, in practice, the enhanced Contextual Cultural Flow connect with complexity, specifically the CADE model -, Contextualizable, Amorphous Dynamic and Elastic? How does an organization's Contextual Cultural Flow enable it to function effectively within this model? The CADE model encapsulates the inherent nature of complexity, underlining the need for organizations to be dynamic in their response to change, evolutionary in their growth, contextual in their understanding, and adaptable in their strategies. To truly embrace these attributes, an organization needs a supportive culture that accepts change, promotes growth, values context, and nurtures adaptability.

This is where the Contextual Cultural Flow comes into focus. It represents a culture that fosters these attributes, empowering an organization to flourish amidst complexity. It's a culture that facilitates the organization's ability to see and connect the dots, acknowledging that complexity is a constellation and aggregation of new beginnings. It's a culture that eschews linear thinking and embraces the multi-faceted nature of complexity, understanding that each situation demands a unique, context-specific response.

Crucially, the Contextual Cultural Flow recognizes that we operate in relative complexity and encourages us to remember this fundamental truth, combatting the phenomena I referred to as **Complexity Amnesia in Chapter 1**. It also understands that success is a byproduct of value generation, emphasizing the importance of Key Value Factors vs. Key Success Factors. In the Contextual Cultural Flow, inclusion is paramount - we cannot foster a culture that values diversity and uniqueness through exclusion. Trust and empowerment are not granted but earned, with the understanding that the organization's role is to create conditions that allow individuals to trust and empower themselves. This culture is adaptable, recognizing that to navigate complexity, we must also help others adapt. It encourages innovation, acknowledging the need for controversy, calculated risk, and incubation. It embodies the principle of slowing down to speed up, understanding that thoughtful reflection and deliberate action are vital to achieving long-term success.

In essence, the Contextual Cultural Flow is a culture that exists for and through its people. It understands the intricacies of operating in a complex CADE environment and uses these complexities as stepping-stones toward continuous evolution and growth. By integrating these central tenets, we can better understand how an organization's culture can equip it to navigate the complexities of the CADE model effectively. This understanding forms a solid foundation to explore the relationship between culture and the Entrusted Empowerment framework in the subsequent sections.

THINKING POINT

Takeaways

Organizational culture is a complex, fluid, multifaceted concept transcending a fixed set of values or attributes. Considering it as "Contextual Cultural Flow" could provide a more nuanced understanding, emphasizing an organization's ever-changing interactions, relationships, and behaviors.

The statement "Culture eats Strategy for Breakfast" isn't about the superiority of culture over strategy. It emphasizes the critical role culture plays in the successful execution of a strategy. Culture and strategy are interdependent and should be harmonically aligned.

The Contextual Cultural Flow and the CADE model (Contextualizable, Amorphous, Dynamic and Elastic) are interconnected. A supportive culture that accepts change promotes growth, values context, and nurtures adaptability, enabling an organization to function effectively within the CADE model.

Reflective Questions

How have you previously understood the concept of organizational culture? How does this understanding change or expand when considering culture as a Contextual Cultural Flow?

Reflect on a situation where a strategy failed to deliver expected results. Could this have been due to a lack of alignment with the organizational culture?

How does your organization's culture support or hinder its ability to be dynamic, evolutionary, contextualizable, and adaptable?

Contextualization Prompt

Think of a specific scenario within your organization where the concept of Contextual Cultural Flow could have been applied to enhance the outcome. How would this shift in perspective have influenced the decision-making process, and what could have been the potential impact?

Leadership Branding and Contextual Cultural Flow

In reconnecting to **Horizon 2**, we can now appreciate how Leadership branding and organizational culture are intrinsically intertwined, each profoundly influencing the other. A leadership brand embodies the unique identity of a leader or a team of leaders, including their skills, traits, values, and practices. On the other hand, organizational culture constitutes the collective behavior of the people in an organization, defined by shared beliefs, values, and practices.

At its core, the leadership brand is the authentic persona that shapes the organization's direction. It drives the vision, the strategy, and the execution within the organization. The behavior and actions of leaders, guided by their leadership brand, significantly influence the development of the organizational culture.

For instance, a leader authoring a brand around collaboration, transparency, and innovation will likely foster a Contextual Cultural Flow that encourages open communication, team cooperation, and creativity. Similarly, a leadership brand authored on performance, competition, and excellence will likely shape an organizational culture prioritizing high performance, competitiveness, and quality. This is how leaders, via their leadership brand, can impact the shaping of the organizational culture if their brand is authored authentically and deployed congruently.

What You Touch, It Touches You as Well

However, the relationship between leadership branding and organizational culture is reciprocal. Just as leaders influence the culture, the existing culture within an organization can also impact the leadership brand. A leadership brand incongruent with the prevailing Contextual Cultural Flow will face resistance and struggle to gain acceptance. Therefore, leaders must ensure their brand aligns well with the existing culture or, if necessary, work strategically to shift it to support their leadership brand.

In this sense, the leadership brand becomes a tool for driving cultural change. Suppose a leader aspires to transform a hierarchical, bureaucratic culture into one that is more collaborative and innovative. In that case, they can model the desired behaviors, reinforcing them through communication, reward systems, and other strategic and value-based actions. This delicate process requires a deep understanding of the current culture, clarity about the desired culture, and strategic thinking about how to close the gap to achieve Contextual Cultural Flow.

Essentially, leadership branding and organizational culture are two sides of the same coin, each shaping and being shaped by the other. To navigate this complex dynamic effectively, leaders must be clear about their unique brand, understand the existing culture, and strategically align the two to foster the Contextual Cultural Flow to operate in complexity. Doing so strengthens their leadership effectiveness and contributes to a vibrant, adaptive organizational culture that can drive sustainable value.

Complexity is Not Optimally Ideal

In the grand scheme of organizational development, one concept from the Harvard Business Review article "Culture is Not the Culprit" by Jay W. Lorsch and Emily McTague proves particularly illuminating: "You can't fix culture, but you can focus on business performance." This perspective provides a valuable bridge between the optimal organizational culture and leadership branding and the practical steps organizations can take to improve, which I will illustrate in the next Chapter with the Entrusted Empowerment framework.

The premise of Lorsch and McTague's argument is that culture, in and of itself, is not a problem that leaders can directly solve. Instead, they propose that leaders focus on changing the business context and critical behaviors that drive performance. In doing so, they contend, culture will evolve as a result. While the article refers to "business performance" and "business context," I would advise reading it as "organizational performance" and "organizational context."

Changing things and the culture will change is the essential message and one that is supported by much of what we have seen in organizations. In 2016, with their intellectual fortitude, Lorsch and McTague gave me a bridge to the work I started in 2015: Entrusted Empowerment. Ok, maybe a rope bridge, but still a bridge. Entrusted Empowerment is about flipping the script and recognizing that while culture may indeed be real as the air we breathe, we first must bring clarity to our organizations and make incrementally intervene in the strategic, operational, and execution dimensions and their interplay nodes to attain the optimal outcomes we desire in our organizations.

I circled back in May 2023 with Dr. Motamedi to compare notes and see where he stood, given that we haven't worked together since the end of 2020. He offered these thoughts. We have no evidence that intervening in culture leads to some specific outcomes, such as performance improvement. Culture is a conceptual filter that is confusing and ambiguous, and it may prevent the deep diagnosis of critical issues in an organization, hence, a clearer understanding of events that are going on around you. Let's suppose there is a village, and people are sick, there have been deaths in the family, and there is grieving and sadness; the solution is not attempting to change the culture but to use the appropriate filters to assess what is causing the sickness among the members of the village. Diagnosing the water, the environment, and aspects that may have been inadvertently brought into the village is needed to assess what is happening. And once a diagnosis is complete and we have identified the critical issue, we can then make changes, and as we make changes by addressing the issues, the village's culture will also change. **Change things, and the culture will change.**

CHAPTER 8

ENTRUSTED EMPOWERMENT

"The essence of leadership is about doing all the science of management says you can with resources, but then taking that extra step and giving it that spark. And that spark comes from getting people to trust you so that they will follow you, if only out of curiosity." — Gen. Colin Powell

The Genesis of the Framework

As James D. White, who at that time was serving as CEO of Jamba Juice, said: "I believe in slowing down to speed up." I do subscribe to his perspective. In this Chapter and the next, we will delve into the concept of Entrusted Empowerment™. During my doctoral studies, I first coined the term to address the need for an integrated conceptual framework in 2015 to offer a holistic perspective. I continued refining and evaluating the framework in battlefields of strategic business consulting, teaching in higher-ed, serving on public agencies' boards, and facilitating executive and leadership development in organizations. It was well-received due to its actionability.

In 2020, I noticed participants' heightened interest in the conceptual framework. Therefore, in 2021, I clarified the framework graphically, wrote a follow-up conceptual paper for clients and other interested parties and openly shared it on our website and social media. Instead of sparking dialogue about the validity of Entrusted Empowerment, the paper led to a series of inquiries about how to "just do it." One particular instance stands out: I sent the conceptual paper to a regional public agency whose executive director expressed interest. After two weeks of silence, I followed up and was informed that they had not only read the paper but were already implementing some of the ideas. This feedback was undoubtedly encouraging.

However, my objective was to research further to establish a methodology that could measure the dimensions and interplay nodes of the Entrusted Empowerment™ conceptual framework and assess the correlation with the projected outcomes. The goal was to determine how we could measure Entrusted Empowerment™ in organizations and set a path to further develop an organization's strategic capacity.

To my surprise, no use of Entrusted Empowerment emerged in organizational leadership. Even domain registrars, those hoarding all those domain names, had not capitalized on the term; EntrustedEmpowerment.com remained available almost two years after my conceptual paper began to circulate.

In Chapter 8, we delve into the concept of Entrusted Empowerment™. We will closely examine this leadership paradigm and how trust and empowerment interact within the framework. Based on qualitative and quantitative research, our exploration will illuminate the empirical relationships underlying these concepts, the links between different dimensions of this framework, and the consequent outcomes. The aim is to demystify the often-opaque subject of leadership, paving the way for it to be participative and inclusive.

Chapter 9 pivots from theory to practice. Using the in-depth survey results, we will explore the actionability of the Entrusted Empowerment framework. We provide practical guidance on operationalizing the tenets of Entrusted Empowerment, demonstrating how these elements can transform your leadership approach. Our goal will be to extend beyond altering individual practices as we aim to induce an organizational culture change by underlining the idea that reshaping behaviors can effectively reshape culture. By the end of these chapters, you will have a comprehensive understanding of Entrusted Empowerment and the means to integrate it into your leadership repertoire.

An Integrated Framework

The Entrusted Empowerment framework allows organizations to diagnose their internal dimensions and interplay nodes to foster the conditions to attain coveted outcomes such as engagement, performance, and adaptability. This is an actionable framework that allows us to diagnose where the weaknesses in an organization are and allocate the proper resources more surgically. John Wanamaker (1838–1922) was an innovative and successful American merchant who is considered a marketing pioneer.

He opened one of the first and most successful department stores in the United States, which grew to sixteen stores and eventually became part of Macy's. His quote, "Half the money I spend on advertising is wasted; the trouble is, I don't know which half," highlights the difficulty of measuring the effectiveness of advertising, a problem that persists even today with more sophisticated analytics and metrics.

I would argue that the same is often true in organizational strategy, leadership development, and culture change initiatives. By diagnosing the organization through the lenses of the Entrusted Empowerment framework, we can assess the conditions quantitatively, benchmark the organization, and then design initiatives to deliver the desired outcomes. Rarely do high-performance organizations result from fortunate circumstances, but they are overwhelmingly the result of intellectually honest organizational design.

"Cultures don't change because we desire them to change. They change because the organization is transformed – the work is transformed." This quote from the HBR article "Culture is Not the Culprit" which we discussed in Chapter 7, clearly shows how organizational culture is often misattributed as the primary factor for a company's failure or success.

This is where Entrusted Empowerment comes into play. Entrusted Empowerment is a concept that emphasizes the importance of strategic clarity, operational clarity, and execution clarity in an organization. It posits that the more explicit an organization's strategy, operations, and execution, the more competent, autonomous, and fair the organizational environment becomes. The key to success lies not in altering an organization's culture in isolation but in diagnosing its current state and implementing changes to its strategy, operations, and execution - the core aspects highlighted in Entrusted Empowerment. The concept of Entrusted Empowerment aligns with the perspective presented in "Culture is Not the Culprit" in that it advocates for a focus on transforming work to effect real, impactful change.

According to the Entrusted Empowerment framework, achieving clarity in the organization's strategic, operational, and executional aspects promotes a higher degree of autonomy, sustained competency, and contextual fairness. These factors enhance entrusted empowerment, as evidenced by how individuals and teams engage, perform, and adapt within the organization.

The bridge between these two perspectives recognizes that an organization's culture is a byproduct of its business model, strategic approach, and operational execution. By concentrating on these aspects, we can transform the work and foster the conditions for the desired culture within an organization. Entrusted Empowerment provides a blueprint for this transformation, pointing to the importance of clarity in strategy, operations, and execution and the positive impact this clarity has on competency, autonomy, and fairness within the organization and on the desired organizational outcomes of engagement, performance, and adaptability.

In other words, culture change is not the solution in itself; it is the outcome of a well-diagnosed and executed methodology encompassing the principles of Entrusted Empowerment. An organization's culture will naturally evolve as strategic clarity, operational clarity, and execution clarity improve, leading to increased autonomy, competency, and fairness – one of the outcomes of Entrusted Empowerment.

THINKING POINT

Section Takeaways

The concept of Entrusted Empowerment emerged to provide a holistic perspective on organizational strategy, leadership development, and culture change initiatives.

The framework is actionable and enables organizations to diagnose their internal dimensions, fostering conditions to achieve engagement, performance, and adaptability.

The Entrusted Empowerment framework emphasizes the importance of strategic clarity, operational clarity, and execution clarity in an organization, leading to competency, autonomy, and fairness in the organizational environment.

Culture change is not the solution in itself; it's the outcome of a well-diagnosed and executed methodology encompassing the principles of Entrusted Empowerment.

Reflective Questions

How does the Entrusted Empowerment framework challenge conventional ideas about organizational change and culture transformation?

What aspects of the Entrusted Empowerment framework resonate most with your understanding of effective leadership and organizational change?

How could the principles of Entrusted Empowerment be applied in your organization or within your team?

Contextualization Prompt

Consider a recent major change or transition in your organization. Reflect on the clarity of strategic, operational, and executional aspects of this change. Did it lead to a higher degree of autonomy, sustained competency, and contextual fairness? How could the principles of Entrusted Empowerment have been better integrated into this process?

If Only Out of Curiosity

We often hear two of the most persistent fallacies: 1. We need to make (or get) people (to) trust us. 2. We need to empower our people. Here is a truth bomb regarding fallacy number 1: Leaders must congruently deploy their leadership brand to foster the conditions for others to trust them. We don't get people to trust us; we must be worthy of their trust. And while not everyone will trust us, we need to understand that we do not control their responses. However, we control how we deploy ourselves in the environment in which we operate. The second truth bomb is that leaders don't empower anyone. Empowerment is a socially constructed process; hence leaders create the conditions for those entrusted in their care to empower themselves. As you may remember from Horizon 2, the word leadership originates in the Indo-European word Leith, which means to cross a threshold. Leaders do guide those in their care to cross that threshold, not out of fear, but because there is a level of reciprocal trust and individuals empower themselves to cross that threshold.

During the Q&A session at the end of a speech by the late General Colin Powell, a White House fellow who was in attendance, Amy Wilkinson, asked this question:

"How would you define the key characteristics of effective leadership that allow you to go and be an advocate for good?"

As the last word was barely through Amy's lips, without hesitation, Gen. Powell replied with one word: "Trust!" He then promptly continued by explaining that the longer he has been in public service, the more people have asked him about leadership and that leadership comes down to creating conditions of trust within organizations. Powell postulated that "good leaders are people whom followers trust; leaders take organizations past the level that the science of management says is possible."

Powell offered a story from his experience at the Infantry School of Fort Benning he had attended as a young lieutenant almost 50 years before. He credited his time at the Infantry School for everything he learned about leadership and recalled one of the sergeants telling him one day:

'Lieutenant! You will know you are a good leader when people follow you, if only out of curiosity.'

As the laughter from the audience subsided, Powell explained that he never had a better definition as it meant that people follow their leaders because they trust them.

Powell continued, "And you've built up that trust. How did you do it? Clear mission and statement, selfless service. People look to you, and they trust you because you're serving selflessly as the leader, not self-serving. Selflessly. And that you prepare the followers, you train them. You give them what they need to get the job done. Don't give them the job if you're not going to give them the resources, and then you're prepared to take the risk with them."

With these words, Colin Powell provided the best definition of the essence of leadership I have ever encountered. I play this video in virtually all my leadership development seminars and courses, and every time, participants are more open to providing the context of their own experiences. Powell concluded his remarks by stating, "So, the essence of leadership is about doing all the science of management says you can with resources, but then taking that extra step and giving it that spark. and that spark comes from getting people to trust you so they will follow you, if only out of curiosity."

In the context of our discussion on leadership branding and organizational culture, the Entrusted Empowerment concept provides an essential bridge. Leadership branding is about cultivating a reputation that attracts and retains top talent because they trust you and want to work with you. Simultaneously, organizational culture is the lived experience of these values and behaviors, reinforcing the brand promise within the organization. Entrusted Empowerment is, therefore, a critical component of both leadership branding and organizational culture in the context of complexity. As we have explored, Leadership Branding is about living the words through congruency. This authenticity is critical in building trust, which is the cornerstone of Entrusted Empowerment. By demonstrating trust in their teams, leaders allow them to self-empower, inspiring them to take more initiative, be more innovative, and be more committed to the organization's value creation.

In a TED video, Michael C. Bush, CEO of Great Place to Work®, shares his insights into what makes workers unhappy, as only 40% of them report being happy at work as of 2019. This was pre-COVID. Bush stated that "There are three billion working people in the world. And about 40 percent of them would say they're happy at work. That means about 1.8 billion, or almost two billion people, are not happy at work. What does that do, both to those people and the organizations that they work in?"

If we think linearly, we can conclude, "Well, it must be the culture, right? We need to go in and create a culture of happiness!" You can now see why we have invested our time in exploring the concept of Contextual Cultural Flow I proposed in Chapter 7. These topics are intertwined in this Horizon as they are relevant lenses in understanding the Organization in Complexity. No framework will provide us with the whole picture, but we can most definitely leverage these concepts to gain the bigger picture while developing our *Inception Mindset*.

Michael C. Bush then continues, "Leaders often say, 'We trust our employees. We empower our employees.' And then when an employee needs a laptop -- and this is a true example -- 15 people have to approve that laptop. So, for the employee, all the words are right, but 15 levels of approval for a $1,500 laptop? You've actually spent more money than the laptop on the approval. And the employee feels maybe they're really not trusted."

Hence, regarding organizational culture, Entrusted Empowerment can be seen as a critical determinant of a healthy and positive culture. Employees who feel trusted and self-empowered are more likely to feel satisfied, engaged, and committed to their work, contributing to a more positive work environment. In this way, Entrusted Empowerment contributes to creating cultures where people want to work and where they tend to stay longer and grow within the company. For instance, Google's fostering of trust and empowerment is often cited as a critical reason for its high levels of employee satisfaction and its success in attracting and retaining top talent.

It is said that "trust is like an eraser; it gets smaller and smaller after every breach." Trust is built over time yet can be wiped out at the drop of a hat or slowly eroded. The word on the street before COVID-19 was that we lived in a global economy. Nevertheless, such a concept has undoubtedly been tested and reshaped as we make sense of the possible scenarios emerging from the worldwide pandemic's aftermath, adding to the complexity of our times. In the age of instant messaging and constant connectivity, the methodologies encompassing strategic and operational implementations have changed much, especially in the context of the massive work-from-home we have been experiencing.

THINKING POINT

Section Takeaways

Leaders must create the conditions for others to trust them; they cannot force people to trust them. Leaders do not empower anyone directly; they create the conditions that allow individuals to empower themselves.

Trust plays a crucial role in effective leadership, as demonstrated by the experience of General Colin Powell.

Entrusted Empowerment forms a critical bridge between leadership branding and organizational culture, fostering an environment of trust and self-empowerment.

Cultivating an environment of Entrusted Empowerment contributes to positive organizational culture, increased employee satisfaction, and better talent retention.

In the context of organizational change, the Entrusted Empowerment framework suggests focusing on changing business strategies and behaviors to cultivate trust and empowerment rather than trying to change the culture directly.

Reflective Questions

How do you create conditions for trust and self-empowerment within your team or organization?

Reflecting on General Colin Powell's experiences, what steps can you take to ensure that your leadership behavior builds trust and encourages others to follow, even if only out of curiosity?

What would Entrusted Empowerment look like in your organization? What strategies and behaviors would need to change to cultivate this environment?

Contextualization Prompt

Consider a recent situation in your organization where there was a lack of trust or conditions for empowerment. How might the principles of Entrusted Empowerment have been applied to improve the situation? How can you use this framework moving forward to build a culture of trust and self-empowerment?

Entrusted Empowerment: The Conceptual Framework

The methods we use to strategize and implement in the contextually complex, globally interconnected world in which we operate are continuously evolving. However, one constant remains. Leaders need to forge and sustain strong connections with their teams. Rapport, the foundation of trust-based relationships, enables leaders to inspire peak performance and reinforce it with sincere appreciation.

Have you ever been handed back a task by a team member who felt unable to handle it? This is a clear indicator of the importance of empowerment. When empowered, employees can improve their decision-making skills, become more versatile within the organization, and make themselves more attractive to potential future employers. Trust and empowerment aren't simply 'nice-to-haves' but essential components of thriving teams. Leaders must serve as the cultural engine of their units by setting transparent practices and personally connecting with their team. This is where Leadership Branding meets the road.

Empowerment also optimizes the synergy between various organizational functions. It helps to clearly define team members' roles and responsibilities, which is critical for effective collaboration. The trend seems to be shifting from the limiting notion of "I am my position" to a more inclusive "We are our department." To foster a culture of entrusted empowerment, leaders need to facilitate communication, establish team processes, and ensure task completion.

However, building trust isn't an overnight process. It requires conscious effort and the right attitude. The regular presence of leaders, signified by both their physical and virtual availability and active engagement, can significantly facilitate this trust-building process. Creating a culture of learning and collaboration allows for more robust decision-making, reducing uncertainty in dynamic environments.

The journey toward trust and empowerment can encounter stumbling blocks despite its importance. Decisions made autocratically, without the team's involvement, may result in subpar outcomes and a sense of alienation among team members. True delegation involves inclusive decision-making, not merely transferring tasks. An autocratic leader creates an environment where conflict is often avoided to maintain surface-level harmony, leading to the loss of valuable insights that come from diverse viewpoints. Avoiding conflicts to maintain team harmony can disrupt the balance within the organization. Sometimes, a level of cognitive conflict can foster innovation and restore equilibrium. If leaders fail to build trust and create the conditions for empowerment in their teams, achieving shared goals becomes doubtful, potentially leading to significant tangible and intangible costs.

Contextually, a conceptual framework emerges. This framework is a roadmap, illustrating the crucial components and their individual and collective contributions toward achieving Entrusted Empowerment. This framework defines three dimensions: strategic clarity, operational clarity, and execution clarity. Four elements further inform these three dimensions. When adequately fulfilled, each dimension contributes to the level of Entrusted Empowerment experienced. However, the dynamic interplay among these dimensions produces a unique node or point of convergence. This node is vital because it directly contributes to the long-term sustainability of Entrusted Empowerment at all levels - individuals, teams, and across entire organizations.

In the following section, we will break down each of the three dimensions and the three interplay nodes to better understand the Entrusted Empowerment framework. See **Image 17** for a visual representation of the framework. Stay tuned as we dive deeper into this exciting leadership paradigm.

Vision
Expectations
Communication
Congruency

STRATEGIC
CLARITY

Sustained
Competency

Contextual
Fairness

ENTRUSTED
EMPOWERMENT

OPERATIONAL
CLARITY

EXECUTION
CLARITY

Processes
Functions
Programs
Action Learning

Autonomy

Responsibility
Accountability
Resources
Incentives

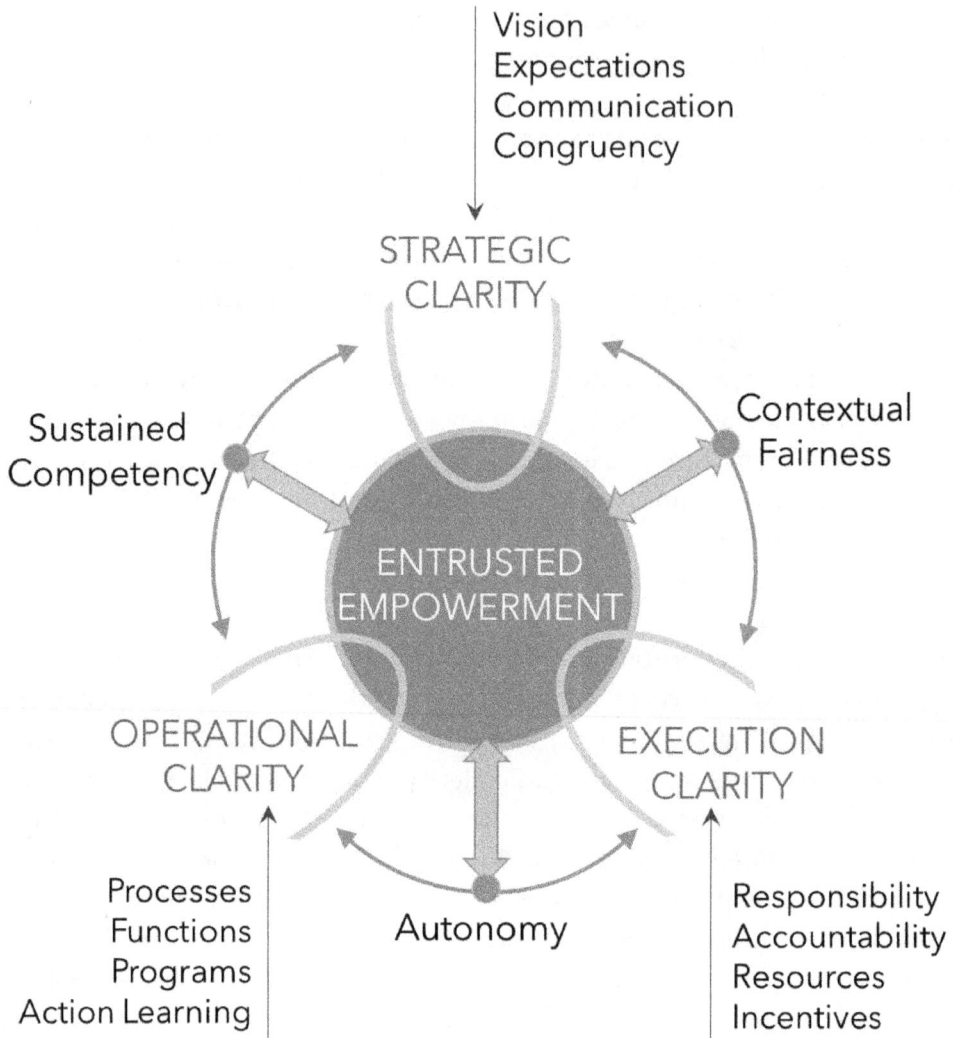

Image 17. Entrusted Empowerment™ Framework (Radi, 2015 - 2023) © Integral Advantage®

The Dimensions and Their Respective Elements

Strategic Clarity: Informed by Vision, Expectations, Communication, Congruency

Strategic clarity is the lighthouse guiding your organization toward its purpose. It takes a tangible, compelling vision to anchor this clarity. Coupled with well-articulated expectations, your team gains a solid understanding of the direction they need to take. However, strategic clarity is not just about setting the vision and expectations; it's also about maintaining clear, consistent communication. Messages must be broken down, disseminated, and tailored to inspire specific actions from different teams or individuals. Finally, actions must be congruent with the vision and expectations to foster strategic clarity. There should be an evident alignment between what is said and what is done.

Operational Clarity: Informed by Function, Processes, Programs, Action Learning

Operational clarity emerges when strategy and operations intertwine harmoniously. Here, processes, functions, and programs align with and serve the organization's strategy. Remember, operations are always tactical, serving the larger strategic objectives. As soon as a strategy is put into action, it is tested by the complex, dynamic reality of the workplace. This is where action learning comes into play - to unlearn, learn, and relearn in the context of actual versus anticipated conditions. Operational clarity, therefore, is about quickly regaining perspective after a curveball, adapting via double-loop learning while staying true to the strategic intent.

Execution Clarity: Informed by Responsibility, Accountability, Resources, and Incentives

Execution clarity stands tall when each team member has defined responsibilities, adequate resources, clear metrics for accountability, and balanced incentives. Ensuring that resources match the magnitude of the task at hand is crucial - as I often remind clients, you would not go to battle armed only with a fork and a spoon. Incentives should not be distributed capriciously or arbitrarily; even worse, they should not be reallocated after promised. The clarity in execution allows for a seamless transition from planning to action, reinforcing Entrusted Empowerment across all levels of the organization.

The Interplay Nodes

Our three dimensions - strategic clarity, operational clarity, and execution clarity - work together, creating a unique dynamic interaction. This interaction forms what we call "interplay nodes." These nodes demonstrate the synergy within the framework and contribute to optimal performance. Let's dive a bit deeper into these nodes:

Sustained Competency: This is the product of the blend between strategic clarity and operational clarity. With a clear vision and well-defined processes, organizations can cultivate a culture of continuous learning and improvement. Sustained Competency is not just about maintaining a certain level of skills or knowledge, it's about fostering an environment where everyone is encouraged to learn, unlearn, and relearn as needed. It keeps the organization nimble and ready to tackle the ever-changing dynamics of the market, ensuring a capacity for reinvention and resilience. Sustained competency is critical in developing an *Inception Mindset*.

Contextual Fairness: When there is clarity about the strategy and how to execute it, the perception of fairness within the organization increases. This Contextual Fairness is not based on a simple notion of everyone being treated equally. Instead, it is a more nuanced understanding that fairness is relative to the overall dynamics at play, including the organization's vision, the roles of each team member, the resources available, and the market demands. It respects that distinct roles may have different requirements, and fairness is seen in providing what is needed for each role to succeed.

Autonomy: The intersection of operational and execution clarity gives birth to a more nuanced version of autonomy. Here, autonomy does not mean complete free reign but a carefully balanced environment where individuals and teams have the space to take ownership of their work while still adhering to the operational procedures and execution strategies laid out by the organization. In this setting, individuals can be creative and innovative, finding ways to reach their goals while aligning their actions with the overall organizational strategy. Autonomy is essential in building self-empowerment conditions where individuals and teams can take ownership of their tasks. Autonomy here also means trust in team members to use their resources wisely and responsibly while still meeting accountability expectations.

The Outcomes of the Entrusted Empowerment Framework

The Entrusted Empowerment framework, at its core, is designed to foster a thriving workplace culture where individuals and teams feel valued, clear about their roles, and fully equipped to perform their tasks. The framework is not just about streamlining operations or increasing efficiency, although these are essential factors. It is about nurturing an environment where people can grow, excel, and adapt in the face of change. This nurturing environment then translates into tangible outcomes that can propel an organization toward value creation. Although not the only outcomes, I have identified three primary outcomes that arise from implementing the Entrusted Empowerment framework: Engagement, Performance, and Adaptability, as shown in Image 18. Let us take a closer look at each of these.

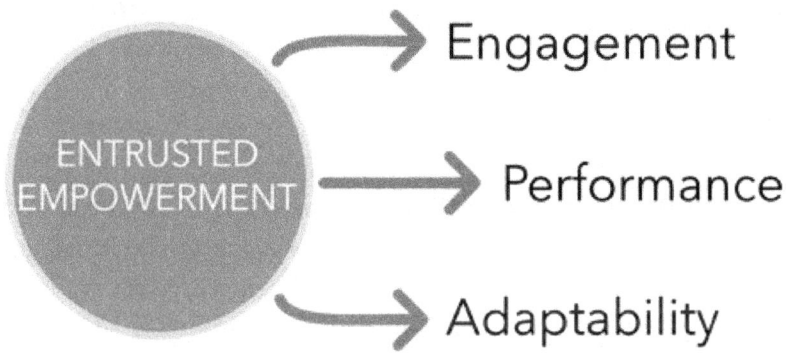

Image 18. Entrusted Empowerment™ Outcomes (Radi, 2015 - 2023) © Integral Advantage®

Engagement: When individuals and teams feel entrusted, understand their roles, see their tasks clearly, and feel they are being treated contextually fairly, they become more engaged in their work. Engagement in this context is more than mere participation. It is about feeling a deep connection and commitment to the work, increasing productivity, creativity, and satisfaction. When an organization implements the Entrusted Empowerment framework, it cultivates an environment that encourages this kind of deep engagement, boosting morale and driving people to strive for excellence.

Performance: Clarity on multiple levels - strategic, operational, and execution - leads to increased performance. When everyone understands the vision, how their work contributes to it, and how their performance will be measured, they can focus on doing their best work. You cannot measure temperature with a ruler or length with a thermometer, you must have an appropriate and objective measurement methodology. This framework ensures that individuals and teams are given the resources, autonomy, and incentives they need to excel, leading to higher organizational performance levels. It means getting things done efficiently, effectively, and in a way that aligns with the company's strategic goals.

Adaptability: Adaptability is crucial in today's ever-evolving business landscape. The Entrusted Empowerment framework increases engagement and performance and encourages adaptability. With clear expectations and a focus on learning and development, individuals and teams can adjust their approaches and strategies to meet the market's changing demands. Adaptability in this framework is seen as a product of understanding the vision, taking ownership of tasks, and having the capacity to learn from experiences. This makes organizations more resilient, enabling them to navigate challenges and seize new opportunities.

A Functional Collaboration

Self-Development and Entrusted Empowerment is a functional collaborative. Trust forms the bedrock of effective collaboration. Constructing it is an iterative process, requiring leaders to consciously foster an environment of transparency and openness. When physical proximity becomes a challenge, the nuanced role of body language in trust-building can be lost, thereby adding another layer of complexity.

In learning communities, functional collaboration goes beyond merely exchanging ideas; it thrives on a culture of entrusted empowerment. This concept catalyzes the social construction of cognitive structures, which guide decision-making processes, helping mitigate uncertainties characteristic of dynamic environments. This higher level of organizational 'networking' decentralizes power and fosters conditions that facilitate self-development.

Entrusted empowerment is a motivator, challenging the organization's abilities like a stress test in a financial institution. It unveils gaps in the organization's learning practices, highlighting areas that require refinement. Self-development parallels individual growth, aligning with the organization's broader learning functions.

A Quintessential Vicious Cycle

We must be aware and remain vigilant about derailing factors in fostering entrusted empowerment. Organizations may encounter obstacles in their quest to foster entrusted empowerment. An autocratic decision, void of participation, can compromise decision quality, while complete delegation may inadvertently lead to an abdication of leadership responsibilities.

Balancing influence in decision-making avoids these pitfalls. Leaders should foster a culture of shared influence, encouraging collaborative ideation. Ideas born from collaborative efforts are more likely to be resilient to criticism, contributing significantly to innovation and experimentation.

However, there exists a propensity towards conflict avoidance, particularly when decisions challenge the status quo. This avoidance, a reaction to perceived discord, threatens the process of trusted empowerment. It generates a cognitive vacuum, marked by superficial collaboration, risking the possibility of shared mental models' development.

Conclusion and a Word of Caution

This chapter journeyed through the prerequisites for an environment conducive to entrusted empowerment. Successful implementation necessitates cognitive alignment among team members, facilitated by a socially constructed foundation of trust and shared values. The Entrusted Empowerment framework serves as a cognitive lens to evaluate the presence of dimensions, the intensity of elements forming each dimension, and the nodes emerging from their interplay. It guides teams and organizations in socially constructing an environment of entrusted empowerment.

However, the journey toward entrusted empowerment is not devoid of caution. Trust, while a function of time, may not always culminate in empowerment. Leaders claiming to empower teams can inadvertently create a deceptive environment that misrepresents genuine empowerment. Such pseudo-empowerment processes often reinforce hierarchical power dynamics under the guise of delegation.

In such instances, the Entrusted Empowerment framework helps diagnose these detrimental behaviors, alerting individuals to potential coercive power tactics. Recognizing these challenges is essential to ensuring the authentic development of entrusted empowerment.

CHAPTER 9

THE PRACTICE OF ENTRUSTED EMPOWERMENT

"Leadership is not defined by the exercise of power but by the capacity to increase the sense of power among those led. The most essential work of the leader is to create more leaders." — Mary Parker Follett

In this chapter, we pivot from conceptual theory to practice. The theory is only as valuable as its implementation. This chapter takes a significant leap from the theoretical realm to practical implementation with the understanding that the practice of Entrusted Empowerment™ is not a one-and-done intervention. We pivot on the insights from our in-depth survey, showing you how to operationalize the Entrusted Empowerment framework effectively, as it is not merely a philosophy but an actionable leadership strategy. It is about redefining our leadership approach's core tenets and shaping how we guide our teams and individuals. It moves beyond words, impacting the daily routines, interactions, decisions, and behaviors that constitute leadership.

However, the implications of Entrusted Empowerment are not limited to individual practices; it aims to induce change on an organizational scale, reshaping the culture that underpins everything an organization does. When leadership behaviors change, cultures evolve. This evolution is central to our objective in this chapter: to provide you with a comprehensive understanding of integrating Entrusted Empowerment into your leadership repertoire. It requires understanding the work that needs to be done and the increments in which it needs to be done.

You will notice that I am reporting the survey results unconventionally to strike a balance between illustrating the compelling aspects of the results and telling an engaging story, as statistical data is inherently dull. We must think about Entrusted Empowerment in conjunction with an *Inception Mindset* by considering the needed awareness of the impact of contextual complexity and the need to engage in developmental steps **to practice** Entrusted Empowerment.

Our journey in the **Four Horizons** continues. While we will explore developmental steps that we can take in our organizations based on the results of our study, we have already explored several essential elements in fostering the conditions for the practice of Entrusted Empowerment in Horizon 1 and 2. As this book is a continuum, we will explore ideas to sustain Entrusted Empowerment in Horizon 4.

The Survey

This study examines the relationship between Entrusted Empowerment and organizational outcomes such as engagement, performance, and adaptability. The Entrusted Empowerment framework includes three dimensions: Strategic Clarity, Execution Clarity, and Operational Clarity, as well as three interplay nodes: Contextual Fairness, Autonomy, and Sustained Competency. A survey instrument consisting of 33 items on a 5-point Likert scale was developed at Integral Advantage® over a period of 18 months to measure these dimensions, interplay nodes, and projected outcomes.

In April 2023, data was collected from n=552 qualified professionals in various United States-based organizations (representing 25 industries) through an independent third party. The largest group of participants were between the age of 45-60 (41%), closely followed by those between the age of 30-44 (37%), followed by some distance by those between the age of 18-29 (14%), and those 60 and over (8%). Of the n=552, one (1) identified as Nonbinary (.18%), 268 identified as Female (48.55%), and 283 identified as Male (51.27%). Ethnically the n=552 participants have identified as follow: American Indian or Alaska Native (0.725%), Asian or Asian American (7.79%), Black or African American (5.25%), Hispanic or Latino (7.97%), Other (2.36%), Prefer not to answer (2.90%), White (66.30%), No Answer (6.70%).

The statistical analysis included Cronbach's alpha and Pearson correlation coefficients. The results showed robust internal validity and reliability for the Entrusted Empowerment framework. The Pearson correlation coefficients revealed significant positive correlations between the dimensions and nodes of the framework, as well as with the organizational outcomes of engagement, performance, and adaptability. The findings suggest that Entrusted Empowerment can lead to positive organizational outcomes and that a focus on the dimensions and nodes of the framework can lead to effective empowerment strategies.

In May 2023, we at Integral Advantage® opened a second survey collecting data organically and longitudinally through multiple channels. At the time of this writing, the data collected mirrors the results attained from the control sample of n=552 professionals in various United States-based organizations.

As always, a word of caution is necessary: correlation doesn't equal causation. However, the correlation principle remains a critical concept. Finding a correlation between two variables can offer significant insights. Correlations help us predict outcomes, identify trends and relationships, and formulate hypotheses for further research. They provide valuable starting points. The relationships we've found offer exciting opportunities for further exploration, improvement, and, ultimately, more empowered, engaging, and adaptable organizations.

To gain a clear perspective of where your organization stands, we can assist you (as a professional courtesy) by providing you with a single organization data collector containing our survey. Individual completion time for the survey is 7 to 8 minutes. Once we have collected the data within the period you establish, we can provide you with a report enabling you to make informed decisions on deploying your Entrusted Empowerment developmental efforts and resources based on the results. More information about the complimentary offer is available at IntegralAdvantage.com.

Validity and Reliability

Are we indeed measuring what we think we are measuring? Validity and reliability form the cornerstone of any research survey, and ours is no exception. We employed Cronbach's Alpha and Standardized Alpha to evaluate our survey tool's robustness.

Cronbach's Alpha is a measure used to assess the reliability, or internal consistency, of a set of scale or test items. In simpler terms, it measures how closely related a set of items are as a group. In most social science research, a rule of thumb is that an Alpha of 0.700 or above is considered satisfactory and indicates good internal consistency. On the other hand, the Standardized Alpha is a version of Cronbach's Alpha that assumes all items have the same variance. It provides an understanding of the reliability of the construct if all items were standardized.

Our findings exceeded the 0.700 Alpha threshold ($\alpha \geq .700$) across all constructs, indicating that our survey exhibits high internal consistency. This level of consistency gives us confidence in the reliability of our results and the conclusions we draw from them. A snapshot of our findings is represented in **Table 4.**

CONSTRUCT	CRONBACH'S ALPHA	STANDARDIZED ALPHA
Strategic Clarity Dimension	0.9102	0.9096
Operational Clarity Dimension	0.8817	0.8816
Execution Clarity Dimension	0.8815	0.882
Interplay Node - Sustained Competency	0.7982	0.7969
Interplay Node - Contextual Fairness	0.85	0.8507
Interplay Node - Autonomy	0.8522	0.8524
Outcome - Engagement	0.8336	0.8335
Outcome - Performance	0.7878	0.788
Outcome - Adaptability	0.7273	0.7361

Table 4. Cronbach's Alpha and Standardized Alpha Analysis

These findings offer robust evidence of the validity and reliability of our survey. The strong internal consistency across all constructs underscores the robustness of our survey tool in effectively measuring the constructs of interest. Consequently, these findings affirm our confidence in the analyses and conclusions drawn from the data.

Moreover, our survey maintains a high level of precision. An independent third-party data collection service calculated the margin of error for our control sample of $n=552$ respondents to be 4.256% at a 95% confidence level. This margin of error indicates the maximum amount by which the survey results might differ from the actual population value, underscoring the reliability of our findings. Based on the margin of error, we can confidently assert that the survey results accurately represent the broader population of professionals in various United States-based organizations.

The Report Card

As our son, Max, moved into Middle School and High School, we humorously (but not too humorously) told him that in our household, we interpret report cards as follows: A = Average; B = Below Average; C = Can't have dinner; D = Don't come home; and finally, F = Find a new family. Thus far, to his credit, he has managed to keep a solid "Average" based on our scale.

However, based on our survey, we "Can't have dinner" (see **Table 5**) given how we score on the dimensions, interplay nodes, and outcomes of the Entrusted Empowerment framework. The results reveal that while respondents generally agree that their organizations exhibit some level of the elements of Entrusted Empowerment, there's still significant room for growth. Complexity underscores the urgent need for organizations to amplify their efforts in enhancing Entrusted Empowerment. Being 'C average' no longer cuts it, but here is where it gets exciting, as there are developmental steps we can take and move into a higher "grade."

ELEMENT	AVERAGE SCORE (MEAN)	EFFECTIVENESS (%)	GRADE
Strategic Clarity Dimension	3.75	75	C
Operational Clarity Dimension	3.76	75	C
Execution Clarity Dimension	3.68	73	C
Interplay Node - Sustained Competency	3.76	75	C
Interplay Node - Contextual Fairness	3.50	70	C
Interplay Node - Autonomy	3.70	74	C
Outcome - Engagement	3.68	73	C
Outcome - Performance	3.79	76	C
Outcome - Adaptability	3.89	78	C+

Table 5. The Report Card: Average Scores (Mean)

From a quick glance, it seems our 'class' is essentially sitting within the 'C' grade territory, with a C- for Contextual Fairness and a C+ for Adaptability. This paints a picture of US-based organizations progressing toward fostering Entrusted Empowerment, but a fair bit of work is still to be done. Achieving a "B- "would sound like a pretty good aim, wouldn't it?

What are the challenges and opportunities for our organizations? To elevate the grades across the board - by turning operational, strategic, and execution clarity into a seamless blend of understanding and action. They also need to nurture the conditions where sustained competency, contextual fairness, and autonomy are the norms rather than the exceptions. Doing so can enhance engagement, performance, and adaptability, propelling their organizations forward in the **Complexity as CADE** –, contextualizable, amorphous, dynamic, and elastic. The goal should **not be** shooting for 'A's all around but instead embracing the practice of Entrusted Empowerment as a discipline for the long-term benefit of the organization and its stakeholders.

Practicing Entrusted Empowerment

The practice of Entrusted Empowerment doesn't come from a set of rigid rules or guidelines but from understanding the inherent links to the Entrusted Empowerment elements. It's a strategic framework that doesn't try to change culture directly; instead, it changes things in the organization and then naturally leads to cultural transformation. If anything is intimidating about the model is its simplicity. The secret of Entrusted Empowerment is that there is no secret. There are no obscure aspects. This isn't about obscure theories or complex methodologies. The elements of this framework are straightforward, relatable, and applicable. They are about gaining clarity in strategy, execution, and operations facilitated by an environment of autonomy, fairness, and sustained competency.

To better grasp the relationships among the constructs of the Entrusted Empowerment framework and develop a high-level approach to developing the practice of Entrusted Empowerment, I have grouped a set of two dimensions and their respective interplay nodes into **"Apertures."** Each Aperture provides us with a digestible approach to developing our practice in each aperture, and it engages us in making sense of the relationships among the constructs of the Entrusted Encompass framework. This approach allows us to evaluate if the salient elements are already in place in our organizations while providing us with some high-level ideas on how to engage in strengthening and enhancing each dimension and interplay node.

It is critical to consider that the practice of Entrusted Empowerment is not a solo act. We must involve, include, and enroll everyone. We cannot get to inclusion by exclusion. Be explicit, and disclose why you are taking actions, as Entrusted Empowerment is everyone's business in an organization.

Lastly, always remember that the journey toward Entrusted Empowerment is not a one-time effort but requires continuous introspection, adaptation, and commitment. Each organization's path will be unique, shaped by its context and dynamics. The leader must ensure this journey is embarked upon with the right tools, determination, and an open mind. Leverage the content provided, and you can chart the way forward.

Entrusted Empowerment: Aperture One

Dimensions: Strategic Clarity & Execution Clarity.
Interplay: Contextual Fairness

The Practice

Aperture One offers a clear view of the importance of Strategic Clarity, Execution Clarity, and the interplay that results in Contextual Fairness. It underscores the significance of a clear vision, expectations, and congruency in fostering Strategic Clarity. Similarly, it emphasizes the role of defined responsibilities, clear accountability measures, adequate resources, and balanced incentives in promoting Execution Clarity. Most importantly, it highlights the intricate relationship between these dimensions and how they collectively create a sense of Contextual Fairness in an organization. By leveraging the insights provided by this aperture, leaders can effectively foster the dynamics to develop Entrusted Empowerment.

Here is a concise description of the two dimensions and the interplay node in question (See **Image 19**).

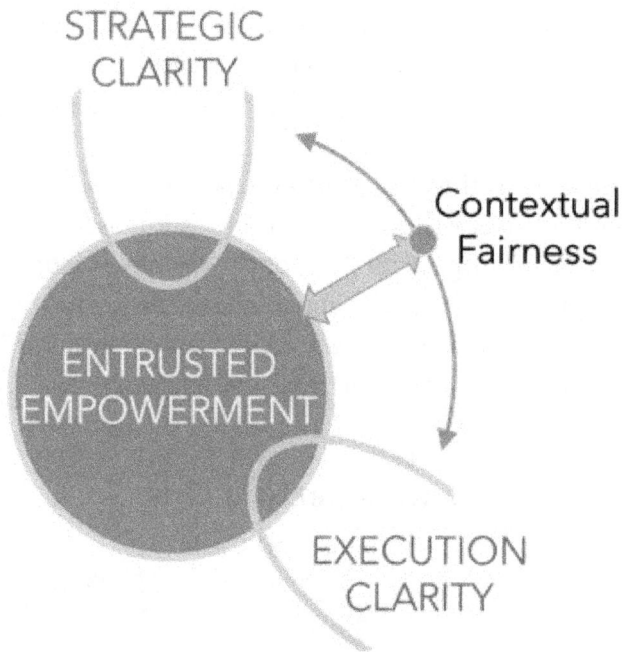

Image 19. Aperture One (Radi, 2015 - 2023) © Integral Advantage®

A high-level approach to developing practice in Aperture One starts with a well-articulated, tangible vision. For example, "A Man on the Moon by the End of the 60's" was such a vision. Hold inclusive sessions to encourage participation from all levels of the organization in defining the vision and setting clear expectations. You can regularly review your vision, update it as needed, and share the updated vision with your employees. **Optoro**, a tech company helping retailers process returned and excess inventory, is well-known for its clear and dynamic vision that adapts to the changing market needs. Do not simply broadcast the vision but communicate it. Develop robust internal communication mechanisms to ensure this vision is shared, understood, and adopted across the board.

Clearly define roles, responsibilities, and the resources required for each. Make sure that everyone knows what they are responsible for. **Gusto**, a company that provides a cloud-based payroll, benefits, and human resource management solution for businesses, has clearly defined roles and responsibilities, enabling the team to work together seamlessly. Provide adequate resources by giving your employees the tools, training, and time they need to perform their tasks.

Do not reallocate resources unless a truly justifiable unforeseen circumstance is at play.

Be transparent about metrics for accountability and ensure incentives are balanced and tied to key performance indicators. Align these resources with clearly defined accountability measures and incentives. Ensure resources and incentives are distributed fairly, considering the varying requirements of different roles. **Buffer**, a social media management company, has a transparent salary policy, which helps promote a sense of fairness. Ensure transparent decision-making by explaining the reasoning behind your decisions so that employees understand them, even if they disagree.

Making Sense of Aperture One

While Pearson's correlation between **strategic clarity** and **contextual fairness** indicates a strong positive and statistically significant relationship ($r = .745$, $p < 0.01$), and the correlation between **execution clarity** and **contextual fairness** also indicates a strong positive and statistically significant relationship ($r = .791$, $p < 0.01$), as anticipated by the conceptual model, the correlation between **strategic & execution clarities** and **contextual fairness** indicates a (higher) strong positive and statistically significant relationship ($r = .807$, $p < 0.01$), clearly suggesting that a higher degree of contextual fairness is achieved when an organization combines strategic and execution clarity instead of solely focusing on individual dimensions.

DIMENSIONS	INTERPLAY NODE	PEARSON CORRELATION
Strategic Clarity	Contextual Fairness	0.745
Execution Clarity	Contextual Fairness	0.791
Strategic Clarity & Execution Clarity	Contextual Fairness	0.807

Table 6. Aperture One: Pearson's Correlations Summary

Imagine you're navigating through the fog. It's thick, you can't see far ahead, and you're unsure which direction to move. You have two tools at your disposal: a lighthouse and a compass.

The lighthouse is our metaphor for Strategic Clarity. Its light pierces the fog, providing a clear, compelling vision and direction for your journey. When the beam from this lighthouse is strong, it significantly and contextually increases the perception of fairness within the organization. How do we know this? Our survey shows a substantial positive correlation ($r = .745$, $p < 0.01$) between strategic clarity and contextual fairness. In other words, the stronger the light from your lighthouse (strategic clarity), the more apparent the landscape becomes (contextual fairness).

The compass symbolizes Execution Clarity. It defines the route, marks your responsibilities, and charts the resources required for the journey. Like the lighthouse, the compass significantly impacts the perception of fairness. Our study demonstrated a robust positive correlation ($r = .791$, $p < 0.01$) between execution clarity and contextual fairness. In short, the clearer your compass points (execution clarity), the more fairly you can traverse the terrain (contextual fairness).

What if you used the lighthouse and the compass together? Could you move through the fog more fairly and effectively? The answer is a resounding yes. When strategic and execution clarity combined, we saw an even higher positive correlation ($r = .807$, $p < 0.01$) with contextual fairness. By shining the light from the lighthouse on the compass's path, your journey through the fog becomes a more balanced and fair adventure.

Remember, improving Strategic Clarity and Execution Clarity independently can result in some progress. However, the fundamental transformation occurs when these dimensions are developed in tandem, contributing to an environment of Contextual Fairness. The resulting synergy will powerfully move your organization towards Entrusted Empowerment.

Entrusted Empowerment: Aperture Two

Dimensions: Execution Clarity & Operational Clarity.
Interplay: Autonomy

The Practice

Aperture Two illuminates the crucial relationship between Execution Clarity, Operational Clarity, and the resulting interplay, Autonomy. It highlights the necessity of well-defined responsibilities, clear accountability measures, sufficient resources, and balanced incentives to cultivate Execution Clarity. Concurrently, it accentuates the role of streamlined processes, clear protocols, and an established decision-making hierarchy in fostering Operational Clarity.

Most importantly, Aperture Two focuses on the complex relationship between these dimensions and how they collectively breed Autonomy within an organization. Autonomy, here, is not unrestrained freedom but a dynamic balance between independence and interdependence, framed by clear operational boundaries and driven by clear execution guidelines. By harnessing the insights provided by this aperture, leaders can nurture an environment that promotes autonomy, leading to Entrusted Empowerment.

Here is a brief description of the two dimensions and the interplay node in question (See **Image 20**).

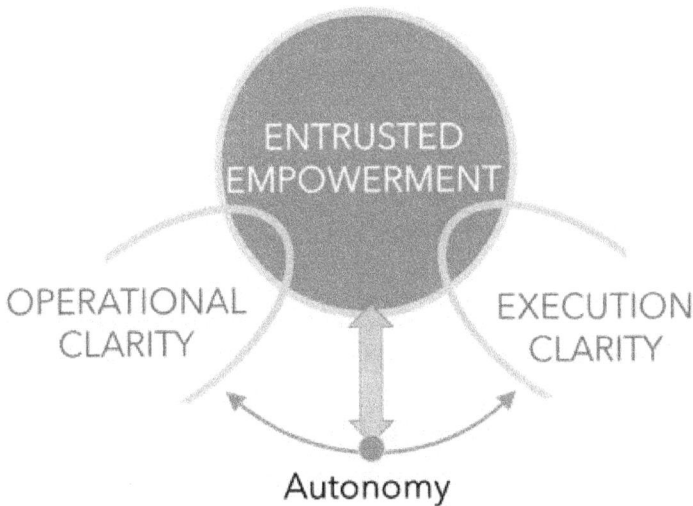

Image 20. Aperture Two (Radi, 2015 - 2023) © Integral Advantage®

A high-level approach to developing practice in Aperture Two starts with enhancing foresight which finds a connection with the CADE model. Foresight is about understanding trends, anticipating future challenges and opportunities, and preparing for them. Companies that excel in foresight tend to be proactive, not reactive. They continuously scan their environment, keep abreast of emerging trends, and position themselves to take advantage of opportunities and mitigate risks. With its focus on electric vehicles and renewable energy, like it or not, **Elon Musk**, through Tesla, has displayed significant foresight in anticipating a shift toward sustainable transportation and energy solutions. In other words, to use a hockey analogy, Elon Musk skated where he anticipated the puck would be.

Cultivating Refined Resilience enables companies to anticipate changes, adapt to shocks, and emerge stronger. It is about 'futureproofing' the business to survive and thrive amidst the change and uncertainty we find in CADE. The practice needs to include a comprehensive review of your current execution strategies. Identify bottlenecks, inefficiencies, and areas of ambiguity that may affect clarity. Work on refining these strategies to ensure they are transparent, well-defined, and effectively communicated across the organization.

Operational Clarity benefits significantly from continuous learning, particularly in terms of action learning. Organizations should invest in training programs and learning opportunities that help employees understand their roles, responsibilities, and the intricacies of the operational processes they're a part of. This investment builds capacity, enabling better navigation of the operational landscape and encouraging reflective practice and learning from experiences. For example, **Etsy**, an e-commerce website focused on handmade or vintage items, has incorporated a blameless post-mortem culture where they analyze their mistakes and learn from them.

Operational Clarity is enhanced when the operational procedures, decision-making hierarchies, and process protocols are transparent and well-communicated, not merely broadcasted. Make sure your teams understand how operations align with the broader organizational strategy. Use tools and technologies that allow for process transparency. For example, **Zapier**, an online automation tool that connects your favorite apps, enables work processes to be transparent with project management tools, making it easy for anyone to understand their operations.

Just as a well-coordinated orchestra delivers a harmonious symphony, an organization achieves higher degrees of Autonomy when Execution Clarity and Operational Clarity are aligned. Efforts should be made to ensure that the operational and execution strategies do not work in silos but are well-coordinated and complementary to each other. Leaders can foster autonomy by allowing employees to innovate and make decisions within the scope of their roles and responsibilities. They can create a safe space where employees are encouraged to take calculated risks, make mistakes,

and learn from them, always within the organization's operational procedures and strategic directions. Delegate decision-making power to your employees where appropriate. For instance, **W.L. Gore & Associates**, the
maker of Gore-Tex and other products, is famous for its lattice structure,
where employees have the freedom to take ownership of their work and
make decisions.

Finally, the process of enhancing Execution Clarity, Operational Clarity, and
Autonomy should be ongoing. Regular reviews and continuous improvement should be built into the operational and strategic plan. This way,
organizations can adapt, learn, and evolve as they work towards achieving
Entrusted Empowerment.

Making Sense of Aperture Two

While Pearson's correlation between **execution clarity and autonomy**
indicates a moderate positive and statistically significant relationship
($r = .676$, $p < 0.01$), and the correlation between **operational clarity and
autonomy** indicates a moderate positive and statistically significant relationship ($r = .673$, $p < 0.01$) once again we see that the need to intervene
on and develop the dimensions and the interplay nodes in the contextual
Aperture. Pearson's correlation between **execution / operational clarity
and autonomy** indicates a strong positive and statistically significant relationship ($r = .714$, $p < 0.01$). It indicates that a higher degree of autonomy is
achieved when an organization combines execution and operational clarity
instead of solely focusing on individual dimensions.

DIMENSIONS	INTERPLAY NODE	PEARSON CORRELATION
Strategic Clarity	Autonomy	0.676
Operational Clarity	Autonomy	0.673
Execution Clarity & Operational Clarity	Autonomy	0.714

Table 7. Aperture Two: Pearson's Correlations Summary

Consider the members of an orchestra, each with their unique instrument.
The conductor symbolizes Execution Clarity. They don't play an instrument,
but they guide the musicians, providing them with the music's tempo, dynamics, and expressive shape. When the conductor's instructions are explicit, the

musicians feel more autonomy in their performance, knowing precisely when and how to play their part. This notion mirrors our survey findings, which show a moderate positive correlation ($r = .676$, $p < 0.01$) between execution clarity and autonomy.

Now, envision the score each musician has in front of them as Operational Clarity. It details each musician's precise notes, rhythms, dynamics, and articulations. When the score's instructions are crystal clear, it empowers musicians to play their part confidently and precisely, increasing their sense of autonomy. This idea aligns with our study's results, demonstrating a moderate positive correlation ($r = .673$, $p < 0.01$) between operational clarity and autonomy.

What happens when the conductor and the music score work in unison? The result is a symphony that is greater than the sum of its parts. When execution (the conductor's guidance) and operational clarity (the musician's score) are combined, the orchestra achieves an even higher degree of autonomy, as our study's strong positive correlation ($r = .714$, $p < 0.01$) suggests.

Essentially, the path to Entrusted Empowerment resembles an orchestra's journey to a harmonious performance. By coordinating clear execution and operation, you allow your organization members to play their unique roles confidently and autonomously, contributing to a collective masterpiece.

Entrusted Empowerment: Aperture Three

Dimensions: Operational Clarity & Strategic Clarity.
Interplay: Sustained Competency

The Practice

Aperture Three unravels the intricate relationship between Operational Clarity, Strategic Clarity, and the emerging interplay, Sustained Competency. It emphasizes the importance of having streamlined processes, explicit protocols, and a well-established decision-making hierarchy to foster Operational Clarity. Simultaneously, it underlines the need for a clear, forward-thinking vision, well-communicated strategic goals, and a comprehensive strategic alignment to nurture Strategic Clarity.

Yet, the most compelling insight from Aperture Three lies in its illumination of the symbiotic relationship between these dimensions and how they collectively contribute to Sustained Competency within an organization. Sustained Competency is not merely about maintaining skills or knowledge over time but about fostering an environment where everyone is constantly encouraged to learn, unlearn, and relearn. It's about keeping an organization nimble, ready to navigate the ever-changing market dynamics, and instilling a capacity for continuous reinvention and resilience.

By harnessing the insights Aperture Three provides, leaders can promote an environment of continuous learning and improvement, leading to Entrusted Empowerment. This nurturing environment primes the organization to embrace the *Inception Mindset*, which is always ready for change, learning, and growth.

Here is a brief description of the two dimensions and the interplay node in question (See **Image 21**).

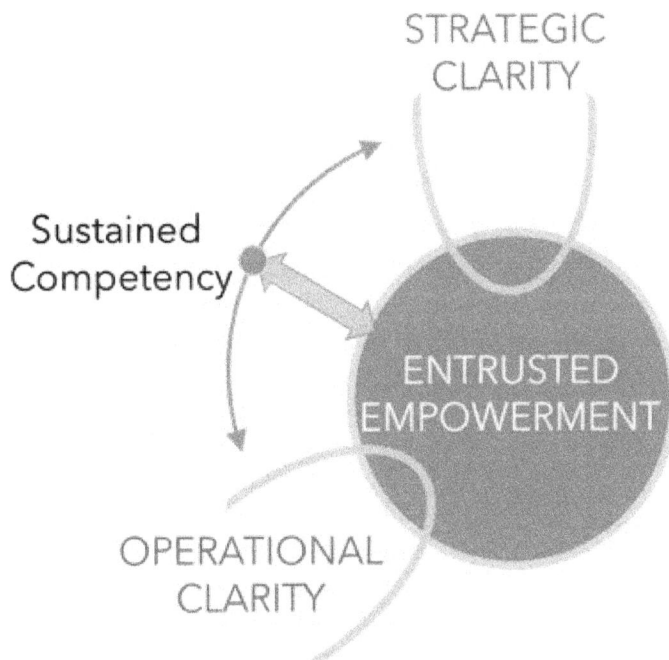

STRATEGIC
CLARITY

Sustained
Competency

ENTRUSTED
EMPOWERMENT

OPERATIONAL
CLARITY

Image 21. Aperture Three (Radi, 2015 - 2023) © Integral Advantage®

A high-level approach to developing practice in Aperture Three starts with revisiting and streamlining your operational procedures. Break down complex processes into manageable steps and ensure that every team member understands their roles, responsibilities, and how their contributions fit into the bigger picture. Make sure all protocols are explicitly defined and communicated. An excellent example of this is seen at **Amazon**, where operational efficiency is critical. The e-commerce giant uses technology and rigorous protocols to streamline its operations, ensuring that all its processes, from warehousing to delivery, operate like a well-oiled machine.

Every team member should understand your organization's vision and strategic goals. They should know where the organization is heading, why, and their role in getting there. Create a shared sense of purpose and reinforce strategic alignment at every opportunity. **Southwest Airlines** exemplifies strategic clarity. The company's vision is to become the world's most loved, most flown, and most profitable airline. Every decision made, every plan drafted, and this clear, compelling vision drives every action. This clarity helps Southwest maintain an engaged, motivated workforce and a loyal customer base.

Leaders can foster sustained competency by promoting continuous learning and improvement conditions. This might mean setting up training programs, promoting knowledge sharing, and encouraging experimentation and risk-taking within the bounds of the strategy and operational norms. In addition, leaders can set a personal example by continuously learning and adapting their leadership behaviors and strategies. The key to sustained competency lies not merely in maintaining a certain level of skills or knowledge but in cultivating an environment where everyone is encouraged to learn, unlearn, and relearn as needed. This dynamic cycle empowers the organization to remain agile, ready to tackle the uncertainties of a volatile marketplace, and ensures a capacity for continuous reinvention. These results underline an urgent call to action for organizations to augment their efforts in fostering a more sustained competency, thereby inching closer to an *Inception Mindset*. After all, in the words of Alvin Toffler, "The illiterate of the 21st century will not be those who cannot read and write, but those who cannot learn, unlearn, and relearn."

Encourage forming a learning community across teams and organizations to foster teamwork and collaboration. By working together, employees can learn from each other, improving their individual competencies and contributing to sustained organizational competency. Encourage employees not just to learn new skills but also to unlearn outdated practices and relearn better ones. Make it clear that making mistakes is essential to learning and that it is okay to fail **if** lessons are learned. **Next Jump**, a tech company, implements a continuous learning and development culture by providing mentoring, workshops, and even a "university" for their employees.

Regularly provide constructive feedback to employees about their performance. Annual evaluations are obsolete. From my perspective, they have very little value, as they are meaningless exercises of a socially constructed norm. Constructive and timely will help team members identify areas for improvement and further develop their skills and competencies. Constructive feedback can help employees improve their skills and adapt to changes. **Huddle**, a project management and collaboration software company, has an innovative 360-degree feedback system that allows for continuous feedback and improvement.

And last but not least, celebrate success and recognize your team's efforts. Recognition can significantly boost motivation and engagement, improving performance and competency levels.

Making Sense of Aperture Three

Once again, we see that a higher degree of sustained competency is achieved when an organization combines operational and strategic clarity instead of solely focusing on the individual dimensions. While Pearson's correlation between **operational clarity and sustained competency** indicates a strong positive and statistically significant relationship ($r = .800$, $p < 0.01$), and Pearson's correlation between **strategic clarity and sustained competency** indicates a strong positive and statistically significant relationship ($r = .798$, $p < 0.01$) we can appreciate that the Pearson's correlation between **operational/strategic clarity and sustained competency** indicates a strong positive and statistically significant relationship ($r = .842$, $p < 0.01$).

DIMENSIONS	INTERPLAY NODE	PEARSON CORRELATION
Operational Clarity	Sustained Competency	0.800
Strategic Clarity	Sustained Competency	0.798
Operational Clarity & Strategic Clarity	Sustained Competency	0.842

Table 8. Aperture Three: Pearson's Correlations Summary

Firstly, envision Operational Clarity as the set of precise, explicit instructions given to an artisan - a step-by-step guide detailing how to create a masterpiece. As they follow these detailed guidelines, their skill level, or sustained competency, naturally rises. Our study's strong correlation ($r = .800$, $p < 0.01$) supports this, suggesting that the clearer an organization's operations, the higher the level of sustained competency.

Next, view Strategic Clarity as the artisan's overall plan or blueprint - it provides a comprehensive understanding of the final product and its purpose. When the blueprint is well-defined and explicit, the artisan gains a deeper understanding of their craft and improves their sustained competency - a concept reflected in our study's strong positive correlation ($r = .798$, $p < 0.01$) between strategic clarity and sustained competency.

What happens when the artisan combines the detailed instructions (operational clarity) with the overarching blueprint (strategic clarity)? Their level of skill or sustained competency is boosted even further. Our research corroborates this, showing a strong positive correlation ($r = .842$, $p < 0.01$) when harmonizing operational and strategic clarity.

The lesson for Entrusted Empowerment? Just as an artisan requires a clear set of instructions and a comprehensive blueprint to perfect their craft, your team members also need clear operational and strategic directives to boost their competency. These twin pillars of clarity empower them to reach new heights of sustained competency, thus driving your organization toward its goals.

The Outcomes of Entrusted Empowerment

Dimensions: Operational Clarity, Strategic Clarity, Execution Clarity
Interplay: Autonomy, Contextual Fairness, Sustained Competency
Outputs: Engagement, Performance, Adaptability

Orientation

The cumulative outcomes of Entrusted Empowerment, as indicated in the comprehensive model of Entrusted Encompass (see **Image 22**), serve as a roadmap to improved organizational outcomes regarding Engagement, Performance, and Adaptability.

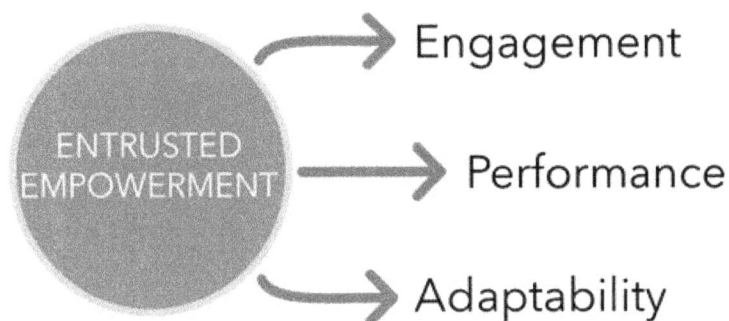

Image 22. Entrusted Empowerment Outcomes (Radi, 2015 - 2023) © Integral Advantage®

The integration of our three dimensions—Operational Clarity, Strategic Clarity, and Execution Clarity—with the three interplay nodes—Autonomy, Contextual Fairness, and Sustained Competency—create the conditions for Entrusted Empowerment. These, in turn, drive favorable outcomes across three crucial indicators:

Engagement: Reflects the level of commitment and dedication employees exhibit towards their work and the organization. Higher engagement levels have been associated with increased productivity and lower turnover rates.

Performance: An outcome metric representing how well the organization or individual meets its objectives and goals. Enhanced performance results in better business outcomes, including growth, customer satisfaction, and increased revenue.

Adaptability: This represents an organization's ability to respond effectively and innovatively to environmental changes. This can include changing market conditions, technological advancements, or internal shifts such as mergers or restructuring.

Making Sense of Entrusted Empowerment and Outcomes

As expected, Pearson's correlation between these combined dimensions and interplays and the outputs of Entrusted Empowerment have been statistically validated. It shows a strong, positive, and significant relationship with engagement (r = .841, p < 0.01), performance (r = .819, p < 0.01), and adaptability (r = .748, p < 0.01).

This indicates that an organization's focus on Strategic, Execution, and Operational Clarity, along with an emphasis on Sustained Competency, Contextual Fairness, and Autonomy, significantly contributes to building Entrusted Empowerment. The outcomes, as manifested in improved Engagement, Performance, and Adaptability, are far more pronounced than when focusing on the organizational dimensions alone.

ENTRUSTED EMPOWERMENT	OUTPUTS	PEARSON CORRELATION
Dimensions: Operational Clarity, Strategic Clarity, Execution Clarity **Interplay Nodes:** Autonomy, Contextual Fairness, Sustained Competency	Engagement	0.841
Operational Clarity + Strategic Clarity + Execution Clarity + Autonomy + Contextual Fairness + Sustained Competency	Performance	0.819
Operational Clarity + Strategic Clarity + Execution Clarity + Autonomy + Contextual Fairness + Sustained Competency	Adaptability	0.748

Table 9. Entrusted Empowerment Outcomes: Pearson's Correlations Summary

A succinct summary of these findings illustrates the value of Entrusted Encompass in enhancing organizational effectiveness and resilience (see Table 9).

As you navigate through the data and observations presented in this section, remember that the journey to Entrusted Empowerment is not linear. It involves a cycle of continuous learning, adjustment, and growth. It's a journey that requires commitment, patience, and an openness to embracing change.

So, we come full circle from where we started at the beginning of Horizon 3 with reframed knowledge and understanding. As we have seen, it's not uncommon for leaders to advocate for a specific culture. We often hear statements like, "We need a culture of innovation" or "We need to cultivate a culture of excellence." These statements, while well-intentioned, are somewhat misguided. The truth is you can't change culture directly. Culture isn't a button you push or a switch you flip. Instead, culture is the result, the by-product, of the systems, processes, and behaviors you put in place within your organization. So, when leaders say they want a culture of innovation and excellence, they're really aiming for heightened performance, engagement, and adaptability.

Envision an organization where each team member feels empowered and entrusted. It is a place where they feel valued, heard, and essential in crafting the organization's future. A place where clarity in strategy, execution, and operations isn't just top-down but a collaborative, co-constructed reality. It is a place where everyone understands their role and impact overall, embodying a sense of shared ownership and accountability. Entrusted Empowerment looks like this, and it's within your reach. As we move into Horizon 4, we will investigate the intersection of the environment, the self, and the organization through the lenses of Adapting and Innovating in complexity.

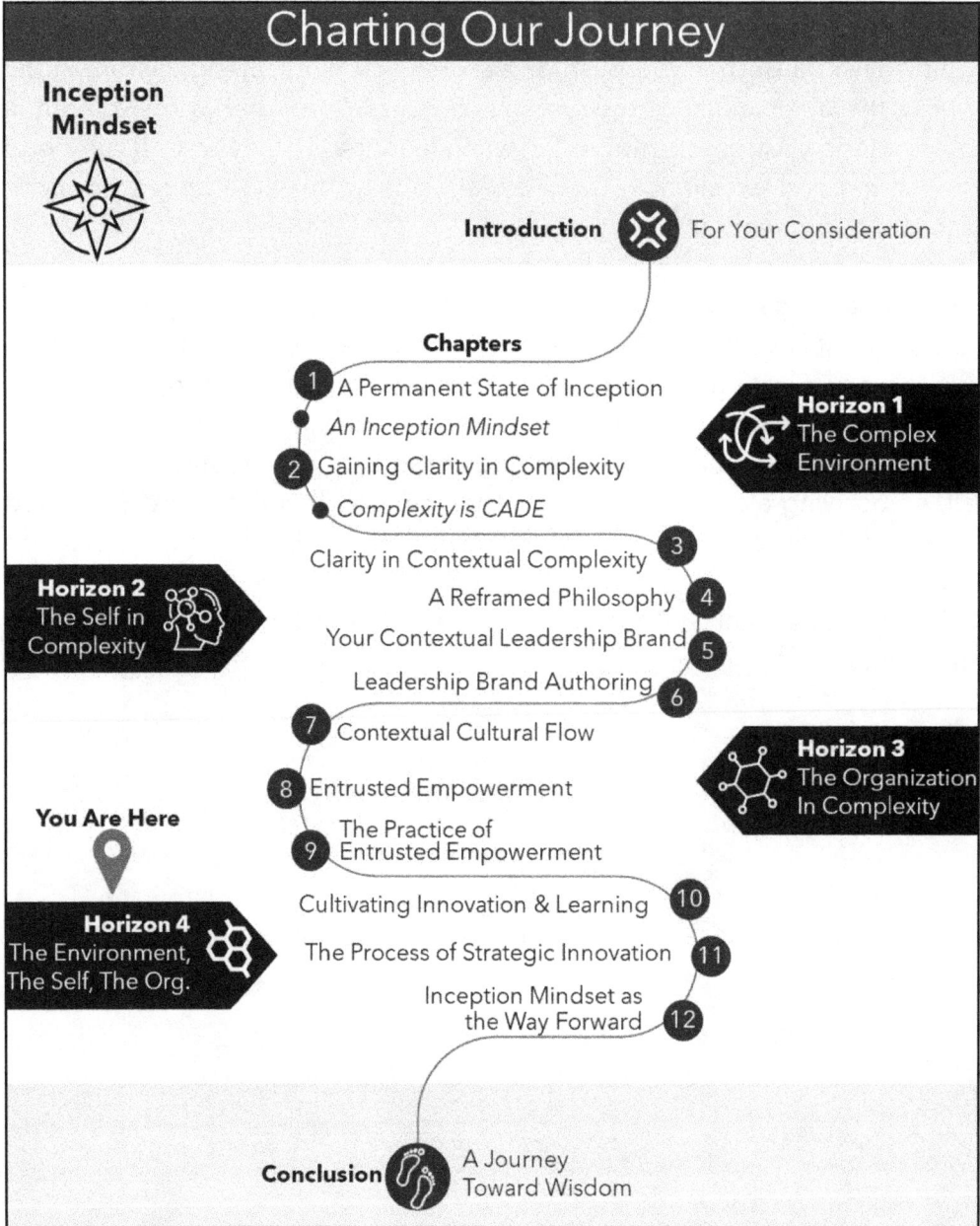

Charting Our Journey

Inception Mindset

Introduction — For Your Consideration

Chapters

1. A Permanent State of Inception
   An Inception Mindset
2. Gaining Clarity in Complexity
   Complexity is CADE

Horizon 1
The Complex Environment

3. Clarity in Contextual Complexity
4. A Reframed Philosophy
5. Your Contextual Leadership Brand
6. Leadership Brand Authoring

Horizon 2
The Self in Complexity

7. Contextual Cultural Flow
8. Entrusted Empowerment
9. The Practice of Entrusted Empowerment

Horizon 3
The Organization In Complexity

You Are Here

10. Cultivating Innovation & Learning
11. The Process of Strategic Innovation
12. Inception Mindset as the Way Forward

Horizon 4
The Environment, The Self, The Org.

Conclusion — A Journey Toward Wisdom

© 2023 Integral Advantage®, Inc.

PART IV

HORIZON 4: IN IT TOGETHER: THE ENVIRONMENT, THE SELF, THE ORGANIZATION.

At its core, innovation is about exploring the new, navigating through the unknown, and embracing uncertainty. It requires agility, flexibility, and resilience. Moreover, it calls for a profound understanding of the external environment, internal organizational dynamics, and individual cognitive aspects. Only then can organizations create and foster an innovation culture that effectively navigates and thrives in contextual complexity.

Innovation is a function of Contextual Complexity. Integrating the previous three horizons propels us to cultivate a fertile learning and innovation environment. It brings together the complex environment, the self in complexity, and the organization in complexity, leading to the birth of the Fourth Horizon, which is the collective innovation effort.

The first horizon helps us understand the complex environment, and the idea of the *Inception Mindset* and CADE model provides the tools to navigate through it. In the second horizon, we learn how to operate in complexity by developing a strong sense of self through self-authoring and leadership branding. In the third horizon, we learn how to practice Entrusted Empowerment in our organization, which forms the backbone of innovation by enabling strategic, execution, and operational clarity, contextual fairness, autonomy, and sustained competency, fostering engagement, performance, and adaptability.

Finally, in the fourth horizon, we combine it to create an environment that encourages learning and fosters innovation. The Fourth Horizon is about cultivating an innovation environment in a contextually complex world by integrating the concepts from the first three horizons. It is about creating an interconnected ecosystem of learning and innovation, where the complex environment, the self in complexity, and the organization in complexity come together to facilitate innovation. It involves reframing our understanding of complexity and our role within it, enabling us to better understand and navigate through the complexities of the modern world.

CHAPTER 10

CULTIVATING INNOVATION AND LEARNING

*"Innovation is the ability to see change as an opportunity
- not a threat."* — *Steve Jobs*

Navigating complexity requires innovation. Creating values for the stakeholders is an essential component of the *Inception Mindset*. A leader in any field must be able to think creatively and foster an environment where new ideas and solutions are part of the organization's fabric. Innovation drives progress and pushes us forward, and those who can embrace it and use it to their advantage will generate value. Human imagination and creativity are what drive the innovation process. While logic and reason are essential for solving problems and making progress, the power of the imagination allows us to envision new possibilities. Innovation often requires exploring uncharted territory with curiosity and a sense of wonder; imagination is the key to unlocking these new frontiers.

Too often, the terms innovation or creative innovation are used to describe a process to develop a product or a service. Innovation encompasses ideation, invention, conception, and other terms that are components of a process of improving, adapting, or developing anew. Innovation is not limited to products and services. It encompasses organizational functions, programs, methodologies, and systems - to name a few - capable of delivering better outcomes and generating value for the stakeholders. Innovation is a critical aspect of organizations, communities, and society at large. Regardless of whether private, public, non-profit, government, or education designations, all organizations must innovate to exist in a complex environment. In this context, the role of leadership is not to use the term innovation as a buzzword but foster the conditions for innovation to occur. We cannot expect innovation as long as nothing goes wrong, as we cannot dissipate risk, but we can mitigate it.

Leaders need to establish methodologies in organizations to unleash creativity and sustain innovation. In 2011, as I was in the process of completing my thesis for my PKE MBA at Pepperdine, I wanted to explore how I could adapt what I have learned over the previous 17 years in consumer product strategy, to business strategy, especially in developing business processes, identifying, and addressing critical issues creatively.

In the strategy context, I simmered down the methodology I proposed to a three-pronged process: **1. Incubation 2. Propagation 3. Maximization.** These are the essential components for innovation in the various contexts we have discussed thus far. Over the many years in consumer product strategy, too often, I witnessed the type of misalignment in organizations causing robust ideas to anticipate changes in the environment to be discarded in favor of the here and now or the "quarterly objectives." I noticed then, and I continue to notice now, that competing interests among members in organizations do not necessarily cause these conditions, although those do play a role. Instead, the lack of common language and shared understanding of a methodology often causes organizations to get stuck in the here and now rather than innovating to anticipate the shifts caused by the complexity of the environment.

Establishing an innovative strategic platform within an organization is essential to fostering an *Inception Mindset*. Leaders in organizations are often seduced by the need for speed, especially when responding to environmental shifts. Then the "we need to innovate drums" are getting pounded, and "speed for the sake of speed" dominates. I believe establishing and maintaining an innovative platform allows the organization to achieve speed by transcending the illusion of speed.

Risk, Failure, Bubbles, and the $10 Million Bet

We cannot achieve innovation without expecting occasional missteps. Developing foresight to anticipate and accept these inevitable shortcomings is a cornerstone of the *Inception Mindset*—an approach to innovation that embraces exploration, challenges norms, and dares to redefine possibilities.

I experienced some spectacular failures while developing a product, a process, or a function. However, thankfully, those failures were self-contained as part of the innovation process and often resulted from pushing the limits to ensure that nothing was left on the table. Innovation is a dance of thinking, experimenting, observing, and learning.

When exploring, we must consider all plausible techniques and method-ologies we can implement. If we are developing a new product, we may be able to model parts ahead of time and test them and learn from those tests before we make additional commitments. We must have clarity about the process by mapping that process. At times we need to decide the ele-ments of a product, a service, a business process, or a functional business program that we sacrifice at the front end in favor of addressing the most salient aspects of what we want to achieve. This is about mapping the cri-teria and organizing them into a hierarchy to identify and anticipate where failure can occur.

Risky Beauty. In 2004, I was at the helm of designing and developing the Neutrogena® Microdermabrasion System handheld device. Radi Design, our firm, was entrusted with developing this cutting-edge skincare de-vice, its versatile attachments, and a neat countertop stand. The late Kelly Preston was featured in its debut thirty-second TV commercial in February 2005, marking the system's entry into retail distribution channels.

The pressure of a stringent timeline was palpable, given the distinct "win-dow to market." Our guidance was spearheaded by Michael McNamara, the Global President of Neutrogena, and Jan Hall, the President, who of-fered us a clear roadmap to our goal, with a degree of flexibility in how we got there.

I brought significant expertise to the table, having previously developed systems under the same U.S. Utility Patent. However, the challenge lay in blending Neutrogena's Iconic brand with functional design, particularly because this was Neutrogena's first foray into battery-operated skincare devices. This intersection of brand design and product functionality was one of our initial potential failure points.

Time was of the essence, and the pressure to meet market deadlines added an extra layer of risk. Meanwhile, we were keenly aware that Neutrogena's impending consumer focus groups could introduce further delays. The project had its fair share of technical complexities, too. We had to ensure ergonomics, water resistance, effective micro-orbit delivery in sync with the skincare regimen, tamper-proofing, and a unique method to prevent competitors' attachments from fitting the Neutrogena® device. Addition-ally, we had to navigate specific engineering criteria from the Johnson &

Johnson® engineering team in Skillman, NJ, and Neutrogena's manufacturing, packaging, and logistics requirements. Amidst all this, I held my ambition steadfastly: to create an enduring, iconic design that maximized performance and user experience through aesthetic and technical innovation.

We achieved our goal by mapping out all these criteria. This approach allowed us to foresee potential failures, manage them proactively, and sometimes shift the risk to more controlled parts of the project or device. Every obstacle that emerged was promptly tackled, allowing us to complete the project within the timeframe.

One of the enduring pleasures of this journey was seeing the Neutrogena Microdermabrasion System on Target's shelves, where it remained until its discontinuation in 2022, some 17 years post-launch. By any measure, this was a testament to a project well-executed by mapping and mitigating risk.

Bubbles and Limit-Pushing. Steve Jobs' anecdote of dropping an iPod prototype into a fish tank exemplifies pushing boundaries for better outcomes, highlighting the importance of challenging the status quo and taking calculated risks for superior results. As the story goes, in the early 2000s, engineers presented Jobs with a prototype of the device during the iPod's development. Jobs felt the device was too big and needed to be smaller. The engineers insisted they had condensed all the necessary components as much as possible and couldn't make it any smaller.

To challenge their assumption, Jobs dropped the iPod prototype into a fish tank. Bubbles started to emerge from the device. He pointed out to the engineers that the bubbles indicated unused space inside, implying that the device could be made smaller. Challenged to reevaluate their work, the engineers managed to reduce the size further. This anecdote highlights two aspects of Jobs' approach to innovation: pushing boundaries and taking calculated risks to achieve optimal outcomes.

Jobs was notorious for demanding what seemed impossible and often made others believe they could do it. He appealed to their self-efficacy, and his legendary approach was defined as *Reality Distortion* Field (RDF), a term first used by Bud Tribble at Apple Computer in 1981 to describe Steve *Jobs'* leveraging his executive presence to make developers believe they could do what seemed impossible.

In terms of leadership and innovation, this story underlines the importance of holding an *Inception Mindset*, challenging the status quo, encouraging creative problem-solving, and taking calculated risks. These are often crucial elements in delivering innovative solutions and attaining superior results.

The Game and the Gamble. Risk and innovation transcend the confines of product design, as exemplified by Dr. Will Roper's experience. He invested $10 million in the Navy interceptor, the Standard Missile 6, which paid off tremendously. However, he raises the question: what if the gamble hadn't paid off? This insight underlines the importance of valuing sound risk-taking, regardless of the outcome.

The journey of Dr. Will Roper, who served as the Assistant Secretary of the Air Force for Acquisition, Technology, and Logistics, is an intriguing exploration of the boundaries of risk and failure. With a yearly budget exceeding $60 billion and more than 550 acquisition programs under his purview, Dr. Roper served as the primary adviser on the Air Force's R&D, testing, production, and modernization endeavors.

In an interview, Dr. Roper candidly shares his experiences of failure and, more importantly, the lessons he's gleaned from these experiences. "I've had a lot of failures in the past," he acknowledges. His resilience stems from encountering failure in non-catastrophic situations, which, had they been otherwise, may have steered his career off its course.

In the Air Force and beyond, a culture that truly embraces risk is yet to take root. As Dr. Roper notes, it's one thing to advocate for risk-taking but entirely another to tolerate the inevitable failures that come with it.

Before joining the Air Force, Dr. Roper was a government employee working for Secretary Carter. Here, he found himself presented with a bet – a bet that would shape his career. He was given just enough money to place a bet on a single system. He invested ten million dollars in a Navy interceptor, the Standard Missile 6, betting on its potential to be reprogrammed for an offensive strike mission. The bet paid off, leading to great advantages for the Navy and an acceleration in his own career.

However, Dr. Roper poses an insightful question – what if the outcome had been different? The risk would've been the same, yet failure could've drastically altered his trajectory. Dr. Roper candidly admits that he might not have been given more opportunities had the risk not resulted in success.

Recognizing a double standard in celebrating risk-takers who get lucky, Dr. Roper points out the hypocrisy in evaluating decisions based solely on their outcomes. He asserts that a good risk remains so, irrespective of the result. To Dr. Roper, a smart choice – one based on sound risk-reward calculus – should be recognized and validated, regardless of the eventual roll of the dice.

One of Dr. Roper's chief aims was fostering a mindset of accepting and appreciating intelligent risk-taking, irrespective of the outcome. He says, "I'm trying to be very mindful with Air Force program managers and people taking a risk, that they get their evaluation and validation from me at the point that they take the risk." The outcomes, he insists, are merely a result of chance and should not define the value of the initial risk. With these reflections, Dr. Roper articulates a critical understanding of risk and failure in innovation – the tale of risk-taking must include not only the winners but also those who dared to roll the dice, regardless of the outcome.

Battling Pirates. Adobe's transition from selling packaged software to providing cloud-based subscription services in 2013 is a striking example of business process innovation. Despite significant risks and initial backlash, Adobe's business model led to a steady revenue stream and substantial growth, demonstrating that holding an *Inception Mindset* can successfully revolutionize business models.

This transition to the "Creative Cloud" was a bold move that drew criticism and resistance from many of its customers, who were used to owning software outright rather than paying a monthly subscription fee. However, Adobe believed that this new business model would provide a more stable and predictable revenue stream and enable them to deliver updates and new features to customers more quickly and regularly.

Despite the initial backlash, Adobe's gamble indeed paid off. Their transition to a cloud-based subscription model has substantially increased their user base and a steady revenue stream. By 2022, Adobe's Creative Cloud had almost 30 million paid subscribers, and the company's revenue had grown from $4.4 billion in 2012 to $17.6 billion in 2022. This example illustrates that despite significant risks and initial resistance, businesses can successfully innovate their business models by holding an *Inception Mindset* and being willing to explore new strategies and methodologies.

Leveraging Thinking in Innovation

The journey of innovation is never a straightforward process. It requires a dynamic interplay of different modes of thinking that work in tandem to challenge norms, provoke novel ideas, and find solutions to complex problems. Three distinct types of thinking often fuel innovation: Critical Thinking, Creative Thinking, and Lateral Thinking.

Critical Thinking: The Debugger of Ideas. Critical thinking serves as the 'debugger' in the innovation process. It entails an organized, systematic approach to understanding and solving problems. It enables innovators to challenge assumptions, evaluate ideas, identify potential pitfalls, and assess the viability of solutions. This process draws on logical reasoning and analytical capabilities to dissect an idea, examining its every facet for errors or inconsistencies.

For instance, when developing a new product, a service, business process or program, critical thinking comes into play when assessing the feasibility of the design, its potential market impact, cost-effectiveness, and technical implications. This rigorous scrutiny helps identify and address potential roadblocks early on, mitigating the risk of failure and saving valuable time and resources. It ensures that the innovative solution proposed is not just novel but also practical and effective.

Creative Thinking: The Genesis of Novelty. Creative thinking is the birthplace of fresh ideas—the very lifeblood of innovation. It's about thinking beyond the boundaries of conventional wisdom, creating new associations, and envisioning possibilities that haven't been explored before. Creative thinking is not confined to artistic endeavors but pervades all areas—from scientific theories to social ideas, business strategies, and new inventions.

A creative mind does not accept the status quo but questions it, seeks alternatives, and imagines different realities. It can reassemble existing elements into new configurations, leading to breakthrough solutions. An example of creative thinking can be seen in the evolution of educational approaches in the digital age.

Consider the development of Massive Open Online Courses (MOOCs). Traditional education models were centered around in-person instruction within physical classrooms. However, with the advent of the internet and digital technologies, innovative educators began to think creatively about how to deliver education to a global audience. They assembled existing elements—video streaming, internet connectivity, virtual discussion forums—into a novel configuration, creating a digital platform that allows learners around the world to access quality education, irrespective of their geographical location.

This creative reconfiguration completely revolutionized education, making it more accessible and flexible than ever before. It challenged the status quo of traditional education models, offering an alternative that caters to the evolving needs of today's learners. So, while the components of MOOCs were not new in and of themselves, their creative application within the field of education was a novel and transformative solution—a testament to the power of creative thinking.

Lateral Thinking: The Pathway to Paradigm Shifts. Lateral thinking, a term Dr. Edward de Bono coined, takes creative thinking a step further. It involves reimagining basic assumptions and looking at a problem from different perspectives to find innovative solutions. Rather than following a linear, step-by-step approach, lateral thinking zigzags is about making jumps, taking leaps, and making unexpected connections.

Lateral thinking breaks away from established thought patterns and explores new territories of problem-solving. For example, Uber's founders didn't just try to improve taxi services; they reconsidered the entire urban transportation concept. They sidestepped traditional industry norms and transformed personal transport through a simple yet revolutionary app-based ride-sharing model.

Innovation thrives at the intersection of critical, creative, and lateral thinking. Each brings unique value to the process—critical thinking ensures the idea's robustness and viability, creative thinking fuels the generation of novel solutions, and lateral thinking enables paradigm shifts. By embracing these types of thinking, innovators can challenge norms, push boundaries, and drive meaningful, lasting change. The *Inception Mindset* is about harnessing these modes of thinking to turn ideas into reality, transform industries, and reshape our world in permanent complexity.

The Myth of the Creative Bone: Unraveling the Neuroscience of Creativity

Creativity is often perceived as a mystical attribute, the sole domain of artists, inventors, or innovative geniuses. "But I don't have a creative bone in my body" - this assertion frequently surfaces in my courses and seminars, despite my reassurances that creativity is an inherent human trait. Indeed, my intuition has always told me that every person possesses a unique creativity profile. This belief has found significant reinforcement as I delved deeper into organizational leadership, behavior, and development and uncovered the robust neuroscience research that validates my intuition.

One of the central theories in the neuroscience of creativity, advanced by Beaty et al. in 2015, involves a complex interplay between different brain networks, specifically the default mode network (DMN), the executive control network (ECN), and the salience network (SN). The DMN involves mind-wandering and daydreaming, the ECN is used for focused thinking and decision-making, and the SN acts as a switch between the two. This underscores creativity's dynamic nature, integrating focused thinking and free imagination.

Further supporting this notion is research emphasizing the role of divergent thinking in creativity, advanced by Gonen-Yaacovi et al. in 2013. Divergent thinking, defined as the ability to generate multiple unique solutions to a problem, is a key element of creative thought. Neuroimaging studies have found that when individuals engage in divergent thinking tasks, there is widespread activation across various brain regions, suggesting that creativity is a whole-brain activity.

The role of environment and experience in creativity is also backed by neuroscience research. Our brains are plastic, continually rewiring based on experiences and learning. As advanced by Schlegel et al. in 2015, regular engagement in creative activities alters the brain's structure and function, fostering an environment that facilitates the generation of novel ideas. Therefore, creativity is not merely an innate trait but a skill that can be developed and nurtured.

Dr. Gerard Puccio is a professor at the International Center for Studies in Creativity at Buffalo State College. His research focuses on creative problem-solving and the development of creative skills. Puccio and his colleagues developed the Creative Problem-Solving (CPS) model, a framework that provides a process for enhancing creativity. According to the CPS model, the creative process involves both divergent and convergent thinking. Divergent thinking is the generation of multiple ideas, while convergent thinking is evaluating and refining these ideas. This mirrors the neuroscience research we have explored, which highlights the interplay between the default mode and executive control networks in the brain.

Puccio's work also emphasizes the learnability of creativity. He posits that creativity is not a fixed trait but rather a skill that can be developed and enhanced through training and practice. This aligns with the neuroplasticity research that suggests regular engagement in creative activities can alter brain structure and function to support generating novel ideas.

Furthermore, Puccio's FourSight Thinking Profile, a tool used to understand an individual's problem-solving preferences, underscores that everyone has a unique creativity profile. This tool identifies individuals as Clarifiers, Ideators, Developers, or Implementers, reflecting different stages in the creative process.

I think I made my case; the "creative bone" myth is a fallacy. Neuroscience research elucidates that creativity is not the privilege of a few but a universal capability. It all boils down to recognizing our unique Creativity Profiles and nourishing them through relevant experiences and continuous learning.

Innovation as Value Creation

In pursuing value creation through creative innovation, we must beware of lingering in the "obvious," the alluring surface layer of existing knowledge and practices. This is where we find incremental improvements or "tweaks" and "hacks," but it's a space that can be deceptive. It gives organizations a false sense of security, keeping them from engaging with complexity and limiting their exposure to risks and potential failures. However, it's in embracing complexity and the willingness to dig beneath the surface where truly transformative innovation resides.

Image 23. Extraordinary Value (Radi, 2015 - 2023) © Integral Advantage®

Aligning innovation with creative problem-solving requires us to delve below the obvious, probing beneath the surface of existing paradigms to uncover novel and non-obvious solutions (see **Image 23**). This concept is exemplified by the US Patent Office's requirement of "non-obviousness" for patentability, pushing inventors to unearth solutions that extend beyond the common knowledge of those skilled in the art. My experience with this? Receiving a letter in 2006 from the U.S. Patent Office rejecting one of my patent applications for being too "obvious." It felt like a bucket of icy water because I was convinced that I met the requirements. From this encounter, I learned a valuable lesson, highlighting the necessity of breaking new ground, not only in the realm of products but across all disciplines of innovation. It got me to think about how often we may remain on the surface and focus our efforts on going the extra mile.

So, what does this journey beneath the surface entail? It's about cultivating a deep, insightful understanding of the problem at hand, challenging existing assumptions, and exploring uncharted territories of thought and practice fearlessly. It's about leveraging the power of technology and data to reveal hidden patterns, connections, and opportunities. But above all, it's about drawing on the distinctively human attributes of intuitions and insights to drive innovation.

As we have explored throughout this book, complexity demands a constant state of inception, a constellation of new beginnings from technology, practices, strategies, and stakeholders' engagement, you name it, it needs to be *learned, unlearned, and relearned*. Complexity demands that we develop an *Inception Mindset* to integrate the constellation of new beginnings. This exploratory and in-depth approach often results in breakthrough innovations that create significant value for organizations and society at large.

Creating the Extraordinary (see **Image 23**) is an ambitious endeavor requiring a systemic shift. It requires courageous leadership, an understanding of complex systems, and resilience to "dig the extra mile." Extraordinary value creation is driven by a purpose or mission that goes beyond pure profit, considering inclusivity and accessibility to ensure that the benefits of innovation are widespread.

In this vein, extraordinary innovation is exemplified by Tesla's mission to accelerate the world's transition to sustainable energy. Tesla's products serve functional purposes and resonate more deeply emotionally by addressing pressing environmental concerns.

Importantly, this extraordinary journey is seldom a solo undertaking. It requires active collaboration with diverse groups - cross-functional teams, partners, customers, and even competitors - to deliver an innovation that truly resonates with all stakeholders.

Despite its challenges, pursuing extraordinary innovation promises considerable rewards: substantial, sustainable value creation that can improve organizations and societies. We can tap into creative innovation's extraordinary potential by venturing beneath the surface.

Busting the Barriers to Creative Innovation

The first step on the path to creative innovation is to acknowledge its necessity. However, this is just the beginning of the journey. You'll inevitably face resistance when you attempt to infuse an innovative spirit into an organization, manifesting as a triangle of barriers: Behaviors, Emotions, and Mindset (see **Image 24**).

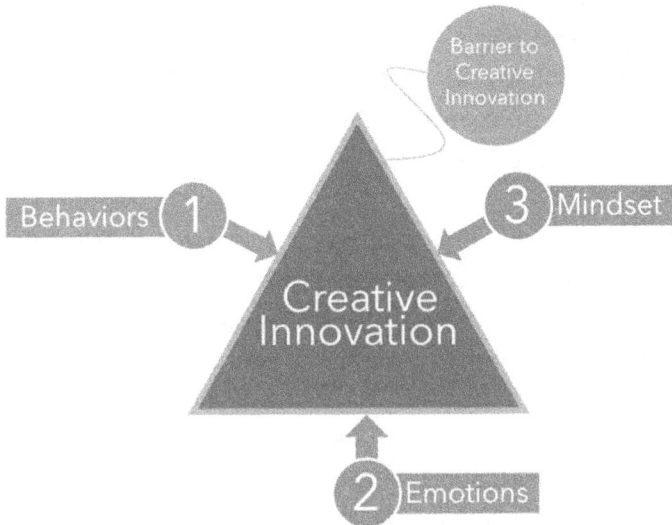

Image 24. The Barrier to Creative Innovation (Radi, 2015 - 2023) © Integral Advantage®

The first side of this triangle is **Behaviors**. These are deeply ingrained habits and actions, hardened by time, tradition, and past successes. They provide the comforting blanket of familiarity but can also stifle the novelty and risk-taking necessary for innovation. To truly spark innovation, an organization must step off the entrenched path and venture into unexplored territories. In the context of debunking the "creative bone myth," this involves recognizing and nurturing our inherent ability to create.

Emotions form the second side of this triangle. The fear of the unknown, a visceral aversion to failure, and an attachment to the status quo can all dampen the innovative spirit. Innovation requires us to step outside our comfort zones, voice unconventional ideas, and even confront the possibility of failure. To counter these emotional barriers, it's crucial to cultivate an environment that celebrates risk-taking, views failure as a stepping-stone to value creation, and values everyone's contributions. Remember, as Dr. George Lakoff, has noted, rational thought cannot exist without emotions. Emotions drive our decisions, and empathy plays a critical role in creating an environment that facilitates innovation.

Mindset forms the final side of this triangle. Carol Dweck's work on growth and fixed mindsets provides invaluable insights into how our beliefs about our abilities can influence our innovative potential. A fixed mindset can stifle innovation, leading people to view their talents as static, making them more likely to avoid challenges and resist change. On the other hand, a growth mindset fosters a love for learning and resilience, both indispensable for innovation. Remember, as leadership expert Ronald Heifetz has noted, resistance isn't to change per se but to perceived loss.

In the context of an *Inception Mindset,* we recognize that constant change and complexity are the new norms. We embrace a constellation of new beginnings rather than resist them. To navigate this triangle of barriers, an organization needs transformation at various levels. Leaders must identify these barriers, understand their implications, and act strategically to dismantle them. They should model the desired behaviors, cultivating an environment that fosters open communication, risk-taking, and creative innovation. In this context, we must also remember what we have learned about Entrusted Empowerment as the framework supports fostering the practice of creative innovation.

The road to breaking down these barriers may be challenging, but it is a necessary part of fostering creative innovation. The struggle can result in rewards in the form of an organization capable of adapting, constantly learning, and continuously growing. By converting barriers into lenses to support exploration, leaders can facilitate the transformation of an organization into one that consistently creates value. The following chapter will explore strategies for turning these barriers into opportunities.

CHAPTER 11

THE PROCESS OF STRATEGIC INNOVATION

"Do the best you can until you know better. Then when you know better, do better." — Dr. Maya Angelou

When navigating through the intricate complexity of our world, it quickly becomes evident that all innovation is inherently strategic. The adage "necessity is the mother of invention" suggests that innovation often emerges from a pressing need or problem requiring resolution. This reasoning naturally leads us to view innovation as innately strategic in nature.

Regrettably, the term 'strategy' is often trivialized and misused in contemporary dialogue. It's casually deployed as a buzzword, frequently associated with operational functions fundamentally tactical, not strategic. This improper usage obscures the true value and nature of strategic thinking and strategy development.

Contrary to common misconception, strategy is not an esoteric practice reserved for an exclusive few. Instead, it represents a practical, pragmatic approach to overcoming obstacles standing in the way of vision fulfillment. Strategy is the critical tool that allows us to navigate and conquer the challenges encountered on our path toward realizing a vision.

Strategy begins with diagnosing a critical issue that impedes progress or creates adverse conditions obstructing our vision. Crucially, understanding that such an issue extends beyond surface-level symptoms is vital. It represents the root cause of the obstacle, and diagnosing it requires a thorough, context-sensitive analysis.

Once the root cause is diagnosed, creativity and innovation enter the picture. A strategy to tackle this critical issue requires innovative thinking and creative solutions. The optimal solution might often hide in plain sight but remains unseen without the right diagnosis. Therefore, strategic thinking in innovation is more than generating new ideas; it's about diagnosing problems and unearthing solutions that may have been present unnoticed. This understanding encapsulates the true essence of Strategic Thinking in Innovation.

In this chapter, we will first explore how the essence of Horizon 1 to Horizon 3 harmoniously coalesce into enhancing our ability to define a vision, devise a strategy, and foster creativity and innovation. We will explore what a vision is and, most importantly, how not to fall into the trap of tunnel vision. We will continue by clarifying how we diagnose a critical issue, develop plausible scenarios, and then establish an innovation platform by leveraging the Incubation, Propagation & Maximization methodology.

Harnessing the Horizons of Complexity

This section delves into how complexity influences leadership, the self, and organizational dynamics, elucidating the harmonious convergence of these elements in enhancing strategic thinking and innovation. To achieve this, we'll revisit the essential core principles of each Horizon, demonstrating their interconnectedness and contribution to advancing strategic thinking and fostering innovation.

The Inception Mindset and the CADE Model (Horizon 1)

At the crux of Horizon 1 are the *Inception Mindset* and the CADE model. These signify the imperative for leaders to navigate the complexities of today's world. The *Inception Mindset* encourages viewing each problem as a new starting point, breaking away from the inclination to apply old solutions to contemporary challenges. This mindset is an invitation to curiosity and resilience, consistently acknowledging and engaging with the world's inherent complexity.

The CADE model—Contextualizable, Amorphous, Dynamic, and Elastic—builds the foundation for this mindset. It paints organizations as fluid entities that flourish amid complexity and underlines that our approach to complexity should be custom, adaptable, and resilient, just like the systems we aim to influence.

The Self in Complexity (Horizon 2)

Horizon 2 highlights the importance of understanding oneself amidst this complexity. Effective navigation of complexity necessitates leaders to grasp their identity, principles, and capabilities firmly. This understanding, manifested through self-authoring and leadership branding, fosters authenticity, resilience, and adaptability. This alignment of personal and organizational values and goals empowers leaders to traverse complexity and drive innovation.

Entrusted Empowerment (Horizon 3)

Horizon 3 emphasizes Entrusted Empowerment, highlighting the need for strategy, operations, and execution clarity to enable a competent, autonomous, and equitable organizational environment. The pillars of strategic, operational, and execution clarity bolster entrusted empowerment, spurring engagement, performance, and adaptability. This empowerment makes the environment conducive to innovation, enabling individuals and teams to tackle complex challenges and drive change.

The Nexus (Horizon 4)

Horizon 4 integrates these concepts into a comprehensive strategic thinking and innovation framework. By understanding and embracing complexity (Horizon 1), developing an authentic leadership brand (Horizon 2), and fostering an environment of entrusted empowerment (Horizon 3), leaders can create an ecosystem ripe for strategic innovation.

Leaders cultivate a contextual understanding of their environment in this framework through the *Inception Mindset* and the CADE model. They strategize effectively by understanding that each challenge is unique, requiring a fresh approach. This mindset promotes innovative thinking, necessitating continual learning and adaptability in the face of complexity.

An authentic leadership brand, honed through self-authoring, aligns the individual's and the organization's purpose. This congruence creates a strong brand identity, encouraging innovation. By understanding their strengths, leaders can leverage them to achieve strategic goals and inspire their teams, fostering coherence and continuity, essential for navigating the ever-evolving business and technology landscapes.

Entrusted Empowerment fosters a culture of trust and autonomy, which is key to nurturing innovative thought. When team members are clear about their roles, responsibilities, and expectations, they feel empowered to take ownership, creating a culture conducive to innovation.

In conclusion, Horizon 4 is the convergence point of these elements, forming a fertile ground for strategic innovation. It provides a holistic framework that encourages embracing complexity, developing genuine leadership aligned with the organization's purpose, and fostering an environment of Entrusted Empowerment. In this ecosystem, innovation thrives not as an isolated occurrence but as an organic process.

Vision: The Ultimate Clarifier

Vision is best defined as a collectively shared and immersive mental model of an optimal future state. It acts as a beacon for an organization or an individual, projecting a clear image of what they aspire to become. By integrating the mission, enacted values, goals, and aspirations, a vision shapes the strategic direction and underpins decision-making processes.

Although potentially distant and challenging, this optimal future state serves as a compelling call to action, driving progress and innovation. Within the context of strategic innovation, a well-articulated vision is pivotal, underpinning the alignment and effectiveness of the incubation, propagation, and maximization stages.

Far from being an abstract concept or a lofty ideal, vision plays a central role in an organization's journey to success. Despite its ambitious nature, the future state encapsulated in the vision is a compelling motivator, inciting progress and fostering innovation. A vision galvanizes an organization's resources and efforts, inspiring individuals and teams to strive for the future they envisage tirelessly.

Strategic innovation requires a clear vision. The guiding principle ensures alignment and optimizes the effectiveness of the three innovation process stages: incubation, propagation, and maximization. A clear vision provides direction and purpose in the incubation stage, where ideas are nurtured. The propagation stage, which transforms concepts into outcomes, relies on vision to maintain focus amid potential setbacks. Finally, during the maximization stage, where outcomes of ideas are scaled, the vision helps measure progress and recognize achievements, reinforcing a culture of innovation.

While a vision defines an organization's desired future state, it should not promote inflexibility. Instead, a well-crafted vision fosters agility and adaptability. It remains a constant, orienting force as an organization traverses the ever-evolving landscape of market dynamics, technological advancements, and societal needs. Acting as a north star, it offers a steady reference point amidst a sea of uncertainty and change while also allowing for course corrections and adaptability. This ensures that the organization remains responsive to emerging opportunities and challenges.

A shared vision significantly contributes to fostering a positive organizational climate. Employees who view their work as part of a larger purpose display increased commitment, motivation, and job satisfaction. Thus, a shared vision can cultivate an environment conducive to collaboration, resilience, and creativity—essential ingredients for innovation.

Avoiding the Positive Tunnel Vision Effect

"The Positive Tunnel Vision Effect" framework (see **Image 25**) unveils a common trap that organizations and individuals often succumb to while crafting their visions. It's crucial to understand that a vision that exclusively focuses on a single "positive" scenario or outcome can potentially be harmful instead of beneficial.

Why is it detrimental? Such a vision hinges on linear thinking and fails to account for our organizations' broader context, environmental nuances, and complex dynamics. It gives an illusion of certainty instead of offering true clarity, narrowing our field of view, and often leaving us unprepared for unexpected challenges or opportunities. It's akin to peering through a spyglass, focusing on a single perspective at the risk of missing the broader panorama.

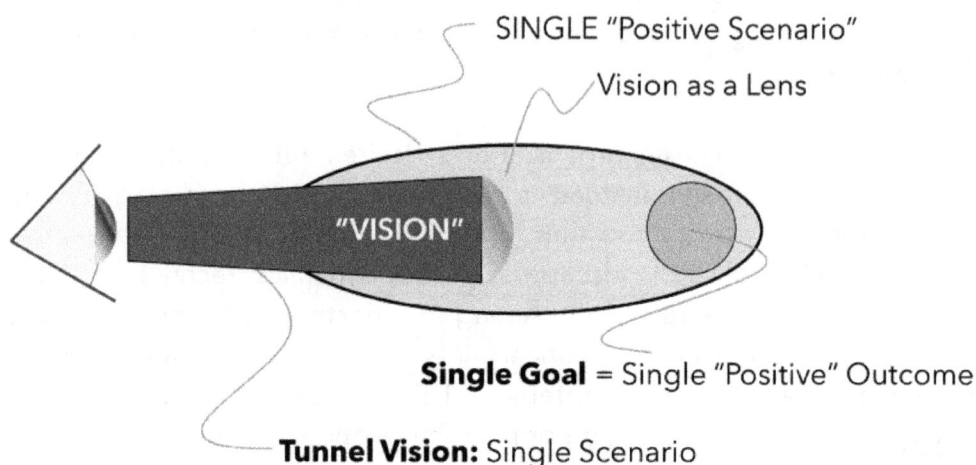

SINGLE "Positive Scenario"

Vision as a Lens

"VISION"

Single Goal = Single "Positive" Outcome

Tunnel Vision: Single Scenario

Image 25. Positive Tunnel Vision Effect (Radi, 2018 - 2023) © Integral Advantage®

Do not get me wrong; I wholeheartedly endorse positive thinking. However, an imbalance between optimism and realism can hamper our ability to assess situations critically and objectively. This can cause problems in strategic planning and execution. This often falls under the guise of "optimism bias" or "overconfidence bias," where excessive positive thinking clouds the ability to craft a vision.

The 'spyglass approach' falls short of fostering a shared vision—an immersive, collective understanding of the future we aspire to. Instead, it creates tunnel vision, a restricted and short-sighted perspective, which often leads to suboptimal outcomes. Such a vision lacks the richness, flexibility, and comprehensive understanding embedded in robust systems thinking. Essentially, it's a closed-aperture approach, disregarding the vast array of possibilities and nuances of viewing the whole picture.

Therefore, the Positive Tunnel Vision Effect serves as a cautionary tale. It underscores that a vision should not be a simplistic, single-scenario projection. Instead, it should be an inclusive, well-rounded understanding representing the optimal state we aim to achieve. This should be grounded in systems thinking and shared by all group members.

Let's take a historical example: In the early 2000s, Blockbuster Video was a colossus in the video rental industry. Yet, their rigid focus on their traditional brick-and-mortar business model made them overlook the emergence of digital streaming services. They declined an offer to buy Netflix for $50 million in 2000, holding onto their singular positive scenario of sustaining physical rentals. This tunnel vision led to its bankruptcy in 2010, while Netflix's value skyrocketed into the billions.

Similarly, Kodak, once a titan in the photography industry, fell victim to tunnel vision. Despite inventing the first digital camera in 1975, Kodak hesitated to transition from film photography, fearing it would undermine its successful film business. This narrow perspective led them to miss the digital revolution, culminating in their bankruptcy filing in 2012. Before the iPhone and Android era, Nokia dominated the mobile phone market. Yet, they failed to recognize the potential of smartphone technology and continued to focus on their traditional phone models. Their inability to see beyond the immediate 'positive' scenario cost them their market dominance.

These historical examples highlight the potential pitfalls of what I defined as the Positive Tunnel Vision Effect. In each case, the companies were so engrossed in their single 'positive' scenario that they overlooked vital industry shifts. Their lack of expansive vision prevented them from anticipating and adapting to change, leading to their eventual downfall.

Strategic Thinking in Innovation

The strategic and creative innovation process must be immersed in a shared vision. For example, Amazon's vision is "to be Earth's most customer-centric company." This vision is shared across all levels of the organization and has driven numerous innovations in e-commerce, logistics, cloud computing, and entertainment. From pioneering customer reviews to launching one-day shipping, Amazon has always been at the forefront of customer-focused innovation. Shared visions are forged, crafted, and pursued through actions. They don't just happen or magically materialize. And it is not sufficient to chisel a vision into a slab of Carrara marble and hang them in the lobby. Years ago, Jeff Bezos stood before his audience, speaking of the early days of Amazon. With a touch of humor, he recalled a time when they were inundated with so many orders that they found themselves woefully unprepared.

"There was no real organization in our distribution center," he confessed. Their system was so rudimentary that they were packing orders on their hands and knees on a concrete floor. He then revealed a humorous yet impactful anecdote. Late one night, amidst the chaos and physical discomfort of packing orders, Bezos turned to a colleague. "This packing is killing me. My back hurts, and my knees are aching on this hard cement floor," he said. In his exhaustion, a 'brilliant' idea struck him. "We need knee pads," he declared earnestly.

The person he spoke to looked at him as though he was entirely misguided, perhaps thinking, 'Great, I am working for this guy.' **"What we need,"** they countered, **"is packing tables."**

Bezos looked at his colleague, struck by the profound genius simplicity of the suggestion. The next day, packing tables were introduced to their operations. Bezos claimed that this single addition doubled their productivity.

Reflecting on that time, he said, "That early stage of Amazon.com, where we were so unprepared, is probably one of the luckiest things that ever happened to us. It formed a customer service culture in every single person in the company."

They had to work close to the customers with their hands, ensuring those orders went out. This intimate engagement with the process helped them establish a culture of prioritizing customer service. His final thought underlined Amazon's vision "to be Earth's most customer-centric company."

With a clear vision, we can move toward strategic innovation, and the **Process of Strategic Innovation** I am illustrating serves as a methodology cemented on clarity (see **Image 26**). Let's break down each element of the process and make them actionable.

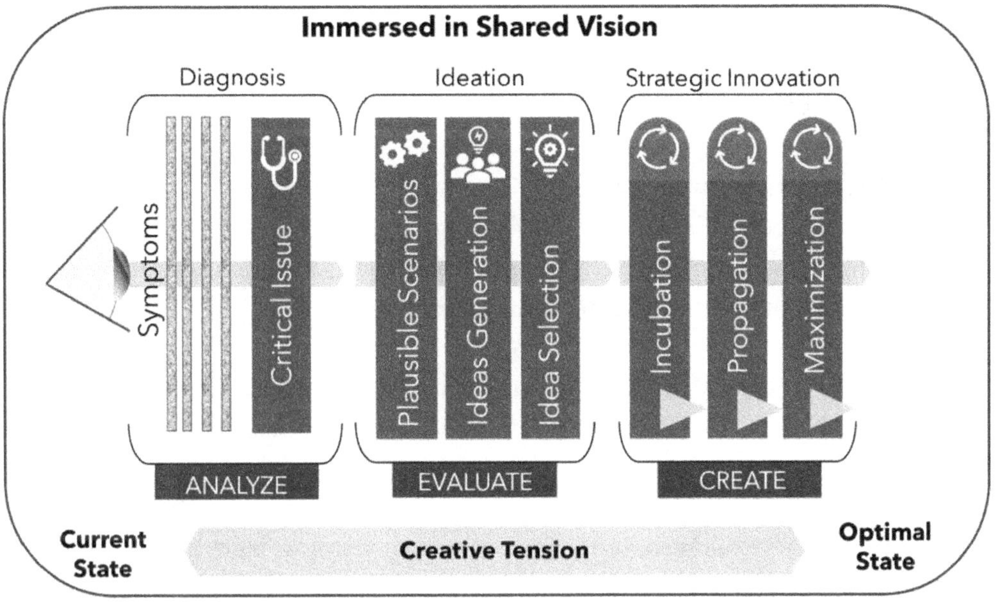

Image 26. The Process of Strategic Innovation (Radi, 2011 - 2023) © Integral Advantage®

The first step in the process is **Diagnosis**. This step, falling under the cognitive lens of 'Analysis,' involves diagnosing the critical issue at hand. We need to identify the need or problem we want to address through innovation. However, it is important to distinguish between symptoms and the underlying critical issues. Symptoms, being more obvious, often distract us from the real problems. It is not about making the complex simple. It is about elegantly addressing the critical issues that are part of the complex system without being seduced by the simplistic answer we may find when we address the symptoms of the issues rather than the critical issue itself. Symptoms of a critical issue are comparable to the alluring singing voices of the Sirens faced by Ulysses.

While addressing symptoms may provide temporary relief, it fails to provide a long-lasting solution. Therefore, we must dig deeper to understand the root causes of our issues. We must see beyond the symptoms.

Next comes **Ideation** under the cognitive lens of **'Evaluate.'** Here, we develop plausible scenarios in the context of internal and external conditions. Instead of relying on simplistic labels like "pessimistic, optimistic, and most likely," we create holistic scenarios considering our environment's contextual complexity. This step also involves generating ideas that address the critical issue in the context of plausible scenarios. The ideas are then refined through an inclusive process, with one idea being selected based on weighted criteria.

The final stage falls under the cognitive lens of **'Create.'** This is where the Strategic Innovation Framework comes into play. It involves the stages of Incubation, Propagation, and Maximization, where the selected idea is nurtured, developed, and implemented at a scale.

This entire process is **immersed in a shared vision**, symbolically represented as a box surrounding the stages in the framework (see Image 26). On the lower left end, we have the Current State, where we begin with diagnosis. Conversely, we have the Optimal State we aim to achieve. In between lies the **creative tension**, a concept popularized by systems scientist Peter Senge. This tension, arising from the gap between our current reality and our vision for the future, drives growth, learning, and change. Harnessing this creative tension is key to moving from our current state to our optimal state through strategic innovation.

Strategic innovation becomes a concrete, actionable process with this framework as a guide. Organizations can navigate the optimal future state by starting with a shared vision, diagnosing critical issues, generating and refining ideas, and progressing through the stages of strategic innovation. Through this journey, they address their immediate issues and foster a culture of continuous learning, growth, and innovation.

Strategic Innovation Framework

I conceived the Strategic Innovative Framework as a comprehensive methodology for innovation. The framework comprises three integral components: Incubation, Propagation, and Maximization. I presented this framework and the methodology at the Sino-U.S. CEO Forum 2011, held on September 27, 2011, at the Global CEO Club in Beijing, China, to a mix of great interest and some puzzlement.

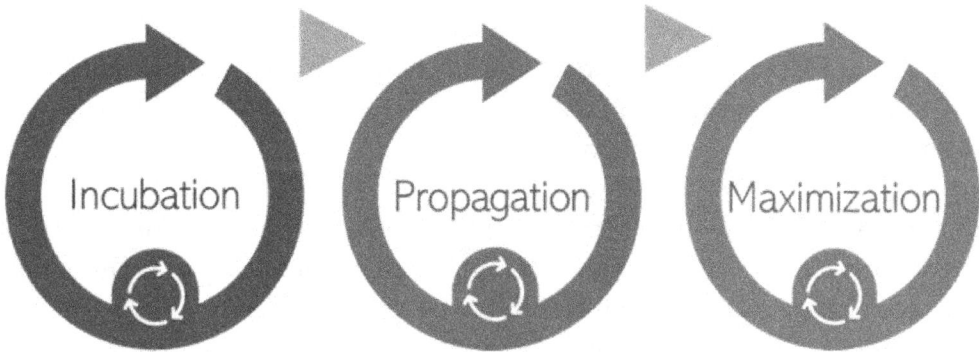

Image 27. Strategic Innovation Framework (Radi, 2011 - 2023) © Integral Advantage®

The initial stage, **Incubation**, sets the tone for the entire process. It fosters an intentional, inquisitive, organic, disciplined, and synergistic atmosphere. The idea is to create a nurturing space that encourages exploration and experimentation, allowing for the birth of potentially ground-breaking refined ideas.

Once these ideas have been incubated, we progress to the next stage - Propagation. Unlike the organic nature of Incubation, Propagation requires a much more structured and systematic approach. It involves sequential and resourceful planning, with a strong emphasis on alignment and competency. The goal of this phase is to have a product or solution that is ready to be deployed. For instance, this could be a citywide camera system installed to aid the police in their duties or any other fully developed and functional product, solution, or service.

The third and often misunderstood stage is Maximization. Many organizations and communities overlook its importance, often resulting in lost opportunities. Maximization involves taking the outcome of Propagation and implementing it most effectively, ensuring sustainability, renewability, and scalability. It requires a cross-functional and encompassing approach that aims to extract the hidden value in the functional interplay of internal processes.

To illustrate this concept, consider the example of a windmill. The windmill, a device designed to harness wind energy and transform it into electricity, is a product of the Propagation stage. However, to achieve Maximization, this technology should be employed in the most efficient manner possible.

The San Gorgonio Pass wind farm exemplifies this. It leveraged the novel idea birthed from the Incubation and Propagation cycles. It applied it to one of the windiest places on earth, as identified by NASA, thereby achieving maximum wind energy production.

This three-part framework of the Strategic Innovative Platform underscores the importance of a well-rounded approach to innovation, highlighting how each stage plays a pivotal role in the overall success of a project. It underscores the need to balance creativity with structure and emphasizes the potential of effectively implemented innovation.

The Essence of Incubation

The incubation process is perhaps the most critical element in the innovation process, (see Image 28) and it cannot be shortened or evaded in favor of the illusion of speed. Incubation cannot be viewed as an impediment; it cannot be "a place where good ideas go to die."

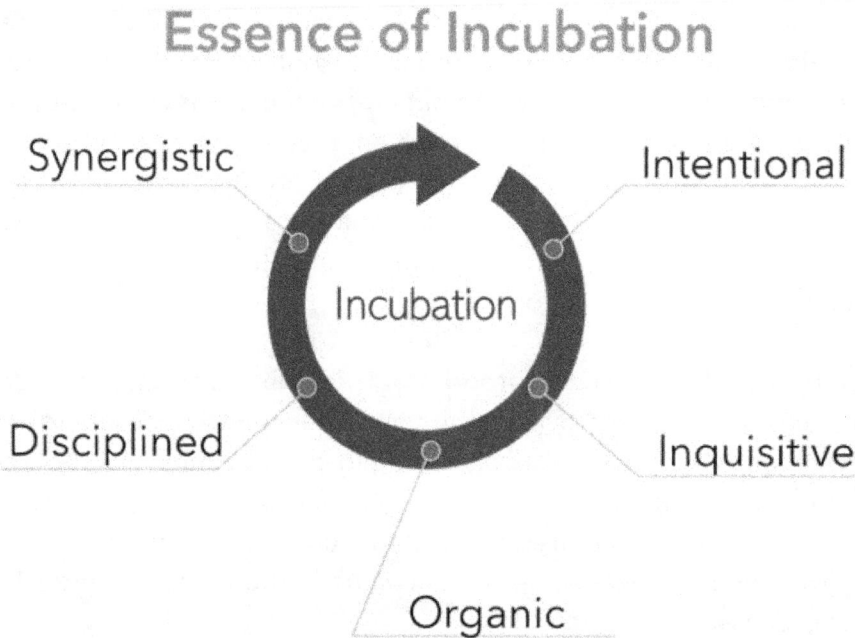

Essence of Incubation

Synergistic · Intentional · Incubation · Inquisitive · Disciplined · Organic

Image 28. The Essence of Incubation (Radi, 2011 - 2023) © Integral Advantage®

Intentional: The process of incubation must be intentional. There needs to be a clear purpose behind the incubation of an idea, and the decision to pursue it must be backed by the organization's vision and strategic object-ives. The intentionality helps align the innovative process with the organizational goals and ensures that the resources invested in incubating the idea add value to the organization's overall mission. When we incubate, we must allocate the appropriate resources for the process and retain that allocation. That means that if we make a commitment to dedicate a certain amount of time per week to incubation, we cannot allow everything else to be a priority over incubation.

Inquisitive: Incubation thrives in an environment that encourages curiosity and questions. Inquisitiveness drives exploration and experimentation, which are crucial for discovering new possibilities and generating innovative ideas. As leaders, we must cultivate an environment that welcomes curiosity, encourages questioning of the status quo, and sees the power of "why" as an asset rather than a threat.

Organic: While intentionality provides direction, the process's organic nature supplies the fuel. Innovation cannot be forced; instead, it must be allowed to develop naturally over time. This means giving ideas the space to evolve, fostering open and honest communication, and creating a safe environment for creativity to flow. The more organic the incubation process, the more authentic and impactful the innovations will be.

Disciplined: While the incubation process needs to be organic, it also requires discipline. This means setting clear boundaries for the innovation process, such as timelines and budgets, without stifling creativity. It involves balancing the need for freedom with the necessity of accountability. A disciplined approach ensures that the innovation process is both effective and efficient, maximizing the return on the organization's investment.

Synergistic: Finally, incubation must be synergistic. This means that the elements involved in the incubation process must work harmoniously. Collaboration, cross-functional teamwork, and diversity of thought are crucial for generating innovative ideas addressing an organization's complexities. A synergistic approach to incubation can lead to ideas that are not only innovative but also holistic and comprehensive, considering multiple perspectives and dimensions.

The Attributes of Incubation

The fundamental attributes of Incubation (refer to **Image 29**) shape the genesis of breakthrough thinking and strategic innovation. These attributes, derived from extensive research and hands-on experience, provide valuable insights into fostering an effective and robust incubation process. They serve as critical building blocks that encourage cognitive conflict, facilitate diverging and converging thought processes, promote collective inquiry, stimulate unasked questions, enable collective sense-making, demand assumption testing, advocate for small experiments, call for integrating perspectives, and harness the power of creative tension. Each of these attributes plays a pivotal role in shaping an environment that encourages the growth and development of ideas, setting the stage for game-changing innovation.

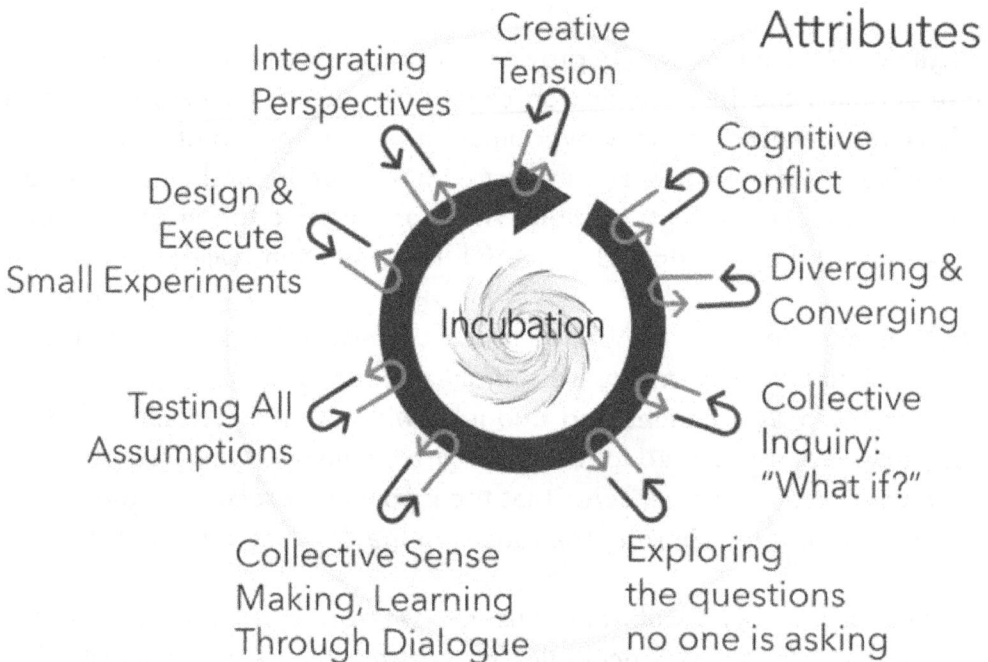

Image 29. Incubation's Attributes (Radi, 2011 - 2023) © Integral Advantage®

Cognitive Conflict: This is the type of conflict we need to mine. The C-Type conflict encourages a healthy diversity of ideas and perspectives. Challenging the status quo or existing mental models can fuel creativity and breakthrough thinking.

Diverging & Converging: This process involves generating a wide range of ideas (diverging) and then narrowing down these options to focus on the most promising ones (converging).

Collective Inquiry: "What if?": This encourages team members to explore alternative scenarios and possibilities, often leading to novel insights and innovations.

Exploring the questions, no one is asking: This approach helps to challenge existing assumptions and to find unique opportunities that others may have overlooked.

Collective Sense Making, Learning Through Dialogue: This involves synthesizing individual perspectives and experiences into a collective understanding. It often involves rich dialogue and active listening.

Testing All Assumptions: This helps to ensure that decisions and strategies are grounded in reality and not based on unchecked assumptions or biases.

Design & Execute Small Experiments: This allows for learning through iterative testing and adaptation, reducing risk and building evidence for what works and what doesn't.

Integrating Perspectives: This involves recognizing the value in each team member's perspective and finding ways to integrate these into a more holistic understanding or solution.

Creative Tension: This exists when there's a gap between the current reality and a desired future state, which can serve as a source of motivation and creative energy.

The Essence of Propagation

Propagation bridges the fertile bed of ideas formed during Incubation and the concrete implementation of those ideas in Maximization. We venture into it after Incubation, where ideas are given a concrete form.

Propagation is, in essence, the act of breathing life into the conceptual outcome of Incubation. To facilitate this process, the propagation stage needs to be intentionally designed. Unlike the spontaneous and organic nature of the Incubation cycle, Propagation is marked by being structured and sequential. It is here that we start shaping ideas into feasible plans. This phase requires diligent, step-by-step planning to ensure that ideas born in the Incubation phase are developed into viable, practical solutions.

The ultimate goal of the Propagation cycle is to produce a tangible outcome that can be implemented. Whether it's an installed citywide camera system to support law enforcement or a finished product ready for the market, the end result of Propagation is a fully developed solution ready to serve its intended purpose. The Propagation cycle (see Image 30) brings us one step closer to Maximization by ensuring we have a viable product that can be scaled and implemented to its fullest potential.

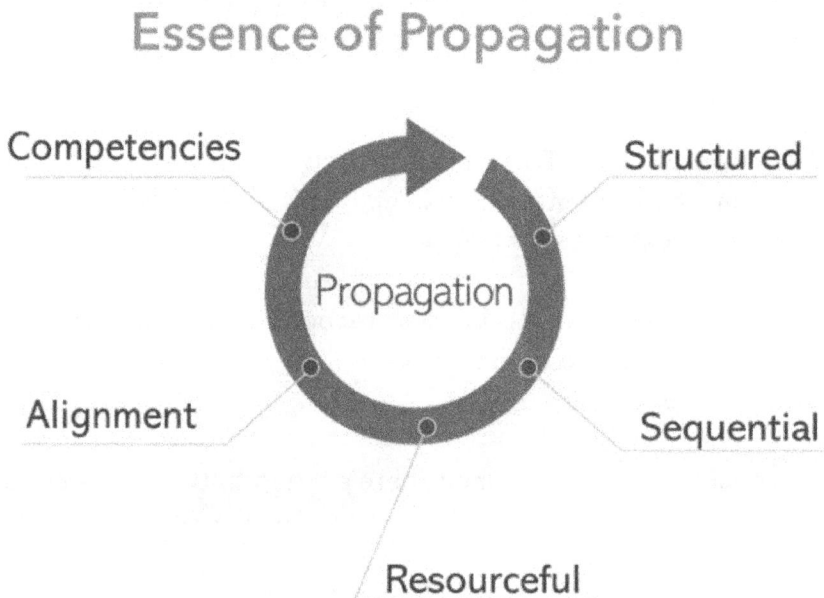

Image 30. The Essence of Propagation (Radi, 2011 - 2023) © Integral Advantage®

Structured: Propagation is a highly structured process, unlike the more fluid incubation stage. Here, ideas that were born and nurtured during the Incubation phase start taking shape into practical plans. The structure provides a clear pathway that guides an idea in development and ensures that progress is made systematically and organized.

Sequential: The Propagation phase follows a sequential order, signifying a progression from one stage to the next. Each step must be essential before moving on to the next. This allows for the meticulous development of ideas, ensuring that no crucial aspect is overlooked.

Resourceful: During the Propagation phase, resourcefulness becomes key. It's about making the most of the available resources – time, talent, and tools – to transform abstract ideas into concrete realities. This also implies finding creative solutions to overcome potential constraints and challenges that may arise in this phase.

Alignment: Alignment ensures that the process of developing the ideas aligns with the larger organizational goals and strategies. It involves checking and re-checking that every action taken, and every decision made, leads towards the overall objectives. This keeps the process on track and contributes to the final product's overall coherence and integrity.

Competencies: Propagation heavily relies on the competencies of the team. Each member's skills, knowledge, and abilities are crucial in shaping the abstract idea into a form ready to be deployed. Competencies facilitate the transition from ideation to implementation, ensuring the final product is effective, efficient, and serves its intended purpose.

Designing the Process of Propagation

The essence of Propagation lies in its structured, sequential approach, coupled with resourcefulness, alignment, and the right competencies. Together, these elements transform innovative ideas into viable outcomes, ready to be launched into the world.

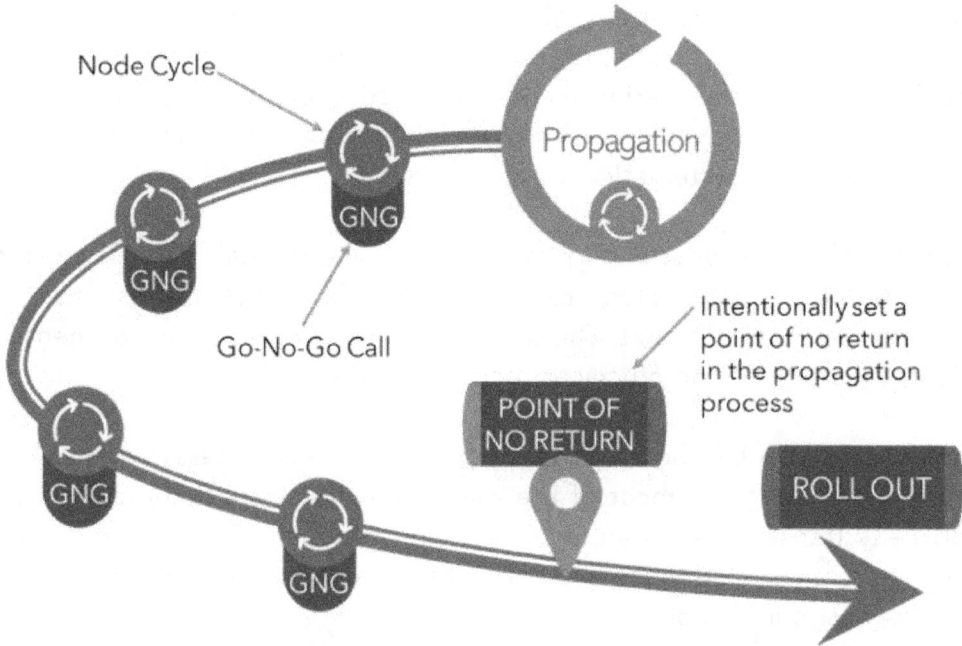

Image 31. Propagation Mapping (Radi, 2011 - 2023) © Integral Advantage®

In the context of designing the process, Propagation must be structured with sequential **node cycles**, accounting for tasks, expenditures, phases, etc. Let's explore the intricacies of the Propagation process within the Strategic Innovation Framework (refer to **Image 31**). The Propagation process is depicted as an arrowed curve to recognize that the process must consider unknowns. Along this curve lie various **node cycles**. These nodes represent critical phases within the process that need to be completed before progressing to the next. This is where we need to design the process intentionally. The number of **node cycles** is informed by the nature of what we are putting through the propagation process. By designing the process, we ensure that we consider all the plausible elements, and the more we see collectively, the more common language we develop, enhancing our internal and external alignments. As previously mentioned, we cannot dissipate the risk of losses or failure, but we can intentionally mitigate risk. This process brings clarity and moderates certainty.

Node cycles, as shown, are self-enclosed cycles. Each node cycle must be fulfilled, with all its tasks and components addressed and satisfactorily completed, before moving on to the next **node cycle**. Each node cycle necessitates a **Go-No-Go** decision (GNG in the image), ensuring that progression through the process is deliberate and thoughtful. By intentionally setting the **Go-No-Go** at the end of each node cycle, we ensure that we make incremental calls and maintain alignment without falling into **Groupthink and Escalation of Commitment traps**.

Groupthink, a term introduced by social psychologist Irving Janis in 1972, is a phenomenon where the desire for group harmony leads to poor decision-making outcomes, as individual critical thinking and differing perspectives are often suppressed. On the other hand, escalation of commitment refers to the propensity of individuals or groups to continue a failing course of action due to substantial prior resource investment, often driven more by emotional factors than logical assessment.

Having Go-No-Go decisions at the end of each node cycle can effectively mitigate these two challenges in your propagation process. These decision points promote critical thinking and debate, helping to counteract groupthink. They also provide a mechanism to objectively evaluate the project status at each stage, which can help prevent escalation of commitment by offering a chance to halt further resource investment if a project is not progressing as expected.

The necessary resources and competencies must be allocated at each node cycle to complete that phase successfully. In certain situations, these node cycles might need to incorporate multiple tasks being completed concurrently or require a degree of flexibility (e.g., time flexibility, research flexibility). These specifications must be clearly outlined within the corresponding node cycle.

By breaking down the propagation process into these distinct node cycles, we create a detailed roadmap that clarifies the process and enhances alignment amongst all those involved. It illuminates the 'dots' that need to be seen and connected, increasing the likelihood of success by reducing surprises and miscommunications.

This mapping process also highlights a critical juncture - the Point of No Return (refer back to Image 31). This point should be intentionally set before a major investment is committed, whether it be the creation of an expensive product mold, allocating resources for a system purchase, or initiating a new program. This point is the ultimate Go-No-Go decision, and it is at this point where alignment regarding the investment is absolutely crucial.

The rigorous planning and diligent progression through each node cycle are designed to reduce risk and build confidence in the process, especially when making the final Go-No-Go decision at the Point of No Return. With this due diligence, if the decision is made to proceed, the team can confidently advance to the final phase of the propagation process - the Roll Out. This methodology serves as a visual guide to navigating the intricacies of the Propagation process, offering a systematic and strategic approach to progress through the Strategic Innovation Framework while minimizing risk and maximizing alignment.

The Essence of Maximization

Maximization is the final cycle of the Strategic Innovative Platform, a crucial component that brings the innovation journey full circle. Often misunderstood and overlooked, Maximization is pivotal in determining an innovation's long-term success and impact. It's here that organizations need to look beyond the immediate results of the Propagation phase and explore how they can fully capitalize on the potential of their innovations. Whether it's scaling the innovation, ensuring its sustainability, or identifying its cross-functional and holistic impacts, Maximization provides the opportunity to drive the innovation's full value (see Image 32). Now, let's delve deeper into the core elements of Maximization, examining what makes it a fundamental part of the innovation process.

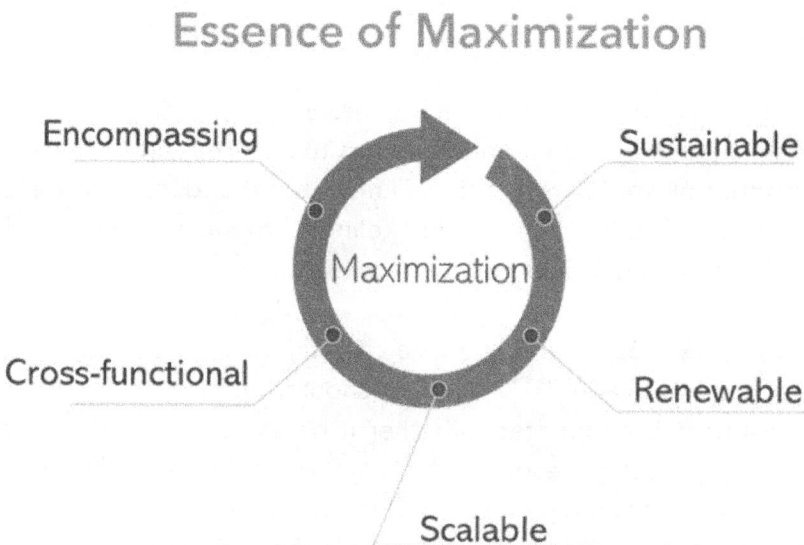

Essence of Maximization

Encompassing

Sustainable

Maximization

Cross-functional

Renewable

Scalable

Image 32. The Essence of Maximization (Radi, 2011 - 2023) © Integral Advantage®

Sustainable: Sustainability is at the core of Maximization. This means that the product, service, or system that emerged from the Propagation phase is not just a one-off success but instead is built to last and remain beneficial over the long term. Sustainable innovation is robust, resilient, and responsive, capable of enduring changes in the market and the wider environment.

Renewable: In the context of Maximization, 'renewable' refers to the capacity of innovation to renew itself continuously. In an ever-evolving world, the most successful innovations are those that can adapt, evolve, and improve over time. This allows for the ongoing relevance and usefulness of the innovation and the potential to generate new opportunities for further innovation.

Scalable: Maximization involves considering the scalability of the innovation. This means looking at whether the innovation can be expanded or replicated on a larger scale. This could be expanding a successful local initiative to a national or even global level or scaling up a pilot project to a full-scale operation.

Cross-Functional: Maximization often involves a cross-functional approach. This means that the innovation serves its primary function and can enhance or support other organizational functions or departments. For instance, a software tool might primarily serve to automate a process, but it may also provide valuable data that other departments can use.

Encompassing: Maximization is about ensuring the innovation is encompassing, or holistic, in its impact. It's about maximizing the innovation's direct benefits and considering and optimizing its indirect effects. This might involve, for example, considering how an innovation can contribute to broader strategic goals or how it might impact various stakeholders.

Unleashing the Hidden Value

In Maximization, we develop foresight to fully understand and plan for the potential of the innovation that has emerged from the Propagation process. Maximization doesn't mean doing more of the same, although that may be desirable in scaling the outcomes of Incubation and Propagation. By unleashing the hidden value stored in the functional interplay of internal processes, the Maximization phase allows us to capture and enhance innovation. This phase challenges organizations to go beyond limited implementation and fully optimize and exploit their innovations' potential instead. However, to unleash the value, we need to name the output of each function and then gain clarity about the synergistic output of the interplay of the two functions.

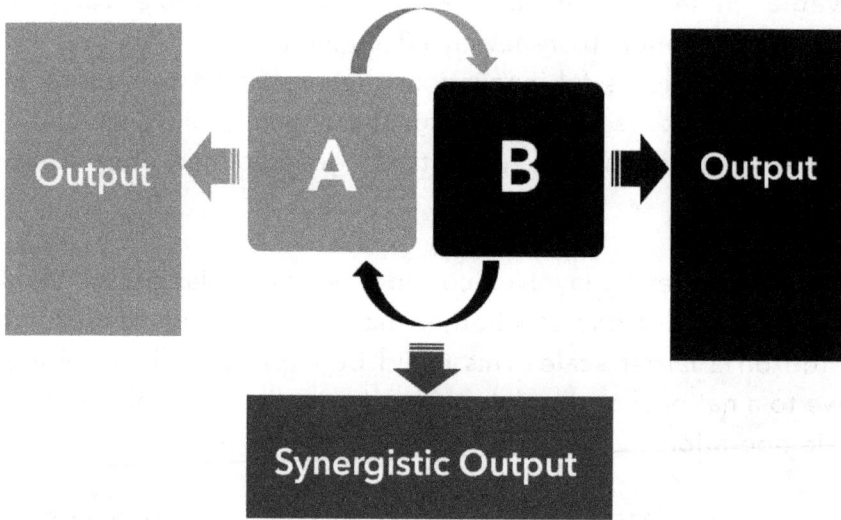

Image 33. Unleashing Hidden Value (Radi, 2011 - 2023) © Integral Advantage®

The concept of Unleashing Hidden Value as part of Maximization in the context of an organization's operations emphasizes the fact that innovation isn't simply confined to the confines of individual units or functions but can be unleashed through the careful examination and utilization of synergistic interactions between different units or processes within an organization (see **Image 33**).

For instance, consider two different divisions within a company, A (Logistics) and B (I.T.). The output of A might be increased logistical efficiency through measures like reduced warehouse dependency, factory-direct shipping to retailers and global partners, cross-organizational training, and vendor expertise development. On the other hand, the output of B might be enhanced IT capabilities, including secure off-site inventory systems, accurate inventory verification, vendor system synchronization for prompt customer shipping, and a two-way alert system for distribution control.

Each division's individual outputs are impressive. However, the real magic happens when we consider the synergistic output arising from the interaction of A and B. By combining Logistics' vendor capacity building and reduced dependency on owned warehousing with I.T.'s advanced methods for securing off-site inventories and ensuring prompt shipments, the organization can achieve the maximization effect. The result is a significant expansion of third-party fulfillment, a substantial reduction in warehousing costs, and improved operational efficiency - this is the power of Maximization.

This example underscores the importance of looking at individual units or processes in isolation and exploring the potential synergies that can be achieved when these units interact with one another. Such an approach enables organizations to fully exploit the value of their innovations fully, driving increased efficiency, productivity, and, ultimately, profitability.

Amazon leverages maximization through the synergistic output of its retail and AWS (Amazon Web Services) divisions. AWS was initially developed to support Amazon's own e-commerce platform. However, Amazon soon realized that it could sell this service to other businesses, which has since become a major profit driver for the company. Additionally, the insights and infrastructure developed by AWS also benefit Amazon's retail division by enhancing its website's reliability, personalizing shopping experiences, and optimizing logistics. This holistic approach to innovation is the crux of the Maximization principle.

In a Nutshell: The Process of Strategic Innovation

In this Chapter, we have explored how strategic innovation is a systematic and comprehensive process, beginning with the Diagnostic phase, where we identify and analyze the underlying critical issues rather than being misled by the symptoms. Understanding root causes is crucial to developing sustainable solutions.

The process continues with Ideation, in which we generate and refine ideas to address identified issues. Here, scenarios are developed with a holistic perspective of internal and external conditions, not confined to simplistic labels. The chosen idea, based on weighted criteria, sets the stage for the next phase of the journey.

The selected idea then advances through the Strategic Innovation Framework's stages: Incubation, Propagation, and Maximization. The idea is nurtured, developed, and finally implemented on a scale to unleash its full potential. The goal is not just to solve an immediate problem but to foster an innovation culture that supports continuous growth and learning.

This journey enveloped within a shared vision, is driven by the creative tension that arises from the gap between the current state and the envisioned optimal state. Leveraging this tension catalyzes progress toward the optimal state through strategic innovation.

This framework provides a concrete and actionable guide for organizations to navigate toward their optimal future state. Starting with a shared vision, diagnosing issues, generating ideas, and navigating through strategic innovation stages, organizations can address immediate concerns and cultivate an enduring culture of innovation. Thus, strategic innovation becomes a transformative journey rather than a sporadic endeavor.

CHAPTER 12

INCEPTION MINDSET AS THE WAY FORWARD

"If you want to go fast, go alone. If you want to go far, go together."
— *African Proverb*

The only way forward is forward. Throughout this book, we have explored various concepts, elements, frameworks, and cognitive lenses directly contributing to developing our *Inception Mindset*. We've recognized the pervasive nature of complexity in our lives and organizations and how the CADE – Contextualizable, Amorphous, Dynamic, and Elastic lenses can enhance our experiences and outcomes. The horizon of complexity that once seemed daunting has transformed into a landscape teeming with opportunities, rich with potential for innovation, discovery, and growth.

We have examined the state of perpetual inception, relentless evolution, and the need to learn, unlearn, and relearn continually. Once an unfamiliar terrain, this state has become an integral part of our reality, a playground where our intellectual, emotional, and creative capabilities come alive. Throughout our journey, we have acknowledged the pivotal role of self-authorship and the importance of developing a contextual leadership brand, pillars in supporting the development of our *Inception Mindset*. We have learned to navigate the stormy seas of complexity, not by battling against the current but by understanding its rhythms and using them to guide our path.

We have scrutinized the role of culture within organizations, understanding the essentiality of a conducive 'Contextual Cultural Flow.' We have seen how it could either facilitate or strangle innovation and how, as leaders, we can direct this flow toward positive, transformative change. Instead of attempting an intervention to change the organization's culture, we have explored how to change things so that the culture changes.

By approaching the Entrusted Empowerment framework with an *Inception Mindset*, we learned how to leverage this practice to foster a thriving, innovative environment and how the outcomes of Entrusted Empower- ment are conducive to organizational cultural change. We've learned to practice it consistently, allowing it to permeate the organizational fabric and fostering an environment where creativity flourishes, and value is cre- ated. We have shed light on cultivating creative innovation, recognizing the barriers that often impede its path. By understanding that behaviors, emotions, and mindset form a triadic barrier to innovation, we have high- lighted the need to bust these barriers and nurture a culture that cele- brates creative exploration.

Throughout our journey, we have shared insights, reflections, and stories, none of which were meant to be a conclusive answer, but rather invita- tions - invitations to ponder, to question, to explore how these ideas res- onate with your experiences, your aspirations, and the context in which you operate.

A Way Forward in a Permanently Complex World

Traditional leadership approaches falls short when we operate in perma- nent complexity. As we have explored, contemporary leaders navigate a realm of realities that constantly shift, presenting new challenges, scenar- ios, and opportunities. This dynamic landscape, perpetually in flux, places us in a permanent state of inception - an intricate maze of interconnected layers, each with its unique characteristics and rules of engagement, which we can see if we develop an **Inception Mindset.**

A mindset of continuous beginnings, of constantly resetting the compass to chart a course through an ever-changing complexity's landscape. In es- sence, our environment is not one defined by fixed markers but a constel- lation of starting points. These points are the nodes of complexity arising from a multitude of factors - technological breakthroughs, shifts in global economies, the emergence of new markets and industries, evolving social paradigms, and our collective sense-making process.

Operating in such an environment transcends addressing operational chal- lenges or following established protocols. Instead, it demands an *Inception Mindset* - a mindset rooted in creativity, agility, and adaptability to build strategic capacity and resilience in an organization. Leaders equipped with this mindset recognize that the past's successful strategies may not hold the answers for the present or future complexities. As such, they continuously explore new nodes of complexity, addressing each as a unique starting point and reframing their leadership approach accordingly.

The concept of an *Inception Mindset* extends to every aspect of leadership. From understanding the broader context to developing a unique leadership brand, leaders must think creatively, make agile decisions, and respond swiftly to change. They need to navigate seamlessly between different layers of complexity, developing and deploying contextual competencies that resonate with the evolving realities of their environment.

This book has endeavored to provide the necessary tools, frameworks, and insights to empower you to thrive in a world defined by complexity. By understanding the nature of the environment, recognizing the interplay between the self and complexity, reframing your leadership brand, and understanding your organization's place in complexity, you will be equipped to lead with an *Inception Mindset*. This final chapter aims to draw together these threads, offering a comprehensive vision for thriving in a permanently complex world. This world calls for leaders to operate in a constant state of Inception.

The Nexus of Navigating Contextual Complexity

Combining the diverse threads spun in the preceding chapters, a comprehensive approach to navigating complexity has emerged. It's an approach that melds understanding and action, theory and practice, the art and the science of leadership in a complex world. It's an approach anchored in learning, resilience, adaptability, and innovation, all culminating in a collaborative culture that is equipped to handle the intricacies and unpredictability of our modern environment and the desired outcomes.

Learning sits at the foundation of this approach. The **Inception Mindset** is characterized by a deep appreciation for knowledge and an insatiable curiosity that fuels continuous learning. This continuous learning is not limited to the leader alone but pervades the entire organization. It transforms the organization into a learning entity where every experience becomes a learning opportunity, whether a success or a setback. By fostering learning, organizations enhance their understanding of complexity and are better equipped to make informed decisions and craft strategies.

Resilience is another critical thread in this tapestry of contextual complexity. The ability to bounce back and persevere in the face of adversity is invaluable. Resilience is not about avoiding failure but learning to cope with it, to learn from it, and to use it as a stepping stone toward value creation. It's about fostering the conditions for a resilient culture that can withstand shocks, adapts to change, and continue to move forward, no matter the circumstances. As we have seen in Dr. Roper's example, we need to redefine what failure is in our organizations.

Adaptability, closely linked to resilience, is another essential component in the approach to navigating complexity. As our discussions highlighted, through the CADE model, the complexity of our world is not static. In such a context, the ability to adapt - to change our strategies, shift our perspectives, and pivot our actions in response to new information or unexpected changes - is paramount. An adaptable organization is responsive and proactive, foreseeing and preparing for potential changes by leveraging the Core-Tangential-Peripheral (CTP) Awareness framework.

Innovation forms the apex of this approach to complexity. As we have explored, cultivating innovation and learning in organizations sets the stage for ongoing evolution and growth. It encourages the generation of fresh ideas, challenging the status quo, and continuous pursuit of value creation. Innovation is not just about product development or technological advancement in this context. It's about innovating the way we lead, the way we collaborate, the way we learn, and the way we adapt. It's about using innovation as a strategic tool to navigate complexity, drive organizational growth, and positively impact our world.

In essence, these threads - learning, resilience, adaptability, and innovation - intertwine to create a collaborative culture capable of effectively responding to and navigating the complexities of the modern world while immersed in a shared vision of the optimal future state. This comprehensive approach, rooted in the *Inception Mindset*, empowers organizations and leaders to not just survive but thrive amid complexity. As we wrap up our journey through the four horizons of complexity, the **Inception Mindset** emerges not as a destination but as a compass, guiding us toward sustainable value through the labyrinth of complexity.

THINKING POINT

Section Takeaways:

Complexity is a permanent state of affairs in modern life and organizations, but this reality is not a hindrance but a landscape filled with opportunities for innovation, growth, and discovery.

Adopting an *Inception Mindset* empowers us to navigate this landscape by learning, unlearning, and relearning continually.

The culture within organizations plays a significant role in shaping innovation and change. As leaders, it's crucial to cultivate a Contextual Cultural Flow that supports positive transformation. When applied consistently with an *Inception Mindset*, the Entrusted Empowerment framework can foster an environment conducive to creative exploration and value creation.

The concept of an *Inception Mindset* extends to all aspects of leadership, encouraging leaders to be creative, agile, adaptable, and capable of navigating different layers of complexity. The foundational elements of learning, resilience, adaptability, and innovation are essential in crafting a comprehensive approach to navigating complexity.

Reflective Questions:

How can you contribute to shaping a Contextual Cultural Flow that encourages innovation and transformation within your organization?

Reflect on how the Entrusted Empowerment framework could be consistently applied within your organization. What barriers might you face, and how could these be overcome?

How can you make learning, resilience, adaptability, and innovation the core of your approach to complexity?

Contextualization Prompt:
Consider the current state of your organization. In what ways is complexity currently manifesting? How might you apply the insights from this book to better navigate these complexities and foster an environment of continuous learning, resilience, adaptability, and innovation? Reflect on the principles of the *Inception Mindset* and how they might be woven into your organizational fabric.

Anticipating Shifts in Complexity

To maintain their competitive edge, organizations must develop a proactive approach that allows them to anticipate and navigate future complexities. The *Inception Mindset* promotes this agility, encouraging creative innovation as a standard response to complexity over merely predicting future trends. Shifts in complexity can be anticipated by adopting, ingraining, and sustaining creative innovation in an organization, as we have seen in Chapters 10 and 11, and by leveraging the CTP Awareness we explored in Chapter 2.

Creative innovation isn't limited to just product development or technological advances; it pervades all aspects of an organization. From strategic problem-solving to restructuring organizational mechanisms to refining communication and interaction with the external environment, creative innovation becomes a crucial tool to navigate the shifts in complexity.

The real power of creative innovation lies in its transformative potential. It disrupts the status quo; challenges accepted norms and instigates change. As the environment grows increasingly complex in reference to our cognitive capacity, the ability to infuse new perspectives into traditional practices becomes vital to ensure adaptability and survival.

Creating the right environment for this innovative thinking to thrive is equally crucial. An inclusive culture that embraces a diversity of thought, learns from failures and promotes an open exchange of ideas can significantly bolster creative innovation. Cross-functional collaboration becomes key, exploiting the combined potential of varying experiences, expertise, and perspectives.

Leadership plays a pivotal role in fostering this innovative culture. Leaders embodying the *Inception Mindset*'s principles of curiosity, acceptance of uncertainty, and openness to new ideas, can stimulate their teams to think out of the box. Leaders can empower their teams to take calculated risks, experiment, and continuously learn by ensuring a psychologically safe environment.

Fostering a culture that thrives on creative innovation is a continual journey. Still, it's a journey that prepares organizations to adapt to the ever-changing dynamics of complexity. Encouraging creative innovation can help organizations shape their trajectory, turning complexity from a formidable challenge into a golden opportunity for growth, development, and transformation.

Adaptability: Helping Others Navigate Complexity

Understanding the organization's context and unique challenges and opportunities is paramount to managing change effectively. The adaptation process necessitates a certain level of creativity and flexibility, akin to a pilot adjusting to varying flight conditions - they utilize all instruments but focus on certain gauges depending on the context. Similarly, adapting to organizational change is not linear; it requires a contextual and individualized approach.

Importance of Adaptability and Agility. The concept of the inception leader is incomplete without the attributes of adaptability and agility. In a complex and rapidly changing environment, an inception leader should anticipate changes, respond quickly, and pivot when necessary. Embracing new ideas, fostering continuous learning, and being comfortable with ambiguity and uncertainty are intrinsic to this role.

Personal Adaptation to Complexity. While strategizing and operational flexibility are important, organizational adaptability's true essence lies in its individuals' growth and evolution. An organization can only adapt to complexity if it helps its people navigate the same complexity. Therefore, fostering an environment that encourages continuous learning and open-mindedness is crucial. This requires a mindset shift towards embracing uncertainty and ambiguity, traits of a complex environment. The objective is to enable individuals to perceive complexity as a springboard for innovation and creative problem-solving, not as a hurdle.

Empowerment and Learning from Failure. Empowerment is a powerful tool to facilitate adaptation. As per the concept of entrusted empowerment, individuals should be granted autonomy and decision-making authority. This cultivates a proactive culture where everyone feels they can contribute to managing change. Adaptation also involves learning from failure. In the face of complexity, not all initiatives will succeed. Hence, creating a psychologically safe environment that encourages risk-taking and learning from mistakes without fear of retribution is critical. Such an environment fosters resilience and a solution-oriented mindset, key aspects of adaptability.

Modeling Desired Behaviors. Leaders need to model the behaviors they wish to see in their teams. This includes showing vulnerability, promoting open communication, and demonstrating a commitment to learning and development. This way, leaders can inspire their teams to adopt similar behaviors. Fostering adaptability in the face of complexity involves cultivating an organizational culture that values learning, encourages risk-taking, and empowers its people. When every individual is equipped to navigate complexity, the organization itself becomes more adaptable, resilient, and poised to thrive.

Mastering the Art of Inception Mindset

Navigating the labyrinth of interdependencies, uncertainties, and continuously emerging realities that make up our complex world requires a significant paradigm shift. It calls for an *Inception Mindset* – a perpetual state of evolution where adaptation, learning, and innovation become intrinsic to an organization's existence.

The *Inception Mindset* can be likened to an artist skillfully crafting a masterpiece on the canvas of complexity. The organization's strengths, weaknesses, opportunities, and threats serve as the palette, its varying strategies, and innovations as the brushes. The artist's vision is reflected in the shared vision steering the organization. Each brush stroke on the canvas symbolizes a decision, action, or strategy, all contributing to the picture of the organization's optimal state in the midst of permanent complexity.

The lifeblood of the *Inception Mindset* is strategic innovation. More than mere ideation or implementation, strategic innovation involves a comprehensive process, starting from diagnosing the key issues to ideation, nurturing, promoting the selected idea, and maximizing its potential. Mastering Inception involves guiding the organization deftly through this intricate process, aligning each stage with the organization's vision, culture, and context.

Integral to this process is the ability to reframe philosophy and leadership branding. A leader's philosophy, values, and beliefs underpin their decisions and actions. In a complex world, however, these must not remain static. Leaders should be ready to reshape their philosophies, question their assumptions, and adjust their beliefs to align with changing realities. Therefore, the *Inception Mindset* requires leaders to demonstrate philosophical agility, openness to new perspectives, and a readiness to evolve their philosophies while navigating complexity.

Leadership branding, and a leader's unique value proposition, is crucial in Inception. It's not about possessing a fixed set of traits; instead, it revolves around a leader's capacity to adjust their style and approach to suit the complexity they are operating within. Therefore, leaders should continuously refine their leadership brands to ensure their relevance and effectiveness in driving strategic innovation within a persistently complex environment.

Mastering the art of Inception is not about perfecting a static set of skills or strategies. It is about fostering a mindset of continuous learning, adaptation, and evolution. It involves welcoming complexity as a constantly changing canvas, employing strategic innovation as the brush, and creating a resilient, dynamic, and always relevant organizational masterpiece. This is the true essence of the *Inception Mindset*.

Deciphering the Inception Mindset: A Scientific Perspective

We have investigated several scientific perspectives in Chapter 3 as we explored the Mindful Vortex. The *Inception Mindset*, also possesses a scientific dimension. It involves understanding the mechanics underlying complexity and the systematic approach to strategic innovation. The intersection of these aspects forms a unique framework, empowering organizations to navigate an eternally complex world successfully.

Csikszentmihalyi suggests that true creativity prompts a fundamental shift in perspective, generating lasting and significant results. This process requires individual inspiration and acknowledgment from society or the field at large. This principle is also integral to adopting the *Inception Mindset*.

Understanding the *Inception Mindset*'s scientific aspects necessitates a profound appreciation for complexity. Complexity science, an interdisciplinary research field, investigates how relationships among parts result in a system's collective behaviors and its interactions with the environment. It delves into how minor changes can create considerable impacts (the butterfly effect), how complexity can emerge from simplicity, and how order and patterns can originate from chaos.

Implementing these principles in an organizational context enables us to refine our leadership and strategic innovation approach. Understanding the butterfly effect can promote more thoughtful decision-making, urging leaders to consider a wider range of potential consequences. Likewise, recognizing that order can surface from chaos can inspire leaders to identify opportunities within periods of uncertainty and disruption.

Strategic innovation's systematic process is a structured, iterative cycle encompassing diagnosis, ideation, incubation, propagation, and maximization. It offers a scientific and systematic approach to navigating environmental complexities and ambiguities. Each phase plays a specific role and feeds into the next, creating a smooth, integrative system propelling the organization from its current state towards its optimal one. This system, grounded in complexity science principles, allows us to convert ambiguity and uncertainty into concrete, actionable plans.

Understanding the interaction between the organization's internal processes and external environment is vital to this scientific approach. By employing tools such as network analysis, scenario planning, and system dynamics, organizations can better comprehend their position within the broader ecosystem, anticipate potential changes, and formulate innovative, contextually relevant, and strategically sound solutions. This scientific approach and the *Inception Mindset*'s artistry can yield potent outcomes.

In essence, the science of Inception provides leaders with the necessary tools and methodologies to comprehend and navigate their environment's complexities. It merges this scientific understanding with leadership artistry, equipping organizations to navigate a perpetually complex world successfully. This synthesis of art and science forms a comprehensive, integrated approach to leadership and innovation, robust, resilient, and adaptive in the face of enduring complexity.

Human-Centric Leadership: The Key to Navigating Complexity

The accomplishment of strategic goals, the spark of innovation, and the navigation of complexity all revolve around a crucial component: people. They are the driving force behind action, the generators of ideas, and the creators of value. Throughout this book, we've explored how leaders can establish practices, processes, functions, and programs to unlock the discretionary energy of the people constituting an organization. After all, our interactions and achievements occur through people, not faceless entities.

In a time when the nebulous nature of A.I. is increasingly prominent in discussing its advantages and disadvantages to humanity, we must steadfastly cultivate a collective *Inception Mindset*. This mindset embraces and celebrates our diversity, capitalizing on it through inclusive practices. We've examined how Entrusted Empowerment, a framework centered around inclusivity, significantly correlates with engagement, performance, and adaptability. As U.S. Navy Admiral John S. McCain, Jr. expressed, "Leadership is the single most important factor as far as achievement, success, and the completion of a job to be done. And furthermore, you have got to tolerate the failings of individuals because all of us have them." Remember, as leadership expert Ronald Heifetz has noted, resistance isn't to change per se but to perceived loss. Cameron & Quinn speaks about the need to have a funeral to retire the old ways. As we have seen, operating in contextual complexity requires innovation, and in order to embrace the new, we need to let go of the old collectively.

As we have seen, the term Leadership originates in the Indo-European word Leith, which means "to cross a threshold" and, more specifically, "to cross a threshold or die." Not necessarily a physical death, but a significant loss. It is more detrimental to avoid crossing the threshold than to face uncertainty on the other side (see Image 34).

Image 34. Essence of Human-Centric Leadership (Radi, 2011 - 2023) © Integral Advantage®

The ability to innovate and adapt is crucial and intrinsically housed within the minds, hearts, and hands of an organization's people. Therefore, we must focus on a human-centric approach to leadership that places people at the core of all activities. Human-centric leadership is not merely about treating people kindly or providing attractive benefits. It's about recognizing and harnessing the unique abilities, perspectives, and potential each individual brings to the table. It demands the creation of an environment where every individual feels heard, valued, respected, and empowered to give their best.

Fostering Entrusted Empowerment grants people, the agency to take ownership and make significant contributions. Encouraging continuous learning and growth helps individuals realize their potential and adapt to evolving circumstances. These practices don't only benefit the individuals; they also enhance the collective capability of the organization to navigate complexity. Additionally, a human-centric approach to leadership entails considering our actions' impact on people beyond the organization, including our customers, partners, and wider communities. By centering people's needs and well-being in our decision-making, we can craft solutions that address complex challenges and generate shared value.

Thus, as we traverse the complexity of the modern world, this fundamental principle remains that nothing gets accomplished without people and for the people. Our strategies' success, solutions' effectiveness, and organizations' resilience hinge on the people who make it all happen. By focusing on people, understanding them, trusting them, empowering them, and serving them, we can navigate complexity and drive sustainable success.

The Intersection of Complexity and the Self: A Crucial Symbiosis

Navigating the turbulent seas of complexity necessitates an understanding of not only the surrounding world but also ourselves - our motivations, biases, strengths, and weaknesses. Self-awareness and comprehension of complexity are two intertwining strands that, when coalesced, forge a resilient and effective leader equipped to guide an organization through the tempestuous waves of complexity.

The leader in the realm of complexity is finely attuned to both their environment and their own values, beliefs, and actions. Such a leader discerns how their behavior influences others and the broader organizational system. They understand that even minor decisions can set off significant ripple effects throughout the organization, mirroring the butterfly effect concept in complexity science.

As discussed in Chapter 3, possessing a self-authoring mind capable of assessing thoughts, beliefs, and actions is vital for leadership within a complex environment. These leaders can question their own assumptions, extract wisdom from their experiences, and modify their behavior to align more closely with their strategic goals. They comprehend the pivotal role authenticity and integrity play in leadership and strive to ensure their actions are consistent with their words.

Moreover, this self-awareness extends beyond individual boundaries. Leaders must be cognizant of their organizational roles and the consequences of their decisions on the broader ecosystem. They acknowledge the interconnected nature of their organization's various functions and teams, striving to dismantle barriers and foster cross-functional collaboration.

Through the cultivation of their leadership brand, as discussed in Chapters 5 and 6, leaders can effectively articulate their vision, values, and purpose. This alignment allows them to rally their teams around a shared vision and nurture a culture that promotes innovation and learning.

Comprehension of complexity and self-awareness aren't isolated concepts but rather deeply intertwined elements. Collectively, they mold a leader capable of navigating and harnessing complexity. A self-aware leader can better discern their role within the intricate system, identify their influence on that system, and consequently make more informed decisions. This symbiosis between comprehending complexity and self-awareness forms the cornerstone of efficient leadership in a perpetually complex world. This is where the art of inception begins to sculpt the landscape of strategic innovation.

Fostering an Inception Mindset in Organizational Leadership

The complexity of today's world presents sizable challenges for organizations but also uncovers vast opportunities for those equipped to navigate and flourish amidst uncertainty. Throughout this book, we have delved into the fundamental elements that enable an organization to succeed within this intricate environment.

Firstly, culture serves as the lifeblood of an organization. It lays the foundation for how members interact, collaborate, and make decisions. As explored in Chapter 7, a nurturing and supportive culture engenders a sense of belonging and purpose among its members, inspiring them to dedicate their best efforts toward the organization's objectives. A culture that esteems learning, adaptation, and resilience is uniquely positioned to thrive amidst complexity. Such organizations perceive challenges not as threats but as opportunities for growth and innovation. They foster a culture encouraging members to take calculated risks, learn from their experiences, and continually adapt to an evolving environment.

Secondly, the exercise of entrusted empowerment, as examined in Chapters 8 and 9, is vital for leveraging an organization's collective potential.

Organizations cannot depend solely on hierarchical decision-making processes in complex environments marked by constant change and uncertainty. Instead, they must empower their members to make decisions, act, and learn from their experiences. This approach necessitates trust in the competence and intentions of their members, reinforced by supportive systems and processes. Empowerment imbues a sense of ownership and responsibility, inspiring individuals to excel and contribute to the organization's success.

Lastly, fostering innovation and continuous learning is integral to an organization's success in a complex environment. As we discussed in Chapters 10 and 11, organizations need to create an atmosphere that encourages innovation and embeds learning into its core. This environment promotes experimentation and idea generation, provides resources and support for innovation, and weaves learning into the organization's fabric. It also involves adopting a systematic approach to innovation, progressing through the stages of ideation, incubation, propagation, and maximization to guarantee the sustainability and impact of their innovations.

In sum, an organization's culture, its practice of entrusted empowerment, and its dedication to innovation and continuous learning are all pivotal elements that equip it to excel amidst complexity. By nurturing a contextual, cultural flow that values learning and adaptation, empowering its members, and fostering a systematic approach to innovation, an organization can weather the stormy seas of complexity and harness them to its benefit. It can transform challenges into opportunities, complexity into innovation, and uncertainty into strategic foresight. Such an organization isn't merely a vessel adrift in complexity but a skillful navigator charting its unique course.

THINKING POINT

Section Takeaways

Mastering the Art of *Inception Mindset* requires strategic innovation and a perpetual state of adaptation, learning, and innovation. This mindset likens to an artist painting a masterpiece in the face of complexity. The *Inception Mindset* has scientific dimensions, including the understanding of complexity science and the systematic approach to strategic innovation. This comprehension allows for a more profound appreciation of complexity and the significant impacts minor changes can create.

Human-Centric Leadership is crucial in navigating complexity. As the term Leadership originates from the word 'Leith,' which means "to cross a threshold," leaders must focus on the human-centric approach that places people at the core of all activities. Self-awareness and comprehension of complexity are intertwined, forging a resilient and effective leader capable of guiding an organization through complexity. Self-aware leaders understand their behavior influences and have the capability to assess their thoughts, beliefs, and actions.

An *Inception Mindset* in Organizational Leadership involves fostering a culture that values learning, adaptation, and resilience, exercises entrusted empowerment, and is dedicated to innovation and continuous learning.

Reflective Questions

How can the concept of crossing a threshold be applied in your leadership practice, and what changes could it bring?

What steps can you take to foster a culture of learning, adaptation, and resilience in your organization?

Contextualization Prompt

Consider your current organization or team. How can you apply the *Inception Mindset* to navigate the complexities inherent in your particular context? Reflect on how you can harness strategic innovation, employ a human-centric approach, and integrate self-awareness into your leadership. What cultural changes might be necessary to promote an environment that encourages continuous learning, adaptation, and innovation? Remember, each organizational setting is unique, and strategies should be tailored accordingly.

The Power of Your Voice

In the multifaceted complexity landscape, leaders must remain steadfast while orchestrating change. They must showcase the resilience of the Lone Cypress, gripping firmly to its granite perch amidst the harshest elements. This tenacity is a cornerstone of the *Inception Mindset*, where leaders must maneuver and adapt to ever-changing realities.

However, in the midst of complex times, resilience alone isn't sufficient. Leaders must do more than merely maintain their position - they must find their voice and become catalysts for change. This need introduces us to the profound role of narrative in leadership and the navigation of complexity.

The Triad of Persuasion: Ethos, Pathos, Logos

In the theatre of persuasive communication, three actors consistently take center stage: Ethos, Pathos, and Logos (see Image 35). It sounds all Greek to me because it is! In "Rhetoric," Aristotle outlined these three modes of persuasion. He believed that in order to be a successful speaker or writer, one needed to appeal to all three.

These Aristotelian concepts have weathered the sands of time, transcending generations, cultures, and technologies, to remain ever-relevant in our discourse today. Together, they form the triad of persuasion, each bringing a unique flavor to the art of convincing others.

Ethos An appeal based on credibility	**Pathos** An appeal based on emotion	**Logos** An appeal based on logic

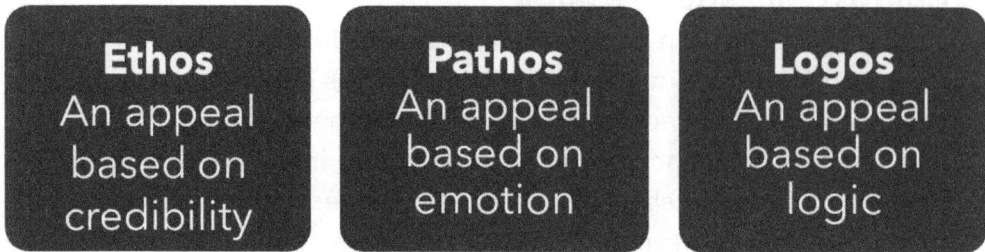

Image 35. Adapted From Aristotle's Rhetoric

Ethos is the credibility factor, the authority you bring to the dialogue, and the trust you instill in your audience. It's like being the keynote speaker at a seminar; your credentials, your reputation, and your character all serve to establish your ethos. It's not just about what you know, but also who you are. Your ethos is the credibility cloak you wear, woven from threads of authenticity, expertise, and integrity. In our digital age, establishing ethos might entail harnessing the power of your leadership branding, thought leadership, and even online presence.

Pathos, on the other hand, is the emotional resonance you create with your audience. It's about appealing to their feelings, fears, aspirations, and values. Think of pathos as the soundtrack to a movie, subtly underpinning and heightening the audience's emotional experience. If your message can touch the heart, it can move the mind. In today's emotionally charged social media landscape, pathos can be elicited through storytelling, empathetic appeals, and powerful visual imagery.

Lastly, we have Logos, the voice of reason. Logos appeals to the audience's rational faculties. It's the scientist in the court of persuasion, calling upon facts, data, logic, and sound reasoning. If ethos gives you the right to speak and pathos earns you the audience's attention, logos deliver the evidence, making your argument compelling. In an era defined by data and information, logos involves wielding credible research, structured arguments, and well-articulated reasoning to persuade.

To weave the triad of persuasion effectively into your communication strategy, envision your message as a three-legged stool, with ethos, pathos, and logos forming the legs. Ethos, the first leg, establishes your right to argue. Pathos, the second leg, ensures your audience is receptive, and their emotions primed. Logos, the final leg, delivers the weight of your argument. If one leg is missing or weaker than the others, the stool loses balance and topples.

Each element of the triad brings a distinct power and, when combined, forms a persuasive force to be reckoned with. Leaders who skillfully integrate ethos, pathos, and logos in their communication are more likely to persuade effectively, ensuring their messages resonate, inspire, and catalyze action.

Personal Leadership Narrative

As you may remember, David Eagleman, a neuroscientist, contends that our brains are wired for storytelling and that new senses might impact our connection and communication with others.

Narratives serve as potent instruments for leaders, enabling them to comprehend their complex surroundings and navigate their role within them. Yet, in adverse circumstances, leaders often grapple to discover their voice, let alone project it effectively. Understanding that our goal isn't about crafting a positive spin on adverse conditions or evading responsibility is crucial. Instead, it's about fashioning a narrative that authentically addresses the complexity at hand. Such narratives penetrate skepticism, resonate with stakeholders, and offer a persuasive, genuine vision for change.

So, how do leaders craft and disseminate these narratives? The answer lies in distinguishing between broadcasting and communicating. Broadcasting typically takes a reactive posture, delivering a message without adequate engagement with its content or audience. Conversely, communicating demands authenticity and centers on active engagement and dialogue rather than simply relaying a message.

Traditionally, narratives have facilitated knowledge transfer. Effective leadership narratives align with stakeholders' values, translating these values into actions. As Marshall Ganz, Senior Lecturer in Public Policy at Harvard University, posits, narrative is a leadership practice that translates values into actions. Thus, narrative serves as a tool for understanding and conveying complex situations and a catalyst for driving change.

Viewed in this light, creating and deploying narratives becomes a critical leadership competency. It's not just about telling a story; it's about aligning the narrative with stakeholders' motivations and emotions and utilizing it as a mechanism to guide and shape change. Consequently, the narrative creation and deployment process holds as much importance as the narrative itself.

This insight adds a vital dimension to the *Inception Mindset*, where leaders operate amidst constant flux and change. By mastering the art of narrative creation and communication, leaders can more effectively traverse the layers of complexity, enact meaningful change, and guide their organizations toward a resilient future. In the subsequent sections, we will uncover the facets of this process and provide practical strategies for their implementation.

Successfully navigating complex environments and tackling adversity calls for strategic communication, thoughtful narrative creation, and robust leadership. Drawing from our research findings, we propose the following roadmap for leaders to communicate effectively under such circumstances:

Environmental Assessment and Awareness: Begin with a clear understanding of your operational environment. This includes comprehending the political landscape, stakeholders' viewpoints, and any internal or external hurdles you may encounter. Evaluate how these conditions influence your role and your narrative.

Identity and Core Values Reflection: Contemplate your identity and personal philosophy. What are the core values that define you and your organization or team? This reflection should underpin your narrative construction.

Reevaluate and Refine Ideologies: Reflect on your current narrative or ideology. Identify elements that may be outdated or not resonate with your audience and focus on those that uphold your core values and reflect your environmental conditions.

Construct an Inclusionary Narrative: Frame your narrative to be inclusive and appeal to a wide audience. Considering your specific adversities, it should detail your goals and the methods to achieve them.

Emotional Connection: Understand the emotional, value-based, and ideological elements that influence your narrative construction. Use personal experiences and shared values to connect with your audience emotionally.

Leadership Behavior: Exhibit leadership behaviors that align with both transformational and transactional dimensions. While transformational leadership can inspire and motivate, transactional leadership can provide structure and effectively manage day-to-day operations.

Adapt and Evolve: Constructing a new narrative is an iterative process. As the environment changes, your narrative may need to evolve. Continually evaluate your narrative's effectiveness and make necessary adjustments.

Effective Communication: Communicate your new narrative effectively. Use accessible language, avoid jargon, and employ all communication channels at your disposal to ensure your message reaches your intended audience.

Embarking on Personal Growth

Your continual evolution in complexity necessitates a constant cycle of learning, adapting, and evolving. It's crucial to acknowledge that the person you were three years ago would not be as equipped to face today's challenges as you are. This acknowledgment is a nod to the journey you've embarked on, the growth you've nurtured, and the wisdom you've gained.

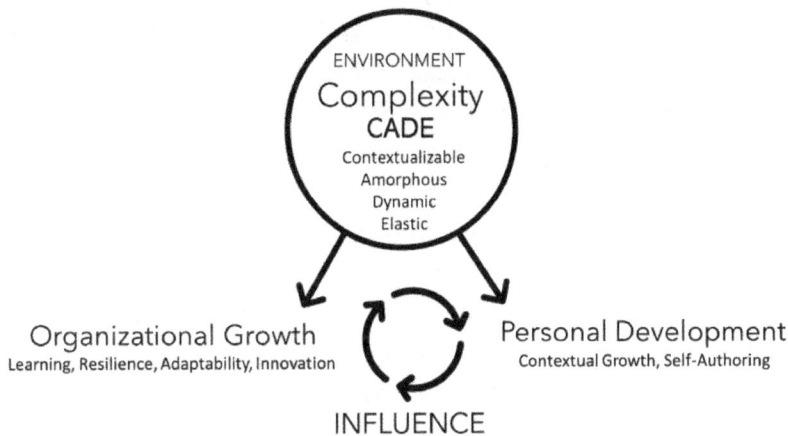

Image 36. Integrating Horizons Perspectives (Radi, 2011 - 2023) © Integral Advantage®

Within the framework of the *Inception Mindset*, such growth is not just desirable but quintessential. Every level of complexity you traverse introduces fresh challenges and opportunities, pushing you to broaden your understanding, hone your skills, and alter your perspective. This journey fosters growth, furnishing you with a more profound arsenal of tools and insights to understand the world's complexity.

However, it's common to overlook or undervalue this personal growth. You might feel like you're simply reacting to an ever-changing landscape, barely keeping pace with change. You could feel overwhelmed by the incessant influx of new challenges, questioning your capacity to manage. Such feelings can breed self-doubt and undercut your confidence.

In these moments, practice self-compassion. Understand that you are not the same person you were three years ago. You've learned, grown, and evolved. You've navigated layers of complexity, confronted numerous challenges, and emerged more robust and insightful. You're constantly reshaping yourself to meet environmental demands, cultivating new skills, and augmenting your comprehension of complexity.

Welcome this growth and applaud yourself for it. Celebrate your triumphs, regardless of their scale. Frame setbacks as catalysts for further growth. Be patient with yourself, acknowledging that growth is a process rather than an instantaneous event.

Your complexity navigation journey is uniquely yours. It's counterproductive to compare your progress with others. The only valuable comparison is against your past self. Therefore, take a moment to reflect on your growth, appreciating how far you've come. Then, focus on the journey ahead, assured that you'll continue to evolve, learn, and adapt.

The 'you' of tomorrow will be equipped to confront challenges that may seem intimidating to the 'you' of today. And this perpetual growth and evolution will empower you to navigate the world's complexity with an *Inception Mindset*. The secret lies in offering yourself the grace to grow, the patience to learn, and the resilience to traverse each new layer of complexity.

THINKING POINT

Section Takeaways

Leaders need to do more than just exhibit resilience. They need to find their voice, become catalysts for change, and use the power of narrative in leadership. The Triad of Persuasion, Ethos, Pathos, and Logos is a potent tool for leaders to use in their communication strategy. Each element brings a distinct power, and their combination forms a persuasive force.

Personal leadership narratives enable leaders to understand complex environments and effectively communicate their vision for change. The process of creating and communicating these narratives is as important as the narrative itself. Leaders can navigate complex situations by using a roadmap that involves environmental assessment, identity reflection, narrative refinement, emotional connection, exhibiting appropriate leadership behavior, and continuous adaptation.

Personal growth is a crucial aspect of navigating complexity, requiring a cycle of learning, adapting, and evolving. Leaders should acknowledge their growth and equip themselves for future challenges.

Reflective Questions

In your leadership journey, how have you seen the power of your voice effect change?

Have you ever consciously used the Triad of Persuasion in your communication strategy? If so, how effective was it?

How do you typically construct your leadership narratives? Are there elements from the proposed roadmap you could adopt in your narrative construction process?

Contextualization Prompt

To make these concepts come alive, let's think about a significant event or challenge in your leadership journey. How did you employ the power of your voice during this time? Did your communication strategy include elements of ethos, pathos, and logos? If not, how might these elements have affected the outcome? Finally, how does this event reflect your personal growth, and how could you use it to guide your future narrative construction and communication strategy?

Charting Our Journey

Inception Mindset

Introduction — For Your Consideration

Chapters

Horizon 1
The Complex Environment

1 A Permanent State of Inception
   An Inception Mindset
2 Gaining Clarity in Complexity
   Complexity is CADE

Horizon 2
The Self in Complexity

3 Clarity in Contextual Complexity
4 A Reframed Philosophy
5 Your Contextual Leadership Brand
6 Leadership Brand Authoring

7 Contextual Cultural Flow

Horizon 3
The Organization In Complexity

8 Entrusted Empowerment
9 The Practice of Entrusted Empowerment

Horizon 4
The Environment, The Self, The Org.

10 Cultivating Innovation & Learning
11 The Process of Strategic Innovation
12 Inception Mindset as the Way Forward

You Are Here

Conclusion — A Journey Toward Wisdom

CONCLUSION

THE FIFTH HORIZON: A JOURNEY TOWARD WISDOM

"By three methods, we may learn wisdom: First, by reflection, which is noblest; Second, by imitation, which is easiest; and third by experience, which is the bitterest." — Confucius

We have journeyed far, through the dense jungles of complexity and onto the shores of innovation. This odyssey across the four horizons has not served merely as an intellectual exploration but as a catalyst for our growth, transformation, and collective quest for wisdom. We have journeyed not from point A to B but along a vast, multidimensional spectrum of ideas, concepts, and paradigms.

Writing conclusions has never been my cup of tea. It is like ending an epic journey with a nagging feeling that we didn't get to see all the sights, and most importantly, we didn't get to eat all the food we could have. At the beginning of this book, I invited you to think with me, with the sincere hope that its content would honor the time and energy you have invested in reading it. I trust that our exploration opened the aperture on the horizons encompassing the complex landscape of innovation and leadership while reflecting on the extraordinary value of embracing and navigating complexity, fostering creativity, and nurturing an *Inception Mindset*.

As we arrive at the end of our journey, we realize it's not an end but rather a beginning. The beginning of a new journey where these insights and perspectives serve as a compass, guiding us through the unpredictability and complexity of our lives and organizations. It's a call to action, to practice these insights, to cultivate our leadership brands, to foster a conducive cultural flow, and for others to self-empower.

We are now standing at the edge of a new horizon, **a fifth horizon**. A horizon that beckons us to continue our journey of exploration, learning, and creating extraordinary value. The fog of uncertainty may still obscure the destination, but the path ahead is illuminated by the wisdom we have gleaned from our journey. As you move forward, remember that leadership is not about the destination but about the journey itself. A journey of continuous learning and growth, of navigating through complexity to creativity, from barriers to breakthroughs, and from ordinary to extraordinary. Continue to grow, learn, and lead with an *Inception Mindset*, nurturing a future of boundless innovation toward extraordinary value.

In our quest for wisdom, Confucius reminded us of three methods: reflection, imitation, and experience. Reflect on the insights gleaned, implement them in your context, learn from the outcomes, and iterate. Share your insights and experiences with others, fostering learning and innovation. Embark on this continuous cycle of learning, unlearning, and relearning, reinforcing the principle that the process of learning is a journey, not a destination.

Remember, it's okay not to know everything. As the great astronomer Copernicus wisely noted, "To know that we know what we know, and to know that we do not know what we do not know, that is true knowledge." Our journey through this book required a leap of faith—an investment of time, energy, and mental resources. I am incredibly grateful for your trust and deeply humbled to have been part of this journey with you. As we close this chapter and open the next, I echo the profound question by Dr. Martin Luther King Jr., 'What are you doing for others?' The knowledge we have gained from this journey becomes truly valuable when it's shared, implemented, and used to make a difference in the lives of others.

So here we are, at the beginning of a new journey, a new exploration across new horizons. A journey guided by the insights and wisdom we have gathered, illuminated by the beacon of our curiosity and our thirst for knowledge. The journey ahead will have its challenges and rewards, its highs and lows. But with each step we take, with each idea we explore, we come closer to understanding the world and our place within it. We gain clarity of who we are to lead others to where we need to be collectively.

The journey is indeed the destination. Let us keep moving forward, carrying with us the wisdom we've gained, the experiences we've shared, and the 'friendships' we've formed. May the road ahead lead us to new horizons of discovery, new peaks of knowledge, and to new vistas of understanding. Let's appreciate that the pursuit of wisdom is a marathon, not a sprint. As we close this chapter and prepare for the next, let us carry these words of wisdom from poet T.S. Eliot: "We shall not cease from exploration, and the end of all our exploring will be to arrive where we started and know the place for the first time."

Remember, the journey toward the extraordinary begins with a single step. Let this book be that first step, the catalyst for a remarkable journey of learning, exploration, and transformation. Take that step today, and let every step thereafter move you closer to your vision of the extraordinary. As we journey ahead, let's hold close to these words from Lao Tzu, "The journey of a thousand miles begins with a single step."

Onward to our next journey, to new horizons, to the extraordinary!

ABOUT THE AUTHOR

Dr. Robert Radi is president and partner at Integral Advantage®, an organization dedicated to developing leadership and strategic organizational capacity in private and public sector organizations. His rich professional journey and personal commitment make him uniquely positioned to offer invaluable insights into leadership, strategy, innovation, and organizational development. Dr. Radi is a seasoned executive, entrepreneur, educator, and former elected official with over three decades of diverse experience in domestic and international markets. Equipped with a Ph.D. in Organizational Leadership from The Chicago School and an MBA from Pepperdine University, he has successfully served as an executive and board member in various private, academic, nonprofit organizations and public agencies.

Before his involvement in executive education, Radi founded a consumer product strategy firm serving global brands for 19 years, structuring iconic consumer product platforms generating over $100 million in annual revenues, receiving numerous awards for innovation excellence, and participating in securing and monetizing multiple patents.

Dr. Radi has collaborated with universities such as The Chicago School, Pepperdine, Benedictine, University of Maryland, and California State University San Bernardino - Palm Desert Campus as an educator. Serving as a faculty member in bachelor, master, and Ph.D. programs, he designed courses and developed frameworks encompassing fundamentals and specialized subjects in executive leadership and integrated strategic management. His work with the U.S. Federal Government has made him a sought-after subject matter expert, lecturer, and facilitator. He has delivered widely recognized lectures and courses to seasoned and emerging leaders from multiple Federal Agencies and U.S. Military.

His civic contributions include being elected Council Member for La Quinta City Council, Board Chair for Sunline Transit Agency, and Coachella Valley Association of Governments' Transportation Committee Chair, among others. His initiatives have led to significant advancements in public safety and economic development.

BIBLIOGRAPHY

Introduction

Johansen, B. (2012). Leaders Make the Future: Ten New Leadership Skills for an Uncertain World. Berrett-Koehler Publishers.

Johansen, B. (2017). The New Leadership Literacies: Thriving in a Future of Extreme Disruption and Distributed Everything. Berrett-Koehler Publishers.

Johansen, B. (2020). Full-Spectrum Thinking: How to Escape Boxes in a Post-Categorical Future. Berrett-Koehler Publishers.

Cooper, J., & Goren, A. (2007). Cognitive dissonance theory. In R. Baumeister, & K. Vohs (Eds.), Encyclopedia of social psychology. (pp. 150-153). Thousand Oaks, CA: SAGE Publications

Day, D. V., Harrison, M. M., & Halpin, S. M. (2009). An Integrative Approach to Leader Development: Connecting Adult Development, Identity, and Expertise. New York, NY: Psychology Press.

McCauley, C.D., Kanaga, K. & Lafferty, K. (2010). Leadership development systems. In Handbook for leadership development (3rd Ed., pp. 29-61). San Francisco: Jossey-Bass.

Senge, P. (2006). The Fifth Discipline. The Art & Practice of the Learning Organization. DoubleDay a division of Random House, Inc.

PART I Horizon 1: The Complex Environment

Chapter 1 - A Permanent State of Inception

Senge, P. (2006). The Fifth Discipline. The Art & Practice of the Learning Organization. DoubleDay a division of Random House, Inc.

Ferguson, N. (2008). The Ascent of Money: A Financial History of the World. New York, NY: Penguin Press.

Peterson, C., & Seligman, M. E. P. (2004). Character strengths and virtues: A handbook and classification. Oxford University Press.

Csikszentmihalyi, M. (1996). Creativity: Flow and the psychology of discovery and invention. HarperCollins.

Duckworth, A. L., Peterson, C., Matthews, M. D., & Kelly, D. R. (2007). Grit: perseverance and passion for long-term goals. Journal of personality and social psychology, 92(6), 1087-1101.

Fredrickson, B. L. (2001). The role of positive emotions in positive psychology: The broaden-and-build theory of positive emotions. American psychologist, 56(3), 218-226.

Snowden, D.J. and Boone, M.E., 2007. A leader's framework for decision making. Harvard Business Review, 85(11), pp.68-76.

Garvey-Berger, J. (2019). Unlocking Leadership Mindtraps: How to Thrive in Complexity. Stanford University Press.

Johansen, B. (2020). Full-Spectrum Thinking: How to Escape Boxes in a Post-Categorical Future. Berrett-Koehler Publishers.

Eagleman, D. (2021). Brains love stories: How leveraging neuroscience can capture people's emotions. Stanford Graduate School of Business. Retrieved from https://www.gsb.stanford.edu/insights/brains-love-stories-how-leveraging-neuroscience-can-capture-peoples-emotions

Bolman, L. G., & Deal, T. E. (2017). Reframing Organizations: Artistry, Choice, and Leadership (6th ed.). Jossey-Bass.

Freudenburg, W. R., & Gramling, R. (2011). Blowout in the Gulf: The BP Oil Spill Disaster and the Future of Energy in America. MIT Press.

Hopkins, A. (2008). Failure to Learn: The BP Texas City Refinery Disaster. CCH Australia Limited.

Broom, G. M., Casey, S., & Ritchey, J. (1997). Toward a Concept and Theory of Organization-Public Relationships: An Update. Journal of Public Relations Research, 9(2), 83-98.

Rehak, J. (2002, March 23). Tylenol Made a Hero of Johnson & Johnson: The Recall that Started Them All. The New York Times. Retrieved from: https://www.nytimes.com/2002/03/23/your-money/23iht-mjj_ed3_.html

Homer. (1996). The Odyssey (R. Fagles, Trans.). Penguin Classics.

Chapter 2 - Gaining Clarity in Complexity

The Future of Jobs Report 2023. World Economic Forum. (May 2023). https://www.weforum.org/reports/the-future-of-jobs-report-2023

Bennis, W., & Nanus, B. (1985). Leaders: The Strategies for Taking Charge. Harper & Row.

See how the future of jobs is changing in the age of AI. (2023). World

Economic Forum. https://www.weforum.org/agenda/2023/05/future-of-jobs-in-the-age-of-ai-sustainability-and-deglobalization/

Csikszentmihalyi, M. (1996). Creativity: Flow and the psychology of discovery and invention. HarperCollins.

PART II Horizon 2: The Self in Complexity

Chapter 3 - Clarity in Contextual Complexity: Self Authoring

Peck, M. S. (1978). The road less traveled: A new psychology of love, traditional values, and spiritual growth. Simon & Schuster.

Frankl, V. E. (1959). Man's search for meaning: An introduction to logotherapy. Beacon Press.

Brown, B. (2010). The gifts of imperfection: Let go of who you think you're supposed to be and embrace who you are. Hazelden Publishing.

Kegan, R. (1994). In over our heads: The mental demands of modern life. Harvard University Press.

Tillich, P. (1952). The courage to be. Yale University Press.

Brown, B. (2010). The Gifts of Imperfection: Let Go of Who You Think You're Supposed to Be and Embrace Who You Are. Hazelden Publishing.

Descartes, R. (1989). The Passions of the Soul. (S. H. Voss, Trans.). Indianapolis, IN: Hackett Publishing Company.

LeDoux, J. (1996). The Emotional Brain: The Mysterious Underpinnings of Emotional Life. New York: Simon & Schuster.

Goleman, D. (1995). Emotional Intelligence: Why It Can Matter More Than IQ. New York: Bantam Books.

Williams, M., & Penman, D. (2011). Mindfulness: An Eight-Week Plan for Finding Peace in a Frantic World. New York: Rodale Books.

Fredrickson, B. (2009). Positivity: Top-Notch Research Reveals the 3-to-1 Ratio That Will Change Your Life. New York: Crown Archetype.

Kahneman, D. (2011). Thinking, Fast and Slow. New York: Farrar, Straus and Giroux.

Covey, S. R. (1989). The 7 Habits of Highly Effective People: Powerful Lessons in Personal Change. Simon & Schuster.

Lencioni, P. (2002). Make Your Values Mean Something. Harvard Business Review.

Brown, B. (2012). Daring Greatly: How the Courage to Be Vulnerable Transforms the Way We Live, Love, Parent, and Lead. Gotham Books.

Dunning, D., Johnson, K., Ehrlinger, J., & Kruger, J. (2003). Why people fail to recognize their own incompetence. Current Directions in Psychological Science, 12(3), 83-87.

Ramón y Cajal, S. (1999). Advice for a Young Investigator. Cambridge, Massachusetts: The MIT Press. (Original work published in 1897)

Chapter 4 - A Reframed Philosophy

Swanson, L.W., & Newman, E. (2017). The Beautiful Brain: The Drawings of Santiago Ramon y Cajal. New York: Abrams.

Dweck, C. S. (2017). Mindset: Changing the way you think to fulfill your potential. Robinson.

Goleman, D. (1995). Emotional intelligence: Why it can matter more than IQ. Bantam Books.

Kolb, B., & Whishaw, I. Q. (2015). Fundamentals of human neuropsychology. Worth Publishers.

Kruger, J., & Dunning, D. (1999). Unskilled and unaware of it: How difficulties in recognizing one's own incompetence lead to inflated self-assessments. Journal of Personality and Social Psychology, 77(6), 1121-1134.

Beck, J. S. (2011). Cognitive Behavior Therapy: Basics and Beyond (2nd ed.). Guilford Press.

Ellis, A. (1991). The revised ABC's of rational-emotive therapy (RET). Journal of Rational-Emotive and Cognitive-Behavior Therapy, 9(3), 139-172.

Neff, K. D. (2003). Self-Compassion: An Alternative Conceptualization of a Healthy Attitude Toward Oneself. Self and Identity, 2(2), 85-102.

Drucker, P. F. (1967). The Effective Executive: The Definitive Guide to Getting the Right Things Done. New York: HarperCollins Publishers.

Peters, T. (1997). The Brand Called You. Fast Company. Retrieved from https://www.fastcompany.com/28905/brand-called-you

Montoya, P., & Vandehey, T. (2002). The Brand Called You: Create a Personal Brand That Wins Attention and Grows Your Business. McGraw-Hill.

Reinventing You: Define Your Brand, Imagine Your Future by Dorie Clark (2013)

Crush It!: Why NOW Is the Time to Cash In on Your Passion by Gary Vaynerchuk (2009)

You Are a Brand!: How Smart People Brand Themselves for Business Success by Catherine Kaputa (2010)

Allis, C.D., Jenuwein, T., & Reinberg, D. (2007). Epigenetics. Cold Spring Harbor Laboratory Press.

Gilbert, J.A., Blaser, M.J., Caporaso, J.G., Jansson, J.K., Lynch, S.V., & Knight, R. (2018). Current understanding of the human microbiome. Nature Medicine, 24(4), 392-400.

Rogers, C. R. (1961). On Becoming a Person: A Therapist's View of Psychotherapy. Houghton Mifflin.

Goleman, D. (1995). Emotional Intelligence: Why It Can Matter More Than IQ. Bantam Books.

Goleman, D. (1998). Working with Emotional Intelligence. Bantam Books.

Salovey, P., & Mayer, J. D. (1990). Emotional intelligence. Imagination, Cognition, and Personality, 9(3), 185-211.

Crossan, M., Gandz, J., & Seijts, G. (2012). Developing Leadership Character. Ivey Business Journal, 76(1), 1-8.

Chapter 5 - Your Contextual Leadership Brand

Covey, S. M. R. (2006). The Speed of Trust: The One Thing That Changes Everything. Free Press.

Northouse, P. G. (2018). Leadership: Theory and Practice (8th ed.). SAGE Publications, Inc.

Kouzes, J. M., & Posner, B. Z. (2017). The Leadership Challenge: How to Make Extraordinary Things Happen in Organizations (6th ed.). Jossey-Bass.

Brown, B. (2018). Dare to Lead: Brave Work. Tough Conversations. Whole Hearts. Random House.

Dweck, C. S. (2006). Mindset: The New Psychology of Success. Random House.

Spector, P. E. (2019). Job Satisfaction: Application, Assessment, Causes, and

Consequences. SAGE Publications.

Bass, B. M., & Riggio, R. E. (2006). Transformational Leadership (2nd ed.). Psychology Press.

Spector, P. E. (2019). Job Satisfaction: Application, Assessment, Causes, and Consequences. SAGE Publications.

Cameron, K. S., & Quinn, R. E. (2011). Diagnosing and Changing Organizational Culture: Based on the Competing Values Framework (3rd ed.). Jossey-Bass.

Goleman, D. (1998). Working with Emotional Intelligence. Bantam Books.

Northouse, P. G. (2018). Leadership: Theory and Practice (8th ed.). SAGE Publications.

Lencioni, P. (2002). The Five Dysfunctions of a Team: A Leadership Fable. Jossey-Bass.

Meyer, J. P., & Allen, N. J. (1997). Commitment in the workplace: Theory, research, and application. SAGE Publications.

Goleman, D., Boyatzis, R., & McKee, A. (2013). Primal Leadership: Unleashing the Power of Emotional Intelligence. Harvard Business Review Press.

Edmondson, A. C. (2019). The Fearless Organization: Creating Psychological Safety in the Workplace for Learning, Innovation, and Growth. Wiley.

Kabat-Zinn, J. (1994). Wherever You Go, There You Are: Mindfulness Meditation in Everyday Life. Hyperion.

George, B. (2015). Discover Your True North. John Wiley & Sons.

Goleman, D., & Davidson, R. J. (2017). Altered Traits: Science Reveals How Meditation Changes Your Mind, Brain, and Body. Avery.

Langer, E. J. (1989). Mindfulness. Addison-Wesley/Addison Wesley Longman.

Avolio, B. J., & Gardner, W. L. (2005). Authentic leadership development: Getting to the root of positive forms of leadership. The Leadership Quarterly, 16(3), 315-338.

George, B. (2003). Authentic Leadership: Rediscovering the Secrets to Creating Lasting Value. Jossey-Bass.

Ibarra, H. (2015). The Authenticity Paradox. Harvard Business Review, January-February.

Luthans, F., & Avolio, B. J. (2003). Authentic leadership: A positive developmental approach. In K. S. Cameron, J. E. Dutton, & R. E. Quinn (Eds.), Positive organizational scholarship (pp. 241-258). Berrett-Koehler.

Senge, P. M. (2006). The Fifth Discipline: The Art & Practice of The Learning Organization. Doubleday.

Hedges, K. (2012). The Power of Presence: Unlock Your Potential to Influence and Engage Others. AMACOM.

Hewlett, S. A. (2014). Executive Presence: The Missing Link Between Merit and Success. Harper Business.

Su, A. J., & Wilkins, M. M. (2013). Own the Room: Discover Your Signature Voice to Master Your Leadership Presence. Harvard Business Review Press.

Collins, J. C. (2001). Good to Great: Why Some Companies Make the Leap... and Others Don't. Harper Business.

Kim, W. C., & Mauborgne, R. (2004). Blue Ocean Strategy: How to Create Uncontested Market Space and Make the Competition Irrelevant. Harvard Business School Press.

Baumeister, R. F., & Finkel, E. J. (2010). Advanced social psychology: The state of the science. Oxford University Press.

Blustein, D. L. (2013). The Oxford handbook of the psychology of working. Oxford University Press.

Bono, E. D. (2010). Lateral thinking: Creativity step by step. HarperCollins.

Chapter 6 - Leadership Brand Authoring

Mueller, P. A., & Oppenheimer, D. M. (2014). The Pen Is Mightier Than the Keyboard: Advantages of Long and Over Laptop Note Taking. Psychological Science, 25(6), 1159–1168. https://doi.org/10.1177/0956797614524581

Mangen, A., & Velay, J. L. (2010). Digitizing literacy: reflections on the haptics of writing. In Advances in Haptics (pp. 385-402). CRC Press.

Marquardt, M. J. (2014). Leading with Questions: How Leaders Find the Right Solutions by Knowing What to Ask. Jossey-Bass.

Kegan, R. (1994). In Over Our Heads: The Mental Demands of Modern Life. Harvard University Press.

Christensen, C., Allworth, J., & Dillon, K. (2012). How will you measure your life? HarperCollins UK.

Warren, R. (2003). The Purpose Driven Life: What on Earth Am I Here For? Zondervan.

Maurer, T. J., Weiss, E. M., & Barbeite, F. G. (2003). A model of involvement in work-related learning and development activity: The effects of individual, situational, motivational, and age variables. Journal of Applied Psychology, 88(4), 707-724.

Day, D. V., Harrison, M. M., & Halpin, S. M. (2012). An integrative approach to leader development: Connecting adult development, identity, and expertise. Routledge.

Rock, D. (2009). Your brain at work: Strategies for overcoming distraction, regaining focus, and working smarter all day long. HarperCollins.

Peterson, C., & Seligman, M. E. P. (2004). Character strengths and virtues: A handbook and classification. Oxford University Press.

PART III Horizon 3: The Organization in Complexity

Chapter 7 - Contextual Cultural Flow

Schein, E. H. (1985). "Organizational Culture and Leadership". San Francisco: Jossey-Bass.

Ouchi, W. G. (1981). "Theory Z: How American Business Can Meet the Japanese Challenge". Reading, MA: Addison-Wesley.

Daft, R. L. (2015). Organization Theory & Design. Cengage Learning.

Coyle, D. (2018). The Culture Code: The Secrets of Highly Successful Groups. Bantam Books.

Cameron, K. S., & Quinn, R. E. (2011). Diagnosing and Changing Organizational Culture: Based on the Competing Values Framework. Jossey-Bass.

Kotter, J. P., & Heskett, J. L. (1992). Corporate Culture and Performance. Free Press.

Schein, E. H. (2010). Organizational Culture and Leadership. Jossey-Bass.

Lencioni, P. (2012). The Advantage: Why Organizational Health Trumps Everything Else in Business. Jossey-Bass.

Groysberg, B., Lee, J., Price, J., & Cheng, J. Y. (2018). The Leader's Guide to Corporate Culture. Harvard Business Review, January-February.

Lorsch, J.W., & McTague, E. (2016). Culture is not the culprit. Harvard Business Review, 94(4), 96-105.

Chapter 8 – Entrusted Empowerment

Radi, R. (2021). Entrusted Empowerment: The Essence of Trust in Empowering Individuals, Teams and Organizations.

Beard, R. (2016). Why Google's Employees Are Its Best Brand Advocates. Adage. https://adage.com/article/agency-viewpoint/google-s-employees-brand-advocates/304531.

Lorsch, J. W., & McTague, E. (2016). Culture is not the Culprit. Harvard Business Review. https://hbr.org/2016/04/culture-is-not-the-culprit.

Gostick, A. & Elton, C. (2010). The orange revolution. New York: Free Press.

Karp, H. B. (1998) Team building from a Gestalt perspective. The Pfeiffer Library Volume 13, 2nd Edition, Jossey-Bass/Pfeiffer, pp. 279-283.

Karp, H., Fuller, C., & Sirias, D., (2002) Bridging the Boomer-Xer Gap: Creating Authentic Teams for High Performance at Work. Palo Alto, CA: Davies Black Publishing.

Laborde, G. (2001) Influencing with integrity: management skills for communication and negotiation. Palo Alto: Syntony Publications

Lencioni, P. (2002). The five dysfunctions of a team. San Francisco: Jossey-Bass

Lewin, G. (1997). Frontiers in Group Dynamics (1947). In , Resolving social conflicts and field theory in social science (pp. 301-336). Washington, DC US: American Psychological Association

Nandhakumar, J., & Baskerville, R. (2006). Durability of online team working: Patterns of trust. Information Technology & People, 19(4), 371-389.

Mintzberg, H. (2009). Managing. San Francisco: Berrett-Koehler Publishers.

Mortensen, M., Caya, O., Pinsonneault, A. (2009). Virtual teams demystified: An integrative framework for understanding virtual teams and a synthesis of research. MIT Sloan School Working Paper 4738-09.

Oncken, W. & Wass, D. L. (November 1999). Management time: Who's got the monkey? In On managing yourself (pp. 21-34, 2010). Boston: Harvard Business Review Press.

Pearce, C.L. & Conger, J.A. (2010) All Those Years Ago in G.R. Hickman (Ed) Leading Organizations, Perspectives for a New Era. Thousand Oaks, CA: Sage Publications.

Pauleen, D. J. (2003). Leadership in a global virtual team: An action learning approach. Leadership & Organization Development Journal, 24(3), 153.

Poole, M. S. and Hollingshead, A. B., Editors. (2005) Theories of small groups: Interdisciplinary perspectives. Thousand Oaks, CA: Sage Publications.

Senge, P. M. (2006). The fifth discipline: The art and practice of the learning organization. New York: Doubleday.

Tuckman, B. W. (1965). Developmental sequence in small groups. Psychological Bulletin, 63(6), 384-39.

Yukl, G. (2010). Leadership in organizations (7th ed.). New Jersey: Prentice Hall. ISBN: 978-0-13-242431-8

Zivick, J. (2012). Mapping global virtual team leadership actions to organizational roles. The Business Review, Cambridge,19(2), 18-25.

Chapter 9 – The Practice of Entrusted Empowerment

Radi, R. (2021). Entrusted Empowerment: The Essence of Trust in Empowering Individuals, Teams and Organizations.

Optoro. (2021). 2021 Impact Report. Retrieved from https://www.optoro.com/about

Basecamp. (2023). How We Communicate. Retrieved from https://basecamp.com/guides/how-we-communicate

Foster, W. (2020). Zapier: How We Work. Retrieved from https://zapier.com/learn/remote-work/how-manage-remote-team/

Allspaw, J. (2012). Blameless PostMortems and a Just Culture. Retrieved from https://codeascraft.com/2012/05/22/blameless-postmortems/

Gusto. (2023). About Us. Retrieved from https://gusto.com/about

Balsamiq. (2023). Our Company. Retrieved from https://balsamiq.com/company/#culture

Next Jump. (2023). Our Culture. Retrieved from https://www.nextjump.com/culture

Huddle. (2023). About Us. Retrieved from https://www.huddle.com/about/

Buffer. (2023). Salary Formula. Retrieved from https://buffer.com/salary

Clevertech. (2023). Approach. Retrieved from https://www.clevertech.biz/

W.L. Gore & Associates. (2023). Our Culture. Retrieved from https://www.gore.com/about/the-gore-story#our-culture

PART IV Horizon 4: In It Together:

The Environment. The Self. The Organization.

Chapter 10 – Cultivating Innovation and Learning

Radi, R. (2011). Strategic Assessment for the Acquisition and Repositioning of ShopNBC. (Unpublished master's thesis). Pepperdine University.

Isaacson, W. (2011). Steve Jobs: The Exclusive Biography. Simon & Schuster.

"How Adobe Got its Customers Hooked on Subscription Software." (2017, June 8). Bloomberg. Retrieved from https://www.bloomberg.com/news/articles/2017-06-08/how-adobe-got-its-customers-hooked-on-subscriptions#xj4y7vzkg

"Adobe Inc." Macrotrends. Retrieved from https://www.macrotrends.net/stocks/charts/ADBE/adobe/revenue

Beaty RE, Benedek M, Kaufman SB, Silvia PJ. Default and Executive Network Coupling Supports Creative Idea Production. Sci Rep. 2015 Jun 17;5:10964. doi: 10.1038/srep10964. PMID: 26084037; PMCID: PMC4472024.

Gonen-Yaacovi, G., De Souza, L.C., Levy, R., Urbanski, M., Josse, G., & Volle, E. (2013). Rostral and caudal prefrontal contribution to creativity: A meta-analysis of functional imaging data. Frontiers in Human Neuroscience, 7, 465.

Schlegel, A., Alexander, P., Fogelson, S. V., Li, X., Lu, Z., Kohler, P. J., ... & Meng, M. (2015). The artist emerges: Visual art learning alters neural structure and function. NeuroImage, 105, 440-451.

Puccio, G. J., Mance, M., & Murdock, M. C. (2010). Creative Leadership: Skills That Drive Change. SAGE Publications.

Puccio, G. J. (2012). FourSight: The Breakthrough Thinking Profile. FourSight.

Chapter 11 – Strategic Innovation Framework

Ehrlinger, J., Johnson, K., Banner, M., Dunning, D., & Kruger, J. (2008). Why the unskilled are unaware: Further explorations of (absent) self-insight among the incompetent. Organizational Behavior and Human Decision Processes, 105(1), 98-121.

Armor, D. A., & Taylor, S. E. (2002). When predictions fail: The dilemma of unrealistic optimism. In T. Gilovich, D. Griffin, & D. Kahneman (Eds.), Heuristics and biases: The psychology of intuitive judgment (pp. 334–347). Cambridge University Press.

Moore, D. A., & Healy, P. J. (2008). The trouble with overconfidence. Psychological Review, 115(2), 502-517.

Stone, B. (2013). The everything store: Jeff Bezos and the age of Amazon. Little, Brown and Company.

Radi, R. (2011). Strategic Assessment for the Acquisition and Repositioning of ShopNBC. (Unpublished master's thesis). Pepperdine University.

Christensen, C. M., & Raynor, M. E. (2003). The innovator's solution: creating and sustaining successful growth. Harvard Business Press.

Kouzes, J. M., & Posner, B. Z. (2017). The Leadership Challenge: How to Make Extraordinary Things Happen in Organizations (6th ed.). Jossey-Bass.

Senge, P. M. (2006). The fifth discipline: The art and practice of the learning organization. New York: Doubleday.

Janis, I. L. (1972). Victims of Groupthink: A Psychological Study of Foreign-policy Decisions and Fiascoes. Boston: Houghton Mifflin.

Staw, B. M. (1976). Knee-deep in the big muddy: A study of escalating commitment to a chosen course of action. Organizational behavior and human performance, 16(1), 27-44.

Staw, B. M., & Hoang, H. (1995). Sunk Costs in the NBA: Why Draft Order Affects Playing Time and Survival in Professional Basketball. Administrative Science Quarterly, 40(3), 474-494.

Tjosvold, D. (1985). Implications of controversy research for management. Journal of Management, 11(3), 21-37.

Turner, M. E., & Pratkanis, A. R. (1998). Twenty-five years of groupthink theory and research: Lessons from the evaluation of a theory. Organizational Behavior and Human Decision Processes, 73(2-3), 105-115.

Chapter 12 - Inception Mindset as the Way Forward

Peterson, C., & Seligman, M. E. P. (2004). Character strengths and virtues: A handbook and classification. Oxford University Press.

Csikszentmihalyi, M. (2013). Creativity: Flow and the psychology of discovery and invention. HarperCollins.

Duckworth, A. L., Peterson, C., Matthews, M. D., & Kelly, D. R. (2007). Grit: perseverance and passion for long-term goals. Journal of personality and social psychology, 92(6), 1087-1101.

Fredrickson, B. L. (2001). The role of positive emotions in positive psychology: The broaden-and-build theory of positive emotions. American psychologist, 56(3), 218-226.

Cameron, K. S., & Quinn, R. E. (2011). Diagnosing and Changing Organizational Culture: Based on the Competing Values Framework. Jossey-Bass.

Radi, R. (2015). The process of political narrative construct: How political leaders construct new narratives while experiencing adverse political conditions (Doctoral dissertation, The Chicago School of Professional Psychology).

Aristotle. (4th Century B.C.). Rhetoric. Translated by W. Rhys Roberts.

Day, D. V., & Dragoni, L. (2015). Leadership development: An outcome-oriented review based on time and levels of analyses. Annual Review of Organizational Psychology and Organizational Behavior, 2(1), 133-156.

Avolio, B. J., & Hannah, S. T. (2008). Developmental readiness: Accelerating leader development. Consulting Psychology Journal: Practice and Research, 60(4), 331-347.

www.ingramcontent.com/pod-product-compliance
Lightning Source LLC
Chambersburg PA
CBHW081459200326
41518CB00015B/2310